Six Lives

Six Lives

A MEMOIR

Dow Marmur

KEY PORTER BOOKS

National Library of Canada Cataloguing in Publication

Marmur, Dow
Six lives : a memoir / Dow Marmur.

Includes index.

ISBN 1-55263-628-3

1. Marmur, Dow. 2. Rabbis—Ontario—Toronto—Biography. 3. Reform Judaism.
4. Jews, Polish—Biography. 5. Toronto (Ont.)—Biography. I. Title.

BM755.M23A3 2004   296.8'341'092   C2004-902775-1

The publisher gratefully acknowledges the support of the Canada Council for the Arts and the Ontario Arts Council for its publishing program. We acknowledge the support of the Government of Ontario through the Ontario Media Development Corporation's Ontario Book Initiative.

We acknowledge the financial support of the Government of Canada through the Book Publishing Industry Development Program (BPIDP) for our publishing activities.

Key Porter Books Limited
70 The Esplanade
Toronto, Ontario
Canada M5E 1R2
www.keyporter.com

Text design: Jack Steiner
Electronic formatting: Heidy Lawrance Associates

Printed and bound in Canada
04 05 06 07 08 09 6 5 4 3 2 1

For my grandchildren
Miriam, Nadav, Gaby, Leone and Ethan

Contents

Preface

A cat, like all God's creatures, lives only one life, but it is equipped to avoid injury in various life-threatening situations, an ability that gives the impression that it can come back from the dead. Hence the saying that a cat has nine lives. I don't mean to suggest that because I've entitled this book *Six Lives*, I've come back again and again from some devastating catastrophe. I do feel, however, that it has been my good fortune to lead very different lives in very different places—and survive them all relatively unscathed. It has been one life in many parts.

But I cannot totally dismiss the feline reference, despite having no particular love for cats. In 1995 the *CCAR Journal*, published by the American Reform rabbinate, carried a piece by Dan Cohn-Sherbock about two kinds of rabbis: dog rabbis and cat rabbis. There are rabbis, he asserted, who, similar to dogs, seem to like everyone and want to be liked by everyone. Cat rabbis, on the other hand, are solitary and much less concerned about others and what others think of them. The congregational rabbinate is for dog rabbis, according to Cohn-Sherbock. That's why, by his own testimony, he was less than successful "in the field" and as a result chose the academic life in which he thrives.

Reactions to Cohn-Sherbock's article appeared in the journal. Several insisted that his distinction was too radical and that it was quite possible to be a successful congregational cat rabbi. I was greatly cheered by these reactions, because in Cohn-Sherbock's scheme of things, I'm decidedly a cat rabbi. Yet I've served three congregations and left each of them on the best of terms and with much affection on both sides. Despite my limited ability to be "one of the boys" and to receive everyone with a cheerful countenance, I think of myself as a successful congregational rabbi.

However, as much as I found the congregational rabbinate satisfying and fulfilling, a side of me wanted to keep my distance from people and mind my own business. In fact, one reason I retired as soon as circumstances permitted was that I was tired of "customer service." Though I find my present cat existence in retirement lonely at times, I have no desire to go back to my previous occupation, for now I can do what I like best—teach and write—even though it's not always obvious that people want to learn and read.

But it's the congregational rabbinate that has made me. Even this book couldn't have been published without the efforts of members of Holy Blossom Temple, the last congregation I served. Despite my confession above, I feel immensely privileged to have served three outstanding congregations, and I'm most grateful to all the contributors for their generosity and support.

Dan Cohn-Sherbock, too, published an autobiography. However, he disguised several individuals with fictitious names, presumably to avoid causing trouble or hurt feelings. The reader needs to know whom the author has in mind to realize that Manchester in the book isn't really Manchester, that Morris isn't Morris, and so on.

Though I've mentioned many names, I hope that I've said nothing to embarrass anyone. When the risk of embarrassment existed, I've omitted the name. And even when I might have had something to tell of those mentioned, if the story doesn't relate to me or isn't relevant to my account, I've chosen to say nothing.

The purpose of this book isn't to tell tales but primarily to give testimony. For I was a witness to certain events during the years of the Second World War, and in the Jewish communities of Sweden, Britain and Canada, and now in Israel. I've tried to be as truthful as possible, and I hope I've succeeded.

I also hope that this account will be of interest to students of Jewish life in general and Progressive-Reform-Liberal Judaism in particular. I was actively involved in it for more than four decades in several different countries. Events as described and reflections as offered may be of interest to some. And I hope that all will enjoy the book.

This book wouldn't have been written without the encouragement of Rabbi John Moscowitz and his wish to put it into the hands of all the members of Holy Blossom Temple in Toronto. And the book wouldn't have been published without the guidance and support of Cynthia Good. I'm deeply grateful to both.

Thanks to Meg Taylor at Key Porter Books, this memoir is more readable than it would have been otherwise. She has also saved this cat rabbi from much cattiness. I'm greatly indebted to her unique blend of professionalism and commitment.

I'm also grateful to Key Porter for having allowed me to include the coda by my wife, Fredzia. "My Luck" first appeared in the Spring 1995 issue of *Manna*, a journal published in Britain, and is reprinted here by permission.

At Holy Blossom, this project was spearheaded by Jack Geller and Sheila Smolkin, the honorary president and immediate past president respectively, on behalf of all past presidents of the congregation. I've been greatly strengthened by the support of past and present leaders of the Temple. Many of them are listed by name below. I'm most grateful for their kindness.

I'd like to thank the following individuals for their generosity, which made it possible for this volume to reach all Temple members: Brenda Spiegler and Mark S. Anshan; Sandra and Gordon Atlin; Marianne and Thomas Beck; Anne MacPherson and Earl Bederman; Thelma and Barnet Berris; Ellen and Murray Blankstein; Gail and Zelik Bocknek; Susan and Barry Borden; Elaine and Stephen Borins; Mimi and Myer Brody; Esther and Theodore Burnett; Debra and Barry Campbell; Henrietta Chesnie; Judith and Marshall Cohen; Shoshana Cole; Esther Zeller and Morris Cooper; Joanne and Richard Cummings; Wendy and Elliott Eisen; Sharon and Lawrence Enkin; Madeleine and Arnold Epstein; Sharyn Salsberg and Hershell Ezrin; Gladys and Lloyd

Fogler; Penny Fine and Hugh Furneaux; Zita Gardner and family; Randi and Alan Garfinkel; Sybil and Jack Geller; Gail and Irving Gerstein; Reva Gerstein; Etta Ginsberg McEwan; Marilyn and Charles Gold; Susan and Marty Goldberg; Karla and David Goldberg; Fran and Bernard Goldman; Cynthia Good; Edwin Goodman; Diana and Marvin Goodman; Sybil and David Gordon; Samuel Gotfrid; Catherine and Robert Grundleger; Sharon and Bernard Herman; Judy Malkin and Elliott Jacobson; Elisabeth and Ivan Jaye; Ellen Karabanow; Ethel and Ron Kellen; Mimi and Malcolm Kronby; Terye and Jack Kuper; Wilma and Monte Kwinter; Lorraine and Donald Loeb; Stefanie Hill and Greg Mahon and the boys; Anne and Ben Marmur; Maxine and Harold Minden; Glenda Mindlin; Audrey and David Mirvish; Edwin Mirvish; Martha and Walter Moos; Freda and Arthur Muscovitch; Lesley and Allan Offman; Sara Pachter; Sandra Papsin; Nancy Pencer; Sheila Pollock; Arlene Perly Rae and Bob Rae; Sandra and Joseph Rotman; Nancy and Sam Ruth; Robert Salsberg; Myrna Sandler; Carol and Lionel Schipper; Elizabeth Wolfe and Paul Schnier; Annalee and Brian Schnurr; Hope Sealy; Mary and Henry Seldon and family; Bonnie Lawrence Shear and Melvin Shear; Janet and Norman Shiner; Wendy and Paul Sidlofsky; Beatrice and Saul Sidlofsky; Carol and Paul Slavens; Sheila and Bob Smolkin; Virginia and Carl Solomon; Evelyn Stagg; Barbara and Hubert Stitt; Arlene and Carl Stone; Francie and Martin Storm; Eleanor and Burnett Thall; Christine and Stephen Tile; Dora Track; Rosie and John Uster; Sandy and Leonard Wise and family; Linda and Gordon Wolfe; Rose Wolfe; Joyce and Fred Zemans; and H.A.B.S.T.Y., the youth group at Holy Blossom Temple.

Poland:
Beginnings

I'm fond of quoting the anonymous professor who, when asked if he came from a distinguished family, replied, "No, but my children do." I know very little about the families of my parents. My father was born in 1902 in Galicia, which at that time was part of the Austro-Hungarian Empire; he was registered on his birth certificate as Maksymilian, the Polish spelling of the emperor's name. He was called Max, and his Hebrew name was Mordechai. When he was two, his mother died and her parents brought him up. He seemed to have had good memories of them. When I was small he would tell me stories from his childhood; I didn't pay much attention, something I now regret deeply. My own childhood, as will emerge from the pages that follow, was totally rooted in the present; neither the past nor the future seemed to matter.

My mother, Zipporah, in Polish Cesia (Cecylia in the documents), was born in Sosnowiec, a town in the province of Katowice in southwest Poland, in 1905 (1907 in the documents). She was the fifth of seven children, five girls and two boys. Her father died in the influenza epidemic toward the end of the First World War, and her mother raised the family by herself, in poverty but with dignity. We stayed with my grandmother during Passover in 1939, when I was four. All I remember of that visit was her *sheitel*, the wig worn by observant Jewish women, which I once saw sitting on a shelf.

We went to see the building where my grandmother and her family had lived when we visited Poland in 1988. Nothing had been done to it in the intervening fifty years. There was still no indoor plumbing. My mother spoke of her childhood home as if it were a palace.

My mother's older sister, Lola, and younger sister, Renia, survived the Holocaust and were taken to Sweden in the last days of the war by the Swedish Red Cross. The other siblings, most of them with their spouses and children, and my grandmother perished by the hands of the Nazis. I'm the only offspring of my mother's side of the family. The Nazis murdered all my cousins. My surviving while they did not is a terrible burden. I've been left with the feeling that I've not done enough for my parents or my surviving aunts. This is by no means the only manifestation of my survivor guilt.

My mother worked as a saleswoman in a Jewish-owned clothing store in Sosnowiec. About a quarter of the town's 100,000 residents were Jews and they seemed to have felt very much at home there. When my father, after serving in the Polish army—something of an ordeal for a Jew, in view of Polish anti-Semitism—came to work in an office in Sosnowiec, he met my mother. There's nothing to suggest a great love between them, and judging by what I witnessed when I was growing up, not much mutual respect and understanding either. But my mother was considered, by the standards of those days, on the verge of becoming an old maid. As she needed someone to boss around and as my father needed to be told what to do, they seemed to suit each other. Happiness was never a factor, it seems. I don't remember either of them ever enjoying life.

What kept them together before they were married was the Party. My father was a member of a socialist Zionist organization called Poale Zion (Left), and my mother joined in its activities. Years later, in Israel, the Party became Achdut Avoda. Politically it was to the left of Mapai, David Ben Gurion's party, and to the right of Hashomer Hatsair. The Sosnowiec branch, which was probably very active, seems to have consisted of young people with relatively little formal education—my father had more schooling than my mother, as evidenced by his greater command of spoken and written Polish—but with a yearning for culture, Jewish and Polish, as a path to self-improvement. My parents would speak of the plays and operas they saw, often travelling to Katowice. It made them feel very sophisticated, especially in the retelling. Unfortunately nothing of their seeming interest in culture survived in their later life. I don't recall them even going to a movie, never mind a play or a concert.

In those days in Poland, despite the occasional visits to the opera or the theatre, it was lectures, given by visiting Party officials and other speakers, that seemed to have been their principal leisure activity. I'm not sure that my parents ever read a book. What they knew, they heard in their youth and, later, what my father read in the papers. My mother's knowledge was always based on hearsay. She pumped people for information and then assimilated it, making it her own. My parents married in 1933 and soon thereafter moved to the small Galician town of Jaslo, where my father was the office manager of a glass factory. They seemed to have led a pleasant middle-class life, with friends and acquaintances. They even had a maid, whom I vaguely remember. Though much smaller than Sosnowiec, Jaslo had a sizable Jewish population, which included factory owners and businessmen who made up the secular Jewish elite. By all accounts, my parents socialized in these circles.

I was born on February 10, 1935. The documents say February 24. To avoid a fine for late registration with the authorities, I was given a later birthday. The delay may have been due to the fact that I was born in my mother's hometown, Sosnowiec; she'd probably wanted to be with her family for the birth. Or the delay may have been caused by the problem with my name. My parents wanted to call me Bernard, but the Polish authorities—in characteristically autocratic fashion—refused to accept the name, declaring it not sufficiently Jewish. They suggested Berl or Berish. But that was too Jewish for my parents, for Jews in Poland climbing the social ladder, as my parents seemed to be doing, wanted Polish names for their children. In the end they settled for the Hebrew name of my grandfather, Dow (the *w* is the equivalent of the Polish *v*), and I've kept the spelling. People called me Belek, but at some point I shed that nickname in favour of Dow.

If Poale Zion held my parents together before they were married, it was I who held them together from the day I was born. My father loved me, even though he had trouble expressing it. My mother was the archetypal woman who married the father and fell in love with the son. For better or worse, I became the centre of their universe. They vied for my attention and my love. My mother knew that I felt much closer to my father, so she smothered me with affection. As late as my early teens, I remember fending off her hugs and kisses. They had no other children, perhaps because of the threat of war. Many Polish Jews of my generation were only children.

My memories of the first four and a half years of my life in Jaslo are pleasant. I remember going with my father to a place that was most likely the local Poale Zion clubhouse, and also once or twice to a coffee shop for cakes. But I don't remember having any friends. In retrospect I wonder whether that was my mother's way of keeping me to herself.

On September 1, 1939, my world collapsed. I mark the date every year as the anniversary of my anxiety neurosis. It was the day Nazi Germany invaded Poland and my mother and I, together with a few others, were taken to the eastern part of the country. The owner of the glassworks where my father worked had a farm outside Lwow (Lviv nowadays) and was prepared to offer us shelter there on the understanding that my father stayed behind to look after the factory. Of course, they all believed that the war would be over in days or weeks and then we would return home and continue life as before.

I recall no details of the journey other than that it was horrendous. The cart that the horses were pulling was full of people and household items. At some point a jar of jam broke and landed on me. It was very sticky and most uncomfortable. I can't bear sticky things to this very day.

That journey marks a rupture and a dramatic end to my childhood. I still long for it.

The Soviet Union:
Exile

I have a distinct memory of standing in the street of the little town of Glinyany, near Lviv, not far from the farm to which we were brought, watching the arrival of refugees fleeing from the Nazi invasion. We were waiting for my father. After what seemed years, but was really only days, he turned up. Like so many others who had stayed behind, he must have realized that the situation was hopeless and decided to save himself. I can still feel the sense of relief when we were reunited, even though I was too young to fully understand what was happening.

Soon thereafter we moved away from the farm. It's not clear to me what my parents did during the year we spent in Glinyany, but I do remember that we lived in one room of a house owned by a woman I knew only as *Di Bassete*. It was apparently the custom in Glinyany that the 2500 Jews who lived there—about half the entire population—call each other by nicknames, not their given names. Our landlady was the widow of a bass player, I believe. Hence her nickname Di Bassete. I recall a man nicknamed *Itche Mensch*. Itche was the diminutive of Yitschok (Isaac), which was his name. He and his father had a dairy. One day the son told his father that one of their cows was sick. He is reported to have said, "*Tate, di kih iz oys mensch,*" which means literally, "Daddy, the cow is no longer a mensch (human being)." To be *oys mensch*

5

in Yiddish is to be barely human, that is, about to die. Since people in general, and Jews in particular, don't like to utter words like "die," *oys mensch* was the euphemism used, in this case even about a cow. A woman I remember was called *Rifke Fuy*. Apparently this Rifka (Rebecca) used to spit at things. The Yiddish *fuy* denotes something negative that imitates the sound of spitting.

Some time in the 1970s, when my wife, Fredzia, and I were sitting at one of the long tables in the guesthouse of kibbutz Ayelet Hashachar, I got talking to the man opposite me. He told me he was visiting from Brazil, but had originally come from Galicia. "Where in Galicia?" I asked. "A place nobody has ever heard of," he replied. "Try me," I urged him. He replied, "It's called Glinyany." When I told him that I had spent a year of my childhood there, he became animated. When I recited the few nicknames I remembered, he was almost ecstatic and wouldn't let me go in the hope that I'd remember more. I became a kind of witness to his past, albeit a poor witness. There are, in fact, several books about the history of the Jews in Glinyany, who settled there in the Middle Ages, as well as records about what happened to them in the Holocaust. Whether or not he knew about these books and records, it was obvious that what he really was looking for was a live connection.

The language I was taught at home was Polish, because my parents had assimilationist ambitions and didn't want me to pollute my Polish with Yiddishisms, something that many bilingual Polish Jews did. One of the many ambitions of my parents' generation of Jews was to speak Polish like educated Poles. Of course, they themselves spoke Yiddish to each other. But Di Bassete knew no Polish, so she taught me Yiddish. Thanks to her, a whole world of culture and wisdom was opened to me. I speak Yiddish to this very day, not very well and with the accent of Jews from Poland, but I speak it and I read it and I feel it, without the romance that some of my contemporaries have attached to it. And I don't giggle each time a Yiddish word is mentioned, which has become the way of many westernized Jews.

I had no sense of what was happening in the world at that time. I still had no friends my own age, so I accompanied my parents wherever they went. We used to spend a lot of time in the home of the Leniower family, who later went with us to Siberia. They must have thought that I was cute and they got me talking. Each time we came home, my mother would read me the riot act, because I had said something I shouldn't have, betrayed some family secret. Of course, I didn't understand what was really going on. She even developed a technique: each time I opened my mouth she would kick me. If she couldn't reach me she would snort at me. She kept this up into my teens until one day I told her that if she did it again, I would announce to those present what she was doing and why she was doing it. She stopped.

Though it took me many years before I could articulate my mother's need to control me, I understood it on some level from my very early years. My father's inability to talk sense into her pained me greatly. In a way it still does, even though he has been dead for more than three decades. As I write this, I become aware that recalling my childhood isn't enough to dispel its demons.

My comparatively comfortable world of Glinyany came to an end one night in 1940, when my parents and I were awoken by a loud knocking on the door. "Who is it?" my mother asked. "The NKVD," was the reply. When the Soviet secret service men entered, they told us: "You've registered to go back home, so we've come to take you to the railway station for the return journey. As you are going home and as there'll be a lot of people on the train, you'll only be able to take very little luggage with you."

My parents, like so many other refugees from German-occupied Poland, had indicated to the Soviet authorities that they wanted to go back to Poland. Because of the concordat between the Soviet Union and Nazi Germany—the so-called Molotov-Ribbentrop pact, named after the respective foreign ministers of the two countries—that divided Poland between them, and placed Lviv on the Soviet side, it was possible to correspond with relatives and friends across the border. Whatever the people on the German side may have written, we on the Soviet side interpreted their words to mean that their living conditions were reasonably tolerable. The fact that the writers feared German censors may not have occurred to us.

So great was their hatred of the Communists that my parents, like many other refugees from Poland, assumed that their situation on the

Soviet side was worse than on the German side. They probably found it incomprehensible that the Germans, who were the model for all Jews who aspired to culture and integration, would turn out to be the perpetrators of genocide. In hindsight, of course, it was utter stupidity. Jews were returning by the thousands to Nazi-occupied Poland, not understanding the horror that awaited them.

Toward the end of 1940 it became clear that the agreement between Nazi Germany and Soviet Russia wouldn't hold. Hitler's plans to conquer the world wouldn't allow for it. So Stalin prepared for war. Because our people had, as it were, chosen the German side, they were considered a security risk and therefore had to be removed to the part of Russia where all security risks, real and imagined, were taken: Siberia.

The NKVD had come to take us there under the pretext of taking us home. I don't remember any elation at the prospect of our leaving Glinyany. The officers insisted that we couldn't take our things with us—so that they could help themselves to them as soon as we were out of the way.

My parents' stupidity in registering to go back saved our lives. Had we stayed behind, as prudence dictated, we would soon have come under German rule when, not long thereafter, Lviv and other regions of the Soviet empire were occupied. We would have perished, as did most of our relatives. Since those days I've come to realize that it's not human wisdom that makes for survival but that strange mixture of divine providence and sheer luck. To this very day, I put my trust in providence, with humility and in gratitude. It's the foundation of my faith.

I was petrified from the moment the NKVD men entered our room. I watched my parents throw a few things into a couple of suitcases. Soon we were on the cart that would take us to the station. By mistake, I'm sure, one of the soldiers who accompanied us put his foot on top of mine. His boot was large and heavy and it hurt. But I was too frightened to say anything. I can still remember the pain of that journey. It was an omen for things to come.

At the railway station I saw many people I had known in Glinyany and what seemed like hundreds of others. We were going "home." The

Russians shoved us into boxcars and sealed them. As we arrived at other stations, more cars were added to the train. It didn't take long for the adults to realize that we weren't going to Poland. So where were they taking us? There was much speculation. "Probably to Birobidjan," some of the adults said. Birobidjan was Stalin's attempt to provide an alleged counterpart to Palestine by creating a "Jewish national home" in the east of his Soviet empire; it didn't attract many Jews. Perhaps taking us there was part of the plan to populate it. After all, Stalin was known for moving populations to suit his political ends.

Then came the humour that I learned to live with in the course of the following years and that turned out to be a reliable tool of survival and sanity: "What happens if we arrive in Birobidjan on the Sabbath? Will the station master greet us wearing a *streimel* (the traditional Sabbath-best hat of Hasidic Jews)?" When the train passed a lake, which turned out to be Lake Baykal, and I asked what it was called, one of the grown-ups replied, "The Sambatyon." (The Sambatyon is a mythical river in Jewish folklore that flows backwards on the Sabbath.) I believed him. This five-year-old knew nothing about either Baykal or Sambatyon.

At some point the Soviet officer in charge of the train was looking for someone to take responsibility for the human cargo being taken to an as-yet-undisclosed destination. My father looked like a natural leader, and so the officer offered him the job. My father refused. It was the first of many such refusals he made. I was disappointed, because I wanted to be the son of someone important. It took me years to realize that, on the one hand, my father needed to be led, not to lead. On the other hand, I've also come to appreciate that to survive in times of crisis, it's prudent to be as ordinary as possible. Not to be given a badge by those in power saves not only one's soul but also one's body, because despotic bosses tend to dispose of gullible collaborators. The fate of the Jewish Kapos in Nazi concentration camps is a case in point. I'd like to think that, in similar circumstances, I'd have acted in the same way, but I'm not sure, for I'm ambitious. Perhaps becoming a rabbi enabled me to be *somebody* and yet remain on the straight and narrow path of decency and morality.

We were finally allowed to alight for short spells, usually to relieve ourselves—until that point we'd had to use a bucket, the stench of which I still recall—and to pick up rations. The most precious of these was *kibyatok*, hot water from the train engine. It gradually dawned on the adults that we were on our way to Siberia. Some six weeks later, we arrived.

I often think of my childhood when I read about the terrible conditions that bring refugees from countries like Cuba or Kurdistan to freedom. I feel that I've been there. The difference is, of course, that today's fugitives believe that they are making their way to freedom and a better life, if not for themselves, then for their children. We, on the other hand, were making the reverse journey, from what seemed freedom to what was certain incarceration.

When we got to the end of the railway line, we were loaded onto trucks and taken another several hundred kilometres into the Siberian taiga, or forest, where the gold mines were. When we finally reached the compound where we were to stay, the local commandant, a Volga German who must have been taken there in "protective custody" too, assembled us and said, "Here you've come to live and here you'll die." I could hear loud crying all around me. The place we were brought to could have been called Hope Abandoned.

In the manner to which I'd get accustomed in the next six years, several families were put into the same hut. The large stove in the middle was to enable us to keep warm and to cook our food. The men would work in the forest cutting trees to provide both fuel and building material. Since our huts were built of wood, when winter set in—which lasted nine to ten months—water was poured over the outside walls. It froze and gave protection from the cold. As a result, it was quite cozy in the huts. There was plenty of wood for keeping the stoves going.

The women were also sent to work. They had to make tightly wrapped bundles of the branches of the trees the men had cut down. These were used to plug leaks in the gold mines. At the time, the grown-ups thought they had literally reached the end of the line, but I myself didn't feel much hardship. I even found a playmate, my first friend. Occasionally he and I would go outdoors for a few minutes, but our parents worried that our faces would freeze in the minus-forty-degree temperatures.

The commandants, both junior and senior to the one who had told us the news about our future, would come and visit, for they were starved of human companionship and we made a nice change from the prisoners they normally had to look after. Our group even organized a little band. We had a klezmer family among us, and they had brought their instruments. When a commandant asked one of the women to dance, the band played the tune of the Hatikva (the Hope), which later became Israel's national anthem. It was a way to counteract the notion of hope abandoned.

On another occasion a very senior commandant came to visit and seated me on his lap; the Russians are notoriously sentimental, especially about little children. He asked me which soldiers I preferred, the Russians or the Poles. Later in life, whenever I had reason to refer to the midrash about baby Moses being exposed to a plate of gold and a plate of burning charcoal, I thought of my experience in our Siberian hut. The Pharaoh's Egyptian advisers told him that if Moses goes for the gold, he is bad news for Egypt; if he goes for the charcoal, the Pharaoh had nothing to fear. As the baby reached out to the gold, an angel pushed him, so legend has it, toward the coal. Thus was his life saved, but because he, in the fashion of babies, tried to put the coal in his mouth, he was left with a permanent speech impediment.

Thank God, I don't have a speech impediment, but my reply to the Russian commandant did endanger our existence, for there was no angel on hand to prompt me to give the "right" answer. I had remembered a picture of a Polish soldier in the characteristic hat of the Polish military—perhaps it was a photograph of my father—and so I told the Russian that I preferred Polish soldiers. In answer to his question why, I told him about the hat and also gave a second reason: the Russians stink. It was true. The material from which Russian uniforms were made had a distinct odour. When soaked in sweat—the soldiers had limited washing facilities—the material, and by association its wearer, emitted a terrible stench. Sitting on the officer's lap made me a victim of it.

As soon as I had finished speaking, the commandant put me down on the floor and left the room abruptly. Our entire group, men, women and children, turned against me, expecting me, at age five, to understand what I had done. I don't remember being comforted by my parents. After the first wave of abuse, I heard a voice of sanity. Someone said, "So what will they do to us? Send us to Siberia? We are already there!" The little mob calmed down and I returned to the bunk that my parents and I regarded as home. Of course, there were no repercussions from the Soviet authorities. The officer was more mature than my fellow inmates.

When the Soviets became partners in the war against the Nazis, Stalin looked for allies wherever he could find them. He even shelved his anti-Semitic measures for a few years. One of his allies was the decidedly anti-Communist Polish government in exile residing in London. In August 1941 its leader, General Wladyslaw Sikorski, negotiated an agreement with Stalin that would allow Polish citizens to live anywhere in the Soviet Union in the hope that this would encourage them to play their part in the Allied war effort. Indeed, acting on behalf of the Polish government, General Wladyslaw Anders was freed from a prison under Soviet control to recruit Polish men to serve in a special regiment to fight the Germans. Many Jewish Poles joined as well, particularly those who had no family ties. I have a vague memory of my father being rejected, to the great jubilation of all concerned.

I also remember that one of the Poles with us in Siberia was Jan Kwapinski, a well-known Polish socialist politician. I have no recollection of him commanding much respect among us. There was no privacy in our lives, and like all of us, he had to submit to frequent delousing sessions. Lice were the only pets of my childhood, but unlike normal pets, these brought me constant discomfort and no pleasure other than that gained by killing them. We were impressed when we heard that later Kwapinski became a member of the Polish government in exile.

As a result of General Sikorski's agreement with Stalin, Polish citizens could now travel wherever they wanted within the Soviet Union. Though the prudent thing would have been to stay where we were, my parents and many others were most anxious to get out of Siberia because of the "end of the world" connotation this region has for people. Perhaps they also had a need to prove the commandant wrong. He told them that they would live and die there. They knew better. Another vindication of Jewish hope. However, if wanting to leave

Glinyany saved our lives, the desire to leave Siberia nearly killed us. Once again, not prudence but providence ruled.

My parents and their friends had two criteria in the choice of the new location: the place had to be warm and it should be close to Palestine. That was how we came to the Soviet Republic of Uzbekistan.

Another long journey, this time in a passenger train. My only distinct memory of it is my foray into another compartment where a group of men were sitting. They looked jolly and friendly and, by then, I must have known enough Russian to respond to their invitation to join them. Soon I had a glass of clear liquid in my hand and they asked me to drink it. I did. It was vodka. The next thing I remember is my distraught parents "rescuing" me from the unwelcome company. Later I was told that they were former criminals who, having served their jail term in Siberia, were now free and on their way home. In the same way as we weren't former criminals returning from Siberia, it's possible that they weren't criminals but political prisoners given their freedom to serve in the armed forces.

Virtually all my memories of encounters with Russians are pleasant. Like a lot of people used to hardships, they had a charming way of enjoying life at every opportunity, despite their burdens. Of course, vodka helped. Though drunkenness has always been a very serious problem in Russia, and still is, most Russians who drink aren't drunks. Vodka for them is a way of coping with life; only for a minority is it a way of escaping life altogether.

After weeks on the train, this time as ostensibly free people, with interminable changes in unfamiliar railway stations and the anxieties that went with each of them, we finally reached Tashkent, the capital of Uzbekistan. Since a lot of people like us ended up in that city, there was no accommodation and no work. I remember sleeping in a park, probably for several weeks. One day I'd like to see the city properly.

The only way for my parents and their circle to get settled in Uzbekistan was to go to a *kolkhoz*, a Soviet collective farm imposed on the hapless Uzbeks. That's how we landed in a place named after a famed Uzbek Communist, Achum Babayev. It was a few kilometres from a little town called Altarik and some twenty kilometres from the

large Uzbek city of Fergana. The authorities removed the owner of
one of the huts in the village, now the *kolkhoz*, on the grounds that he
had another home, and we were placed there. The hut had one large
and one small room and nothing else. In the large room stood three
bunks; in the small one was a fourth, and this was where the Sznall
family lived—a mother with a daughter, Chaya, and two sons, Szloyme
and Szulem, all three children unmarried adults.

In the larger room with my parents and me lived the Leniower family, our friends from Glinyany. The family consisted of Mr. and Mrs.
Leniower, their three daughters—the twins Fryda and Hanka and a
younger daughter, Ella—and Mrs. Leniower's brother-in-law, Mr. Ajzen.
As was customary in those circles, people addressed each other by
their surnames. When they were formal with each other, they prefixed
the surnames with *Pan* for men and *Pani* for women, the Polish equiv-
alents of Mr. and Mrs. That's why I don't remember the first names of
most of the adults we knew; I probably never heard them.

Also in the large room lived Mrs. Sidwerts and her adult son. That
made eleven of us in the large room and four in the other room, all of
whom used the wood-fuelled stove in the larger room for cooking.
Whatever possessions we had were stored under our bunks, except the
food, because the rats would eat it. So the provisions, mainly grain,
were hung in sacks from the walls. I can still see the hut now and I
know exactly where everybody slept. I even remember waking up on
occasion because of my parents' panting. It took me years to understand what they were doing. I assume that if I heard it, so did the others. Lack of privacy deprives people of their dignity.

There were other similar huts where Polish-Jewish refugees were
billeted (unlike in Siberia, there seems to have been no non-Jews here).
I remember going to visit at least two such places in our village, but the
inhabitants were less central in my universe.

Our hut was my cosmos, and it was not without discord. I recall
especially one almighty fight over the hanging sacks of grain. Mr.
Leniower was caught helping himself to our supply. Of course, there
was no way of breaking off relations as a result, because we lived in
the same room. On another occasion I recall a row between Mrs.
Leniower and my mother. I've a vague memory that the reason was the

threat of our moving somewhere else. The grown-ups may have hated each other, but they couldn't live without one another. The years together turned us into a kind of family, albeit a dysfunctional one. The thought of my parents and me going elsewhere seems to have been perceived by those doomed to stay behind as something of a betrayal. It took me years to realize that the quarrels and the fights in our hut were not manifestations of hatred but only expressions of frustration, even despair.

In the rainy season, the situation worsened, because the rain came through the roof and made sleeping in the hut impossible. Also, the provisions had to be taken off the walls for protection. The hut did have a dry niche. I was allowed to sleep there, as long as I was small enough to fit. In the summer, we had to sleep outdoors because of the bugs, which seem to be far more menacing inside. But there were other dangers in the open air—scorpions, for example. One once bit my father.

The hut stood at the edge of the village and was surrounded by some fruit trees and cultivated fields. Whatever grew there didn't belong to us, yet we helped ourselves to what was available, mostly fruit, usually before it ripened, when its owners—either the collective or an individual farmer—would come to claim it. I doubt whether they ever found any fruit to claim. Since there was hardly any work for the adults, we all lived on what they could steal. Our only contribution was the natural manure we provided, for needless to say, there were no toilet facilities. Another manifestation of the lack of privacy.

The most successful thief was Szulem Sznall. He could climb trees like nobody else and he could find things in places no one else was looking. He was my hero. The closest I came to him was when he shaved my head periodically. (In view of the lice that plagued our existence, long hair wasn't prudent.) Despite the pain, for the cutting tool was blunt, I enjoyed Szulem's attention. Many years later I met him on one of his visits to his sister, Chaya, in Toronto. I had remembered him as a giant, but now he was a short, shrivelled man who addressed me as Rabbi. He earned his living as a plumber in Philadelphia. Probably he was one of those people in whom the hardships of war brought out the best, whereas ordinary living reduced him to the ranks.

My parents weren't adept at stealing, so my mother worked as a cleaner and night "watchman" at a men's hostel some distance away; my father tried to help feed us by transporting stolen goods. Once a week he walked during the day to Fergana, where he knew people who worked in the local plant turning the cotton that grew in the area into oil, soap and cloth. Some of what they stole he would carry back during the night, and my mother and I would sell it in the weekly market in Altarik the following day. That, too, was dangerous, so my father would stay away from the market area and lie low in a secure place. Neither my mother nor I ever carried more than one item of stolen merchandise, so that if it was stolen from us, or if the police caught us, the loss wouldn't be total. Whenever we sold an item, we'd find my father and get more.

I was particularly adept at selling. Soap was my specialty. Because I was a kid, the Muslim women would lift their veils and allow me to negotiate face to face. This enabled them to spit on the small pieces of soap to see if they were genuine before they decided to buy. I also learned the Uzbek language quickly and must have been sufficiently cute to charm them. For security reasons I stuffed all cash received into one of my boots before going to my father to prepare for the next sale. If I had a successful day, walking became increasingly uncomfortable. I can still feel the relief when, at the end of the day, I would sit down on our bunk at home, my father would pull off my boots, and the bundles of money would fall out. Of course, we had to be as discreet as possible, because the envy of the others knew no bounds.

Knowing the language had other advantages. In one of the neighbouring huts lived Dr. Perlberger, a physician, and her son, Rysiek. (He and I were the same age and we played together—not with toys, for such things didn't exist.) Like all the other refugees, including her son, the doctor didn't know Uzbekish, which made communication with her patients difficult. She therefore offered me the opportunity to accompany her—on foot, of course—around our village and the surrounding villages as an interpreter. Apparently it worked well, even though I had no idea what I was interpreting. I felt very important and loved it.

The locals greatly appreciated the doctor's ministrations, even though, I imagine, there wasn't much she could do for the patients, most of whom had to drink the polluted water from the brook that flowed through the village. One of my tasks at home was to walk upstream a distance to make sure that no animal was standing in the brook defecating while one of the adults was fetching water.

The Perlbergers had, by our standards, a wealthy household. The doctor had a housekeeper and nobody there seemed to go hungry. One painful incident stands out in my mind. The housekeeper was frying meat and the smell was beguiling. I'd eaten hardly any meat from the day we'd left our home in Jaslo years before. Rysiek offered to steal a piece for me. The housekeeper caught him and we were both severely reprimanded. I was made to feel like a criminal. I had known that, in order to survive, virtually all of us refugees stole from the state or engaged in selling stolen goods from state-owned enterprises, as I myself did, and it had never occurred to me theft as something to be ashamed of. But neither the smell of that meat nor the pain of being caught has ever faded from my memory.

My knowledge of both the Uzbek and the Russian languages turned me, at the tender age of six, into the public relations officer for our little group of Polish Jews, a position I held till we left when I was eleven. My knowledge of Russian came from a Russian novel, the middle part of which I'd found when we were still in Siberia. I remember going around asking people to tell me what the letters meant. In the end I could read the text and I read aloud, mainly to myself, what I found on the pages. Since neither the beginning nor the end of that novel were extant, I never knew the title, author or full content of the book. But knowing Uzbekish and being able to read the Russian Cyrillic script, I could now read the local Uzbek newspaper. Uzbekish, being a Turkish language, had followed the motherland and abandoned the old script in favour of the current one. Like the Turks, the Uzbeks are Muslims with a taste for modernity. Although by now I'm sure that most Uzbeks can read and write, at the time it appeared that I was the only one who could. As a result, the locals would come to our hut and bring the latest issue of the newspaper, asking me to read it to them so that they could know what was going on in the world. I have a feeling that this, together with the presence of a doctor among us, greatly improved the relationship between the villagers and the aliens who invaded their territory, which is what we must have seemed.

Being treated as an adult was a mixed blessing. I remember particularly one incident when someone wanted to know where Ella Leniower was. I volunteered the answer: "I saw her and Szlojme Sznall go behind the bushes over there." Her sisters turned on me with unheard-of ferocity, which I couldn't fathom. Someone had asked a question. Being accustomed to provide answers, I said what I knew. It was many years before I worked out the cause of the sisters' ire.

I had Uzbek playmates in the village. With their help I could be a child now and again. One of them had reached the age of circumcision, according to Muslim practice, and I was part of the pack of kids who roamed the village in anticipation on the day of the evening ceremony. We spent time watching the village barber, who was to perform the ritual, sharpening his knife. It looked gruesome. The fact that I was already circumcised gave me considerable status among my peers. In the evening we all gathered around the barber and watched him do his job. The only antiseptic he had was tar. I saw my freshly circumcised friend a few days later. He had survived the act, but said he was very sore.

I don't remember a mosque in our village and I don't remember much Jewish practice either. Mr. Ajzen and Mr. Sidwerts were observant and put on tefillin, phylacteries, regularly at their morning prayers. I also remember at least one Passover celebration, even the baking of matzah. Being the youngest in the group I was to recite the traditional *Mah Nishtana*, the four questions that challenge the grown-ups to tell why the night of the Passover Seder is different from all other nights. Szloyme Sznall taught them to me by rote in Ashkenazi Hebrew with Yiddish translation. My first Jewish text!

Being hungry is my most persistent memory of the five years we lived in Uzbekistan. There was never enough to eat, even though the situation eased a little with time. The hunger was probably more bearable because everybody was hungry, locals and refugees alike. When I was nine or ten I was allowed to ask for a birthday present. I asked for an egg. I can still recall the taste of that egg. No food has ever tasted that good since. The end of war, the adults told me, would mean that there would be enough to eat. They insisted that that was all they wanted in life. My father argued with the others, suggesting that once they had enough to eat, they'd want other things. Of course, he was right. The arguments about things other than food started on the train back to Poland.

Being lonely was my next most persistent memory of the war years. Other than Rysiek Perlberger and a few boys in the village, I had no friends. The adults, my parents included, were too preoccupied with their own problems to pay much attention to me other than when I was useful to them. The life my family led wasn't normal in any sense, nor was my upbringing. Though I was too young to grasp everything that was going on, I understood some of what I read in the newspaper to the local villagers, and I listened to the conversations of adult refugees, both in our hut and in several neighbouring huts. So I was aware that things were bad, even though nobody tried to explain why they were bad. I had vague memories of my pre-war childhood, but no real sense of what was normal.

The world baffled me and frightened me. It baffled me when, for example, some of the younger adults took me to see a film based on Chekhov's *The Three Sisters*. I couldn't understand how the actors could hide behind the screen and never come out at the end of the performance. None of the adults had the patience or the knowledge to explain to me the rudiments of film.

But mostly the world frightened me. I recall especially a few weeks when my parents, together with many other adults in our circle, went to prison. They were jailed for refusing to become Soviet citizens out of fear that this would prevent them from ever returning to Poland. I remember being left with Mrs. Sidwerts and Mrs. Leniower; there may have been others too, but I don't recall any. I do remember walking a few miles every day to stand outside the prison in the hope of hearing some news or catching a glimpse of my parents. Visitors were not allowed to go in, so we stood on the road. Some brought food to give to their imprisoned relatives; I hope some was shared with my parents, for I was obviously in no position to feed them. Writing about it now, I'm surprised at not having been particularly traumatized by the experience. The dysfunctional extended family in the hut provided a kind of security, I suppose.

My parents and the other prisoners finally realized the futility of their protest and became Soviet citizens. As a result, they were freed and I was greatly relieved.

The end of the war didn't bring immediate changes. I well remember the day, probably May 10, 1945, when an Uzbek came to our hut to tell us that the Second World War had come to an end. He had heard it on the only radio in the village, near the *kolkhoz* office. I was the only one at home; the others were out in the fields picking sugar beets. I ran to tell them the news and was surprised that they weren't more excited. In retrospect I understand why. First, they had followed the news sufficiently to know that the end of Nazi Germany was nigh. Second, they would also have surmised that the end of the war didn't necessarily mean the end of our exile. It had always been relatively easy to get into the Soviet Union, but not to get out.

It took another year of anguish, speculation and negotiation with the authorities before we were on our way back to Poland. There were bureaucratic delays, and the fact that we had become Soviet citizens by then may also have caused complications. But finally, almost a year to the day after the end of the war, we were on a train heading home.

It was on that train journey that the relationship between the members of our group began to change. During our five years together, the Sznalls had dominated. Though seemingly less educated and less urbane than the others, they had more survival skills than the rest of us and so did relatively well. Chaya even acquired a wristwatch in some barter deal. She wore it proudly, albeit on a piece of string. The Nussbaums, who'd lived in one of the neighbouring huts with their relatives, the Mondscheins, were probably the least adaptable and may not have survived without the help of people like the Sznalls. The Nussbaums had been wealthy before the war, but in times of crisis hadn't any idea how to manage things. They had a nephew with them, Heniek, who would have been in his twenties at the time and whom they treated as their son; they may even have adopted him formally. I remember once going into their hut and seeing Heniek standing stark naked on the family bunk while his aunt washed his lower body. It made a great impression on me, for I didn't know that an adult could be treated like a child. But it seems that Heniek had never had to do things for himself, so that even now his aunt was his nursemaid. This fact gave rise to a lot of mirth, perhaps even contempt, on the part of the other refugees in the village.

Now on the train the roles were being reversed. In Uzbekistan we'd always treated the Sznalls with respect and the Nussbaums with ridicule, not least because of the way they doted on Heniek. But during the journey home I heard a bitter quarrel between Chaya Sznall and Mrs. Nussbaum. "I've always been a lady and I'll always remain a lady," Mrs. Nussbaum said to Chaya. "You were always a peasant and you'll remain a peasant." By the time we disembarked a couple of weeks later, the various families dispersed and had little future contact with one another. Even though Chaya Sznall, the husband she married a few weeks after our return and their children and grandchildren now live in Toronto, we don't have any sort of relationship, because all we have in common is a past that by now has largely faded from memory, at least from mine.

My memories of these squabbles between the various individuals and families pale in comparison to the experience of entering Poland again. As we arrived to Przemyslany, the first Polish town the train came to after crossing the border, many Poles were standing at the station and staring at us in apparent disbelief. They hadn't come to greet long-lost compatriots but to voice their displeasure that so many Jews had survived, after all. Though the overwhelming majority of Poland's three and a half million Jews had been annihilated by Hitler, Polish anti-Semitism seemed to have remained intact, for you don't need to know Jews or live with them to hate them. Many years later I had reason to object to blanket condemnations by Jews of all Poles as anti-Semites, yet the memory of that border crossing has stayed with me. My liberal attitude came from my head; my prejudices are stuck in my gut.

Until the time of our return to Poland, the adults seemed to believe that many of our relatives had survived. When the Red Army was advancing into Poland and we heard stories of German atrocities against the Jews, my parents and their friends refused to believe the stories and tended to say they were just Soviet propaganda designed to stir up hatred of the enemy. Even then my parents and their friends were prepared to trust the Germans rather than the Soviets. The truth, I suppose, was too painful for them. Hope may have sustained them during the war years, but the despair that now replaced it devastated them. For they could now see with their own eyes that the only ones waiting for them were disappointed Poles.

At age eleven, despite the fact that the war had robbed me of a normal childhood, I found it difficult to fathom what was going on, but I could *feel* what was happening. I could sense the despair and I could see the fatigue. My parents and their friends may have had enough inner resources to withstand the almost seven years of exile and pain, from the day they fled Poland in September 1939 to the day they returned there in June 1946, but it was by no means certain that they would find the strength to continue. That those whom they had left behind, those whom they'd wanted to rejoin, had perished was almost too much for them.

The only pleasant moment I recall during the days our train moved across Poland was a stop at a station where members of a Zionist youth group greeted us with singing and dancing. They were preparing to go to Eretz Israel, the Land of Israel—in those days still called Palestine and understood to mean the Zionist homeland—to start a new life. It took me many years to realize that that was the moment I became a Zionist. Much of what I've written about Zionism in later years goes back, it seems, to that experience.

In all the years in the Soviet Union, and perhaps even before, I don't remember anybody being happy, including myself. But the young people on the train platform exuded joy and hope. It must be, I assumed, because they were on the way out to a better life in another place. I wished I could join them, but I was only eleven, and soon the train continued toward the city of Szczecin, formerly Stettin, in Lower Silesia.

The defeat of Nazi Germany and Communist domination of postwar Poland, resulted in Eastern Poland becoming part of the Soviet Union and some of Eastern Germany becoming part of Poland. Because the indigenous German population in the new Polish territories had been expelled, the authorities were anxious that the new arrivals from the Soviet Union should settle there. That was why our destination was the city of Sczecin. It had been heavily bombed by the Allies during the war and all I remember of it are ruins. We lived on the ground floor of a house the rest of which had been destroyed. We couldn't imagine a future there. So my father travelled to Sosnowiec as soon as that was possible. He found there an old friend from his Poale Zion days who arranged a job for him in the Jewish Community Council. He returned to take us back.

I remember that train journey too. My mother told me not to speak lest I said something that might betray my Jewishness. That was the climate those days in Poland. Nowadays when I travel in Poland, I make a point of wearing a *kippa* or skullcap, which I normally don't do, to almost flaunt my Jewishness. So far nobody has attacked me. Perhaps things have changed in the intervening half century.

Formally, this chapter describing our seven years in the Soviet Union should now come to a close. But I feel that though we had come back, we hadn't come home. We were still refugees, albeit now in our native land. Therefore, the description of our almost two years in post-war Poland belongs to this section. Physically we were in Poland; emotionally we remained in Uzbekistan. My life was still a life of danger.

A remnant of the Poale Zion group to which my parents belonged before they were married seemed to have been fairly active in the region. It had a makeshift kibbutz in Sosnowiec and a kibbutz for children in nearby Katowice. The purpose of these kibbutzim was to prepare young people for life in the Land of Israel. They would engage in menial work, for that was the kibbutz ideal, and they would learn Hebrew, for that was the language of Zion restored. Poale Zion also had at its disposal an apartment where two families already lived in its two rooms. My parents and I were now housed in the kitchen where the three of us would also share a bed. The toilet was outside and there was no bathroom.

To ease the congestion, I was sent to the children's kibbutz in Katowice to prepare for life in the Jewish homeland. I was extremely miserable there and so was allowed to come home after a few weeks. Nothing of the joy I had observed at that railway station could be found here. Though I was well accustomed to collective living, I had not been taught how to live even semi-independently. During my stay in Katowice I would write to my parents from time to time; telephones had yet not reached my orbit. First I wrote in Polish, which suggests that at some point I was taught to read and write the language, though

I have no memory of it. But after a while I began to write in Yiddish, which I must have learned in the children's kibbutz. My parents objected. It seemed that even now they wanted me to know Polish well; they hadn't yet quite given up their assimilationist ambitions.

Since there was really no room for the three of us in the kitchen during the day, we spent most of our time in the small kibbutz apartment in the centre of Sosnowiec, where there was hardly enough room for the residents. When I came back from Katowice, I slept in this kibbutz, another joyless place. A young man, David Szwimmer, allowed me to share his bed. I wetted it often. Why he let me in, I don't know. Today I would have suspected him of less-than-pure motives, but I have no memory of any sexual impropriety. As the residents in the other rooms of the apartment where my parents were staying moved out, we were allowed to occupy them. For the first time in seven years I had a bed of my own.

Soon after I returned from the children's kibbutz, a Hebrew-speaking school, in the tradition of the pre-war secular Zionist *tarbut* schools, was established in Sosnowiec. This was the next attempt to educate me. I had been a pupil in the school in Altarik, the town next to our *kolkhoz* in Uzbekistan, but only for a few months and, as I recall, sporadically. Now I was to go to a proper school. Because of the anti-Semitism in Poland, my parents wouldn't send me to the local state school. The Hebrew school was considered more appropriate, especially since we, too, were planning to leave for Palestine as soon as circumstances permitted.

The school was one room, and there were two teachers and a dozen or so children of different ages. Though arithmetic and the Polish language were part of the curriculum, the emphasis was on Hebrew, Jewish history and the geography of Palestine. When I started learning Hebrew, I forgot, almost immediately, all my Uzbekish. To this very day, I recall only a few words of a language I spoke freely for almost six years. The only phrases that seem still to stick are the profanities.

The one-room school in Sosnowiec couldn't sustain itself, because very few children had survived, and those who had soon left the country with their families, mostly for Palestine. After a few months the school merged with its counterpart in Katowice. I now had to take the streetcar from Sosnowiec to Katowice every day. Travelling on public transport was apparently considered safer for a Jewish child than attending a local Polish school.

My clearest memory of that school is my friendship with a boy called Chilek, the diminutive of Yechiel. He, his older brother and I were inseparable. Theirs was an observant family and their home was my first experience of traditional Judaism. Chilek and his brother went to the local heder, the traditional place for Jewish religious education for children, a few afternoons a week. I joined them. It was a makeshift establishment consisting of a few rooms in an old building—all the synagogues in the city had been destroyed, of course—with an old-fashioned teacher who was strong in corporal punishment but weak in almost everything else. He calculated the day of my bar mitzvah and began to instruct me in anticipation. I have no memory of learning anything, but I remember creating something of a problem for the teacher and the other Jews who were sitting around the little *Beit Hamidrash*, the House of Study. The only Hebrew I had learned was at my school, and it followed the modern, so-called Sephardic pronunciation used in Eretz Israel. The heder used the Ashkenazi pronunciation of Polish Jewry. Since I couldn't master both, I was allowed to say my blessings in the Hebrew I knew. The teacher made fun of my "goyish" way of speaking. He was less than happy about this concession to modernity. In the fashion of the ultra-Orthodox, even after the Holocaust, he was also opposed to Zionism, which my pronunciation epitomized.

A couple of weeks before the designated day for my bar mitzvah, I informed my parents of what was about to take place. They were stunned. It had never even occurred to them to expose me to Judaism. Like so many in their circle, they wanted me to know Hebrew, but not to pray. They wanted me to be Jewish, but not to practice Judaism. My parents now asked me if they were expected to attend the ceremony. I didn't know. Since it was to take place on a Monday or a Thursday (I no longer remember which) and women didn't attend such services, my mother said that she wasn't coming. My father decided to come and, as an afterthought, took with him a bottle of vodka to celebrate the event. I don't remember much of what happened during the Torah reading, other than that everybody was pleased, especially once the vodka had been consumed.

My most vivid memory is leaving the room that served as a synagogue. Its rabbi, Rabbi Engelhard, walked between my father and myself with one arm around each of us, saying to all who wanted to hear that "this boy will one day be a rabbi." It was perceived, probably by all three of us, as a joke. Rabbi Engelhard left for what was to become the State of Israel soon thereafter and settled in the ultra-Orthodox community of Bnei Brak, where he was regarded as something of a sage, with several claims to prescience. He knew of my existence because his friend from Sosnowiec, the late Dr. Jacob Maitlis, whom I knew and often visited in London, told him about me. But there is no evidence that he ever included my career in his record of prophecies come true.

I recall no other celebration, but I got my first watch as a kind of bar mitzvah present. I may have been excited, but I don't think I was happy. Happiness was not part of our lives.

The few moments of pleasure that I recall from those days were linked to my membership in a youth group of the Poale Zion party, known in Yiddish as *Borochov Yugend* (Borochov Youth). Ber Borochov, a Zionist revolutionary in Russia, was the founder of Poale Zion. We were told that we were his heirs and had to complete the work he had left undone due to his untimely death in the influenza epidemic in 1917. I read his magnum opus in Yiddish, *Di klassn interessn un di natsionale frage* (Class Factors in the National Question), but I didn't understand much of his effort to combine Marxism with Zionism. Yet, it may have influenced my socialist Zionism more than I've been conscious of.

The most memorable activity from that period was the march we made on May Day 1947 through the main street of Sosnowiec, dressed in blue shirts with red ties and holding a red flag. I'm not sure we were allowed to display the blue-and-white flag too, for Soviet Communism was taking hold of Poland. The anthem of Poale Zion also made a great impression on me, especially the phrase, *Mir shvern, mir shvern, mir shvern, a shvue fun blut un fun trern* (We swear, we swear, we swear, an oath of blood and tears). Membership in the group gave me a sense of belonging, at least for a few months.

The letters my parents coached me to write in Polish were primarily to Lola and Renia (Regina), my mother's two sisters, who now lived in

Gothenburg, Sweden. In the last weeks of the war, in April 1945, the Swedish Red Cross had obtained permission to rescue Jewish women in the concentration camps. It was Himmler's attempt to save his skin as the end of Nazi Germany was nigh. Two of those women were my aunts. The Red Cross must have enabled my parents to find them.

Both aunts had been married, Lola long before the war, Renia during the war. Both had lost their husbands. Lola's husband, Romek Potasz, whom I only vaguely remember, went to the gas chambers with their only son. Renia married a man called Altman, who also died at the hands of the Nazis. The two sisters now worked in factories, as did so many other rescued women.

They were befriended by Ingrid Segerstedt-Wiberg, who later served in the Swedish parliament. Her father, Torgny Segerstedt, had been the editor of the most liberal Swedish newspaper, *Handelstidningen*, of Gothenburg and during the war had been the most vociferous critic of Sweden's ostensible policy of neutrality. He informed his readers of the duplicity of their government and its implicit collusion with the crimes of Nazi Germany. His daughter shared his views and saw in the rescue of the Jewish women an attempt at Swedish atonement. She worked tirelessly among the refugees and on their behalf. With her help, my aunts obtained permits for us to go to Sweden. My parents decided to go, abandoning the Zionist party platform and, in a sense, their previous life. Unfortunately they didn't make a new life for themselves, but that's another story.

Two months after our arrival in Sweden, the State of Israel was proclaimed. I have often speculated how different my life would have been had the Swedish papers not come through and we had carried out our original intention of going to Israel. Either way, however, it would have meant the end of our seven-year exile.

Sweden:
Refuge

We arrived in Gothenburg on March 24, 1948, having travelled from Katowice to the Polish port of Swinoujscie (formerly the German Swinemünde) across to Trelleborg in Sweden and onward to our final destination. The train journey was very different from those that took us first to Siberia, then to Uzbekistan and finally back to Poland. This time we travelled like proper passengers sitting in proper train compartments with proper tickets and proper travel papers.

I don't remember the reunion with my aunts Lola and Renia being very emotional, but the reception seemed warm. When we got into their apartment, I was particularly impressed by the presents that were laid out for each of us. Before we could enjoy our gifts, however, or even inspect them properly, they disappeared, never to be seen again. Like much else in their lives, Lola and Renia lived for show, not for real. They had assembled several items from among their personal belongings for each of us without ever intending to part with them. It's tempting to suggest that it was their war experiences that warped them, but I surmise that it was part of their character and culture, perhaps even upbringing. Even now, almost five decades later and when they are no longer among the living, I still find their behaviour peculiar, though over the years both had been extremely generous toward my family and me.

Another manifestation of the make-believe world Lola and Renia inhabited was their pretence of being Orthodox. Probably to impress the rabbi who worked among the women refugees in Sweden after the Swedish Red Cross liberated them from the camps, they made themselves out as coming from Orthodox stock. There's nothing to suggest that either of them, as adults before and during the war, had been observant. They now imposed the charade on us. Their apartment was on the ground floor, and each time friends came to visit unexpectedly—when we may have been eating non-kosher food or cooking on Shabbat—we had to lie down on the floor under tables or beds, because the visitors, not getting a response at the door and rightly suspecting that we hadn't gone out, would look through the windows to see if we were at home. Needless to say, I was instructed to keep my mouth shut about this.

Like so many other refugees from the camps, the sisters had found work in local factories, made new friends and generally tried to put their lives together. By the time we arrived, they had been in Sweden for almost three years and ostensibly had made their way in the new country, even speaking Swedish. We were not convinced. The aunts definitely hadn't found a way of living in harmony with each other. For example, only a couple of days after our arrival, they were discussing how much money they had saved. Lola, or maybe it was Renia, mentioned a sum. The other sister thought it was higher. They took down the bundle to count it, for nobody trusted banks. It turned out to be less than either had indicated. As a result, one blamed the other for stealing. What followed was a very ugly scene with Renia becoming hysterical and needing water and smelling salts to recover.

Both Renia and Lola had lost their husbands in the Holocaust. Renia married during the war and had no children. I didn't know her husband and never heard her speak of him. But I have a vague memory of Lola's husband Romek and their son, an only child also named after my maternal grandfather. Though she would rarely talk about them in my presence, I learned from my parents that Romek refused to be separated from their son, so father and son had gone to the gas chamber together. I don't think she ever recovered from their deaths, and she carried a deep sense of guilt for having survived. I always felt implicitly accused in her presence. Why had I survive and her son didn't? Why, indeed?

The sisters' apartment consisted of two rooms, a cooking facility and a toilet on the landing. There wasn't enough room for five people. Therefore my parents found an apartment for the three of us: a hovel on Husargatan 12 in the slum district of Haga in the centre of the city. It consisted of two rooms, one of which had a cold tap and a sink. A table, three chairs and a primitive cooking appliance were acquired for it, probably bought second-hand. It became our kitchen. There was a communal toilet in the courtyard, which nobody kept clean. It was a dark and very cold little place, and I found it impossible to use. I soon learned that the public toilet a few hundred yards away was warm and clean, so I trained myself to go there at a given time every day. If circumstances dictated otherwise, I did my utmost to control myself and only went to the toilet in our building in extreme emergencies. We all urinated into a pot that emptied into the sink in the kitchen. Visits to my aunts were, therefore, most welcome, for they had a warm and clean toilet.

Having lived all those years in places with no washing facilities, we didn't miss them much here either. Once a week, however, on a Saturday afternoon when my father came home from work, he and I would go to the public bath nearby. I don't know what my mother did, but I still have vivid memories of naked men at the bathhouse.

We stayed in that hovel for seven years. The three of us slept in the main room, where there was also a large table and chairs. It was our living room. I had a bed of my own and my parents had a bed. Apart from a cupboard for clothes, I recall no other furniture. We ate in the makeshift kitchen. The table in the living room was used almost exclusively by me for homework. While I worked, my parents sat in the kitchen. The only luxury was a radio, mainly to listen to the BBC Polish broadcast. It was years before my parents could understand enough Swedish to listen to local news.

Although there may have been some justification in moving into the hovel when we first arrived—we had no money—there was no reason to stay there for more than a few months. For soon my parents earned enough to enable us to move to a more appropriate modern apartment in a suburb, but my mother wouldn't hear of it. She didn't enjoy life and she was going to make sure that my father and I didn't either. Living in a hovel was a manifestation of poverty of spirit, more than of lack of money. The only thing that ever gave her pleasure was saving money she didn't know for what. As usual my father wasn't able to go against my mother's wishes. This meant that, throughout my seven years of school in Sweden, I could never have a shower on my own or invite a friend home. I still harbour these old resentments, even though I've been blessed with comfortable homes for almost fifty years in four different countries. Significantly these homes have always been open to visitors, including house guests—with very ample washing facilities. I'm still compensating for the privations in my youth.

The few occasions that the three of us ate at the table on which I normally worked were to celebrate a semblance of a Seder, the meal on the eve of Passover. Other than a packet of matzah and an improvised Seder plate, I don't remember anything else that would make it a Passover meal. My father would mumble through the Haggadah, the little book giving the order of service, and I may still have remembered the four questions that Szloyme Sznall had taught me in Uzbekistan. Our Seder had no festivity, no joy, no explanation, no effort to affirm life and celebrate the Jews' exodus from Egypt. And, of course, no guests. I now know that my parents never felt that they had left the house of bondage. The festival of freedom that's Passover wasn't really for them.

In our early days in Sweden, my parents very occasionally invited people to our place. (God help them if any of them needed a washroom.) Normally, because the apartment was so small, the cooker in the kitchen heated the whole place, but when guests arrived, the stove in the other room, fuelled with charcoal, would be lit. Because it was badly ventilated and never cleaned, the stove emitted a most unwelcome smell. On one occasion when we had guests, several of us felt unwell because of the smell. I know now that it was carbon dioxide and we were indeed being poisoned. At the time someone decided that our discomfort was evidence of the *ayin hara*, the evil eye. He volunteered to rid us of it by waving a corner of his shirt that he produced from his trousers. Ignorance breeds superstition.

Within a week or so of arriving in Gothenburg, my parents found work. Mother got a job at the coat manufacturer where my aunts worked, and my father got a job in a factory that produced tins for the food industry. I was to go to school. My parents had calculated that I had had two years' schooling so far—I was thirteen at the time—and therefore arranged for me through an intermediary, probably one of my aunts, to be enrolled in a third-year form in the local primary school. I'll never forget my first day there. I didn't understand a word of what was going on in class. At recess my new classmates, all three or four years younger than I was, surrounded me. Their question, spoken with the characteristic Gothenburg lilt, still rings in my ears: *"Vad heter du?"* (What's your name?) Since I didn't understand what they were saying, I just stared at them. They stared back at this enormous lump of humanity, me, towering over them, grossly overweight, dressed in heavy Polish winter clothes, totally out of keeping with the new surroundings. They must have thought that I'd come from another planet. In a sense I had.

At around eleven in the morning on my first day at school I saw my classmates leave the building. I did the same and went home. My parents were surprised to learn that school finished so early, but who were they to question the system in the new country? And whom could they have asked? The following morning, Mr. Olsson, the teacher, stood in front of me and moved his pocket watch to twelve o'clock. He tried to tell me something, but I couldn't understand. A few days later, having nothing to do, since my parents and my aunts were at work, I went for a walk. When I passed my school I saw my classmates there in the yard, even though it was afternoon. I waited till the school bell rang and followed them in. They went to a room where they all produced socks they would now darn. As I didn't bring any, I sat through the hour totally bewildered.

But I realized now that there were activities in the afternoon and so returned to the school every afternoon from then on. The children had only been going home during the lunch break. Now I also understood why the teacher had moved his watch to twelve o'clock. The following week, on the same day that I discovered the afternoon activities, I even brought a sock to darn. I haven't darned one since.

Because I was growing out of my Polish winter clothes and the Swedish summer was still months away, I was given a new overcoat. It was Lola's. Whatever little self-respect I may have had before had now gone. A thirteen-year-old boy wearing a woman's coat! When, many years later, in the days I still argued with my mother, I mentioned this to her. She denied it and said that like so much else I was saying, it was untrue. When I persisted, she added, "Anyhow, we couldn't afford anything else." I've reason to doubt the truth of that statement, but I've long given up trying to understand my mother's parenting skills or my father's acquiescence.

The Swedish school year ends in June, which means that I would only have been in the third form of Annedalskolan in Gothenburg some ten weeks. During that time, however, I learned enough Swedish to make myself understood and to grasp what was being said to me. Not that I was *taught* the language, for this was long before the government instituted Swedish as a second language for newcomers from abroad, but having previously learned Yiddish, Russian, Uzbekish and Hebrew, I had developed good imitating skills. They call it an ear for languages, I believe.

The school authorities realized that neither my school nor I benefited from my presence there and decided to send me to an institution where I could be with boys my own age. As I didn't know much, I was sent to a small unit designed for youngsters with behavioural and learning problems. The teacher, Mr. Nilsson, was delighted to have me in his class, for bad behaviour wasn't my problem and I wanted to learn. In the year I was there, whenever higher-ups came to inspect the facility, Mr. Nilsson would show me off as one of his great successes. Contrary to expectations, my fellow students didn't seem to resent it. They were indifferent to an outsider. In those days, much more than today, foreigners were alien species of humanity in Sweden. When I was beaten up, which did happen from time to time, it was usually by a boy from another school. Needless to say, I didn't know how to defend myself. My schoolmates, though not belligerent toward me, weren't prepared to shield me from such attacks. Swedish neutrality, I suppose. The culture of the schoolyard all over the world is, I believe, that he who is beaten up by others deserves it. Many victims come to believe it too. I may have been one of them.

I no longer remember how Fred Forchheimer "discovered" me, probably at some gathering in the Jewish community centre. He must have taken pity on the little boy among the grown-ups. Perhaps I reminded him of his own youth, when in the 1930s, as a refugee from Germany, he came to Sweden. He realized how inappropriate my present school was and decided to help me to get into a regular high school. Under normal circumstances I should have started there the year I was sent to Mr. Nilsson. The only way to remedy things now without falling behind was to let me have private lessons in English to catch up so that I could enter the second year of high school. My parents agreed to pay for the lessons because, like so many Jewish refugees, they saw education as the key to integration in the new country. Though they knew that they couldn't obtain it for themselves, they wanted it for me.

I just about scraped through to be allowed to enter the second year at Burgårdens Samrealskola, a coed middle school that three years later would get me something called *realexamen*, a certificate that assured me of a place in a high school. Three years thereafter I could do the university entrance examination. The moment I entered that middle school, I never looked back. I had found the right path—thanks to Fred Forchheimer. An engineer, he continued to tutor me, particularly in mathematics and the natural sciences—without payment. When in my second year at Burgårdens, we had a hobby fair that encouraged students to share their interests with others, I declared my hobby to be chemistry and spoke about it to the school. If I was ever interested in the subject, the interest has long gone.

My real passion became the Swedish language. I had now discovered that a language has a structure and was governed by rules called grammar. The principal of Burgårdens, Ejnar Lilje, was also the author of the grammar book we used, and I devoured it. Soon I became something of a phenomenon: I spoke Swedish like a Swede, because of my imitative skills, and I wrote it better than most of my peers, because of my fascination with grammar and vocabulary. I began to participate in debates and, before I left the school, I chaired its debating society. My earliest printed words appeared in the school magazine.

Not having a life outside school and no home to which I could take friends, I found that being a good student was my window to the world.

I read a lot and I prepared well. Though there were no books in my home, the public library was close by—next door to the public bath— and I spent much of my free time there. As a result, by the time I left Burgårdens in 1952 with my *realexamen*, I was the recipient of a record number of prizes. One of them, a history of world literature that I got for excellence in Swedish, is still on one of my bookshelves. I also realized that my only way out of the slums was through schooling. And reading was my window onto the world; whatever I learned about real people came from fiction.

I was also fascinated by psychology in general and Freud in particular. I read as much as I could about both. If fiction helped me to grasp reality, reading books on human behaviour provided me with tools with which I could defend myself against my mother. I sometimes tried to tell her what she was doing to me and to my father, but to no avail, of course. Reading books on psychology also gave some kind of meaning to my loneliness.

It's customary in Sweden that for the *realexamen*, and even more for the university entrance examination, the *studentexamen*, the graduates are cheered by family and friends with garlands of flowers as they leave the school with their diplomas. Since the world of my school, where I shone, was totally divorced from the world of my home, where I suffered, I feared that I'd stand there on the day totally alone. I therefore cajoled my parents and my aunt Lola—Renia had moved to the United States by then—to show up at these events with flowers. Like everybody else, I was photographed on the occasion. It shows a rather cheerful boy of seventeen I hardly recognize now.

But one of my teachers at Burgårdens did, of sorts. In 1980 the Jewish community in Gothenburg invited me to fulfill rabbinic functions. The community was celebrating with much pomp two centuries of existence. As they didn't have a rabbi—a very common condition there—I was invited to preach and make speeches. After all, I was a product of the community and I spoke Swedish like a Swede, which their rabbis didn't. One day during the visit, I was strolling along the main street in Gothenburg when I saw my class teacher at Burgårdens, the one who had seen me showered with all the prizes. In a rare moment of exuberance, I accosted him and told him that I had been his student some three decades earlier. He asked my name, thought for a moment and then said he remembered: "Jewish, fat." He was right on both counts. I don't think I've ever approached any of my Swedish teachers since.

While I was making my way at school, my parents settled down to a humdrum existence of work and minimal household chores. Relaxation meant not working and doing a lot of bickering; leisure activities, such as going to the movies, were considered frivolous and wasteful. If my parents' bickering was restrained, it was because I was studying in the living room while they had to sit quietly in the kitchen. They had respect for education and wanted me to get on. It was years before they realized that my education also alienated me from them, because it transported me into a world they perceived to be hostile.

Apart from my education, my mother's main interest was in marrying off her sisters. I don't know whether it was out of love for them or because of her need to control the lives of others. Anyway, Renia soon found a partner. Abram Praga was visiting from Helsingborg in the south of Sweden. He, too, was a survivor of the Holocaust, in which he lost a wife and child. He and Renia met and got on well. He moved to Gothenburg and they were married. I've no memory of the wedding.

Abram's intention was to go to the United States as soon as possible. He had found an uncle there who had provided the necessary papers. But before he could enter the Promised Land of California, he and his new wife had to produce birth certificates. They tried to argue with the official in the American Consulate that because they were both born in Poland, there was no way of obtaining such things. But the official insisted that they had to write to the authorities in the places where they were born. Only if the authorities wrote back to say that their records were destroyed could he take action.

I was told that Renia was born in the 1920s and wasn't more than a dozen years or so older than I was. Since I remembered her as an adult before the war, for she came to stay with us once in Jaslo, I questioned the information, but having been instructed to keep my mouth shut, I said nothing further. The fact that her father had died in the influenza epidemic in 1916 or 1917 further confused the issue. Abram was allegedly only a couple of years older.

After some time Renia's birth certificate arrived, giving what must have been her correct age. She was beside herself, insisting that trying to show that the Jews were older than they were was characteristic of Polish anti-Semitism. Of course, Renia's older sisters knew that the birth certificate was accurate, but said nothing in case Abram decided to leave for America without his bride. But shortly thereafter, his birth certificate arrived, giving his correct age; he, too, was much older than he had intimated. Instead of laughing at themselves, Abram and Renia held on to their respective younger ages till the end of their days. In view of the fact that so many second marriages of Holocaust survivors turned out to be quite disastrous, theirs seems to have been reasonably harmonious despite the absence of full disclosure, or perhaps because of it.

Many years later, when the pair—now Abe and Renee Prager of Los Angeles—came to visit my young family in London, where we lived at the time, Abe collapsed during a visit to Madame Tussaud's. In the ambulance taking him to the hospital the attendant wanted to know the patient's age. My aunt, prudently, gave his real age. Abe, who until then had appeared to be unconscious, sat up, mumbled his younger age and immediately returned to his catatonic state.

He recovered and lived many more years, but predeceased his wife. When Renee died, we discovered that she had arranged for a double grave and a double tombstone on which not only were Abe's particulars carved in stone, but also her name and the date of birth that would make her younger. I assume, however, that for pension purposes, both she and Abe used their real dates of birth, perhaps concealing the dates from each other. When, a few months before her death, I had to arrange for Renee to go into a nursing home, I asked her for her date of birth, because I needed it to fill in the application form. Her reply was unforgettable: "I've got so many. Use whichever you wish."

Many Holocaust survivors, perhaps most, who had become single or were never married, made themselves younger than they were in the hope of attracting a partner. They often came from a culture where disclosing one's age, especially if you were a woman, was considered vaguely indecent, and looking young was very important. Those who had been through the war under Hitler also felt that they had, literally, lost years and so, having survived, these should be discounted.

When Abe and Renee married they were long past child-bearing age. I was never much of a son substitute, though I did my best to stay in touch with them, but I was the heir to their modest savings and my children have been among the beneficiaries.

Lola married another Holocaust survivor. Abra(ha)m—Avrum Yitschok Wajsbort—had been married before. He, too, had lost his family at the hands of the Nazis. Lola and he were very different people, he an honest but simple tailor, she a devious and complicated former lady of leisure, now a factory worker and victim.

I remember their wedding because of its drama. Like so many Holocaust survivors, once they found a partner, they wanted to get married as soon as possible. To satisfy the civil authorities, a lot of documentation was needed and it took time. Therefore, they would get a suitable individual to marry them according to Jewish law, because the local rabbi wouldn't contravene state regulations. The official marriage would take place later, when circumstances permitted, often in front of a local rabbi. In the case of Lola and Avrum Yitschok, the officiating person was the man who conducted worship services in the little Orthodox synagogue that served as an alternative to the main Liberal establishment in Gothenburg, which was frequented at that time by virtually all Holocaust survivors, especially someone as ostensibly pious as Aunt Lola.

Liberal Judaism was very alien to Jews from Eastern Europe. Whether or not they themselves were Orthodox, or even believers, the only Judaism they considered authentic was Orthodoxy. It's still like that today in Eastern Europe and in Israel. When I told my parents that I wanted to be a rabbi, they found it difficult to accept. My father was particularly opposed to my becoming a Reform rabbi. He wanted me to be Orthodox on the grounds that "you can always become Reform."

A few minutes before the unofficial marriage ceremony that would bring my aunt Lola under the *huppah*, the man scheduled to officiate "discovered" that, as was the case of virtually all who perished in the Holocaust, there was no eyewitness evidence that Lola's husband had actually died. So therefore he, as a "pious" Jew, might be an accomplice to an act of bigamy, which Jewish law tolerated for a man but not for a woman. So he refused to officiate and suggested instead that my father tell them to consummate the union nevertheless. I recall a lot of consternation among the assembled crowd, but the couple went on to live together, alas not very happily. Of course, the man could have officiated without the inquisition, because the demand of an eyewitness to a death at Auschwitz is absurd. According to my mother's prejudiced opinion, the officiant was a Hungarian and Hungarian Jews will do all they can to put stumbling blocks in front of Polish Jews. The couple married formally some time later, when their papers came through, in front of the local rabbi—but not for long.

The fact that theirs was a bad marriage had nothing to do with the way they got married. They inhabited different planets and stayed together as long as they did, I think, because Avrum Yitschok had started a business and was quite successful. (He drove a car, which was unheard of in those days in our world of Holocaust survivors.) I surmise that Lola expected financial security, if not affluence, whether or not she was happy. His expectations were low. Having a home may have been sufficient for him, even with a nagging wife. When they finally decided to divorce, they squabbled endlessly about money. Avrum Yitschok had to be careful, lest Lola's claims about his alleged wealth reached the ears of the tax authorities. Soon after the divorce, he went to Israel, where he had two brothers, and was never heard from again. I believe he died quite young. Lola reconnected with some friends in Brooklyn and went to the United States, first on a temporary basis and then, after she met her new husband, Sol Spielman, she settled there permanently.

Sol is a splendid person and has been an exceptional husband to Lola. When we visited them in Brooklyn not long before Lola's death, she was singing his praises. "Sol does everything," she said. He agreed and explained in his characteristic pithy way, "When we married, I said 'I do'—so I do." He is younger than Lola. When I called him a day or so after she went into the hospital for the last time, on New Year's Day 2003, to tell him that my mother had died that night, he mumbled something about the doctor telling him that his wife was a hundred years old. This seems correct, according to what my mother had told me. When I spoke to Sol a few days after Lola died and, in an effort to console him, said that at least she'd lived a long life, he was indignant. "Eighty-seven isn't that long a life," he said. It seems that, even after thirty-seven years of marriage, he may never have known his wife's real age.

Throughout their years together in Gothenburg, Lola and my mother had long spells of not talking to each other. As usual my father played the middleman. Whenever the opportunity arose he would tell me about it, invariably making Lola the culprit. Renia, because she lived far away, was considered to be the perfect sister.

Once, around 1985, my mother went to visit Lola in Brooklyn. They had a terrible time together. My mother had intended to continue on to Los Angeles to visit Renia, by that time a widow. But Lola signalled Renia to find an excuse not to receive my mother, and so my mother returned to Toronto, where we had moved by then. I don't think that Lola and my mother spoke to each other after that. Like my father, I became the intermediary, bringing greetings from one to the other, but only when asked. The sisters died within ten days of each other.

Being Jewish was an inescapable part of my parents' destiny, but Judaism itself meant very little to them. Nevertheless they made sure I attended the classes in religious education offered by the Jewish community in Gothenburg. The rabbi soon discovered that I was a rarity among his students: I could read Hebrew. It was arranged, therefore, a few months after our arrival in Sweden that I'd read from the Torah at the Simhath Torah service, the celebration of concluding one cycle of readings and starting the next, even though I wouldn't be able to chant. When the time for the festival approached, the rabbi asked me if I had a suit. Of course I didn't. So he arranged for a local firm, owned by a member of the community, to equip me for the occasion. The rabbi would pay for it, presumably out of a discretionary fund. It was my first suit, but instead of enjoying it, I was embarrassed because it meant accepting charity. But I did enjoy being the centre of attention in the synagogue.

The only instruction the religious school offered was in Jewish history, primarily biblical. Though the congregation was Liberal, the underlying assumption of the curriculum was that all the events described in the scriptures actually happened. We were taught about the Jewish festivals, but that teaching had virtually no meaning for me, because we didn't celebrate the festivals in our home. The school had no Hebrew and I don't remember ever being exposed there to a classic Jewish text in any language. There was no joy in any form for Rabbi Hermann Loeb, the spiritual leader of the community and my teacher, a dour man who was more concerned about our behaviour in class than about transmitting the drama and the joy of being a Jew. It never occurred to him that had he been a little more interesting, we students would have been far better behaved. In retrospect, I don't think he liked being Jewish or teaching young people, but it was difficult to know, because what he said was mostly incomprehensible. Allegedly he gave fine sermons, but as a native of Germany, he had never quite mastered the Swedish language. In fact, he was something of a laughingstock in the congregation, not only because of his lack of oratorical skills but also because of his bachelor life with a housekeeper. Nobody I knew had ever been in his home.

After leaving the city I'd still visit Hermann Loeb in his office periodically. Though he didn't say much about himself, I gleaned that he had received his rabbinical training in his native Germany and soon after his ordination landed in the Jewish community of Gothenburg, where there was a respectable Liberal pulpit. He felt stuck there, perhaps because of the Second World War. Now he was a bitter man. His only triumph came after his retirement: his successor didn't last long and he was called back. It was during his second period in office, when I myself had decided to become a rabbi, that he said to me, "I always thought of you as a bright and sensible boy, but now I've changed my mind." When I asked why, he told me that since I wanted to be a rabbi, I obviously couldn't be up to much. I felt very sad that a rabbi should regard his life as a failure and a mistake. Later on I'd meet another embittered rabbi in Sweden.

Some two years after I'd come to Gothenburg and been a student of Rabbi Loeb's, my class was being confirmed with a ceremony in the city's main synagogue. The Liberal movement in Judaism, in an attempt to imitate the Protestant Church as well as keep teenage students learning, has always regarded confirmation as an important event in the synagogue calendar. Virtually all my Christian school friends would be confirmed in their respective churches and so would I.

But I had no idea what confirmation meant. I had never attended such a ceremony before and didn't know what was expected of me. When I now look back on the event, this time attended by my parents and many members of the congregation, I realize that in the two years between my bar mitzvah and my confirmation I had traversed two centuries. The ramshackle room in which I was called to the Torah in Sosnowiec was on a different planet from the ornate and magnificent synagogue in which I now stood. Though I don't remember what actually happened during the ceremony, I know that the dramatis personae in the Polish *stiebel* must have been in my eyes a different species of humanity than those who surrounded me now. I think that I, too, had undergone a metamorphosis, changing from a hapless refugee boy to an aspiring member of the Jewish community of Gothenburg. I think I felt that at last we had found refuge.

Whereas my bar mitzvah didn't leave me with much enthusiasm about Judaism, the confirmation seems to have had a positive influence. I stayed connected to the community, participated in the activities of the youth group and attended worship services fairly regularly. A few years later I became a member of a small group of young people, though most of them much older than myself, who after the Friday evening service in the synagogue would go to the home of one of the members, not for *Kiddush* and not for a meal, but for coffee and talk. Another window was opened to me. I was a regular participant, even though I could never host the group in my own home.

I was active in the Jewish community and, in the land of the Jewishly ignorant, I was considered knowledgeable. Hence the invitation from the local B'nai Brith Lodge to come speak to them about the Jewish dietary laws. I accepted, but a few days before the due date, one of the leaders of the lodge came to see me—we had no telephone—to tell me that the meeting had been cancelled. I took the message at face value. Only years later did I understand what must have been the true reason for the cancellation: they had realized that I didn't observe what I was going to talk about, and therefore found it unseemly that I should speak on the subject.

They were right. *Kashruth* was not on my family's agenda. Since both my parents were at work all week, I did the shopping. It was always the same routine: bread, cheese, sausage, ham and eggs for the sandwiches they took to work and meat for the evening meal—which three times a week was ground beef, and twice pork chops. On Saturday mornings my mother would go to the market in the centre of town to buy a chicken for the weekend and fruit and vegetables for the week. Cooking wasn't her strong point. Usually I found the school lunches we received courtesy of the Swedish welfare system much more to my taste: pea soup with pork on Thursdays, blood pudding on another day, and so on. Not exactly a diet that reflected a Jewish dietary discipline.

The real impetus to Judaism came to me from a different and quite unexpected source. After my *realexamen*, I was admitted to one of the better schools in the city, Vasa Högre Allmänna Läroverk. Both Fred Forchheimer and my parents wanted me to go there, because the school was strong in natural sciences and between them they had decided that I was destined to be an engineer. Gothenburg has a very good technical university, Chalmers, and I was urged to prepare myself for it. The natural sciences, however, were my worst subjects at school. I had neither aptitude nor interest. Instead, I concentrated on the humanities: first and foremost Swedish, but also English and German, as well as history and religion. The man who taught religion, which was really basic Christianity, was also our class teacher. Ove Nordstrandh made a deep impression on me. Unlike the other committed Christian teachers and students in the school, he was open and urbane, a real man of the world. He joked with his students, even about religion, and he didn't try to be overtly pious. He gave me a special task: to write a description of Judaism to be presented to the class, even though the curriculum didn't allow for it. By all accounts, I did a good job, but more important, it whetted my appetite to study my tradition. I've never looked back. I now began to think about the rabbinate as a career. What my parents and even my rabbi couldn't do for me, this doctor of Christian theology did. God works in mysterious ways.

I was active in the life of my new school, not only as a clown in various shows—the entrée into society for every outsider—but also as the president of the debating society and ultimately president of the student council. I don't think they had ever had a foreigner occupying the position, which carried with it much status among students and teachers alike. More than ever, school was my life. I couldn't share any of it with my parents.

From mid-June until the end of August, when we were off school, I'd work in an office. My mother was known as an excellent worker in the factory that employed her from the time we had come to Sweden. My father also went to work in the same firm. Both stayed there until their retirement. Because of my parents' record, I got a summer job in the office and rose, in the three or four summers I worked there, from office boy to assistant in the accounts department. On one occasion I was even deputized for the chief accountant while he was on holiday. Of course, every krona I earned went into the family kitty.

When I was sixteen, I heard that the Scandinavian-Jewish Youth Association was sponsoring an essay competition. I decided to enter. Months later I was informed that the first prize went to Arne Melchior, my senior by a decade, the son of the chief rabbi of Denmark and subsequently a politician of note in his country. Still, the organizers invited me as the association's guest to a youth leadership course in the southern Swedish town of Kristianstad. It was a rewarding experience. For the first time, perhaps, I realized that there was a life beyond our hovel and my school and that I might be able to function in it.

At the time I thought I did very well at the course. In retrospect I realize that I behaved abominably, using my debating skills from school to speak often and at length on every conceivable subject. I had a lot of growing up to do, and I didn't know it because there was nobody to tell me.

The following summer my parents allowed me to go the annual convention of the Scandinavian-Jewish Youth Association, which that year was held in Trondheim, Norway. For me it was a great adventure because, since coming to Sweden, I had been out of the country only once—on a school day trip to Frederikshavn in Denmark. In the course of the convention I got to know some young Jews from Oslo; one of them even invited me to stay with him and his parents in the Norwegian capital. I came back energized, happy and a little more self-confident.

In 1954 the same convention was to be held in Uddevalla, a town in the vicinity of Gothenburg. Our Jewish group was responsible for the local arrangements. I was assigned to help out with registration and greeting the out-of-town delegates. One of them was a girl from Stockholm, beautiful and elegant, by the name of Fredzia Zonabend. I had heard of her before. One of the participants in the Kristianstad meeting had written to me suggesting that, as there were so few young Jews in Sweden, we should form a correspondence club to get to know each other. He asked me to write to Fredzia and I did, introducing myself by way of a short autobiography. I received no reply. After we got to know each other, I found out that the idea of the correspon-dence club was Fredzia's ploy to fend off the young man who was very keen on her and interest him in one of her girlfriends. Fredzia had, in fact, written to me in response, but had spilled coffee on the letter before it was mailed and so abandoned the project.

Not knowing any of this when I met her, I was apprehensive. Being shy and awkward in the presence of girls at the best of times, with vir-tually no experience of the opposite sex beyond adolescent banter, I felt rejected by her even before we met, having received no reply to my letter. But in the course of the week, we got talking and went for walks. On one occasion I even put my arm around her shoulders. She told me that the only reason she let me do so was that it was chilly. We spoke freely to each other. When she asked me what I wanted to do when I left school, I told her—hearing myself say it for the first time—that I wanted to be a rabbi. She was interested and supportive.

After the residential part of the convention, the delegates went to Gothenburg for business meetings. Fredzia stayed with a family not far from where we lived. She wasn't going to the ball that ended the fes-tivities, but she was having a little party afterwards by permission of her hosts and would I come? At the party it was decided that the fol-lowing day a group of us who were still in the city would go together to Liseberg, Gothenburg's amusement park. Walking to the amusement park along Gothenburg's main street, one of Fredzia's friends made a point of talking to me about Fredzia. I told her how I felt about Fredzia and how apprehensive I was to get to know her better. The friend encouraged me to take the plunge and hinted at a favourable response.

The following morning I called Fredzia. When we met, I proposed. She accepted. I now know, and knew it perhaps then, that that day in July my real life began. She was eighteen and I nineteen. This book should really start with the story of meeting Fredzia, then the title would be *beshert*. It's a Yiddish word used to describe two people finding each other and falling in love. In my case, I found not only Fredzia but I also found myself. I wish I had the skills of a poet to describe my feelings for her then and now. She remains to this very day the centre of my universe.

Fredzia is the only child of Fela and Isaac Zonabend of Stockholm. She was born in Lodz, and after the Nazis invaded Poland, she was taken, along with her parents, to the large ghetto in her home city. Her father was in charge of a factory and so the family wasn't sent to the camps until relatively late. In fact, they were due to leave on an earlier transport, but Fredzia was ill at the time, so the departure was delayed. Later Fredzia and her mother were sent to Ravensbruck concentration camp and her father to another camp. All three survived. Fredzia and her mother came to Sweden the same way my two aunts got there, thanks to the Swedish Red Cross, and her father returned to Poland after his ordeal. The family was reunited in Sweden about a year later. In time Isaac brought to Sweden three of his four surviving brothers.

Fela was very anxious that her only daughter should marry soon and marry well. With this in mind, Fredzia was introduced to an about-to-become-a-doctor from a good Jewish family from Poland; "good" in the language of these Holocaust survivors from Poland may have meant that the members of the family spoke Polish well and had money. For reasons I fully understand, the young man fell in love with Fredzia. By all accounts, she was less keen. Her coming to the convention was a way to gain some perspective. Now she had to tell not only him but also her parents that things had changed. I think that when my lack of credentials as a suitable marriage partner became obvious, Fredzia's mother was even more upset than the young man. When I went to visit a few months later, Fela told me not to speak Polish to their friends, because my vocabulary and grammar didn't measure up to her standards.

My parents weren't thrilled either, albeit for very different reasons. It now became obvious that I was about to leave Gothenburg at the earliest opportunity, which would be in another year when I would get my *studentexamen*, the certificate that would allow me to go to university. This meant that the control my mother had over me would come to an end. As far as my father was concerned, he was about to lose the only ally he had. The two of them being left to themselves must have constituted a real threat to him. I felt guilty, but not guilty enough to sacrifice my life.

The same morning Fredzia and I decided to get married, I told my parents that I had invited her to dinner in our hovel. She would be the first and last friend I ever invited to our place. My mother was beside herself and insisted that this wasn't possible and I should call off the visit. I insisted too, and she gave in; normally when nothing else worked, she would throw a hysterical fit and I'd yield, but not this time. My parents should have been thrilled and enchanted; this beautiful young woman came from the same background as they did and spoke their language, and she was about to make their only son very happy. As usual my father said nothing. My mother on the other hand spent the next year, before I moved to Stockholm, telling me how treacherous and unreliable women are and how I'd be exploited and abused.

Nevertheless, during the winter holidays I was given fare money to visit Fredzia in Stockholm. From the time she and I parted we wrote to each other at least once a day and often more. As we had no telephone at home, I called from public phone booths. Our conversations were, therefore, very unsatisfactory, but our letters were rich. We kept them for a number of years, but they finally got lost in the attic of our first home.

My visit to Stockholm was successful, even though Fredzia's mother viewed me with suspicion. Fredzia's maternal uncle had died a few weeks earlier, which may have contributed to the low-key reception I received. For the two of us, being together was bittersweet. We were overjoyed to discover that what we felt then was genuine, but sad that we would have to part again in a few days. My own insecurity further complicated things. I found it totally unbelievable that this magnificent person who, in my eyes, was endowed with only the best human qualities, really wanted to marry me, with my awkward body, lack of experience of life and a family that was nothing to write home about. It took me many years to accept the fact that Fredzia really loved me. There are moments when I still find it difficult to believe. I ascribe the tension in the early years of our marriage largely to this insecurity. I now know that people who don't regard themselves as lovable find it very difficult to love.

My next visit to Stockholm came during the spring vacation, this time at the expense of a Swedish national newspaper, *Stockholms Tidningen*. Every year, the paper held a nation-wide public-speaking competition for high schools. In view of my debating experience and fascination with the Swedish language, I was to represent my school in the local qualifying round. I scraped through to win. This was enough for the local papers to make much of the boy who came to Sweden six years earlier knowing no Swedish and with only two years of formal education and who had so excelled in the language of the land that he was proclaimed the best public speaker among high school students in the city. As far as I was concerned, my real reward was a free trip to Stockholm.

Once again I stayed with the Zonabends. Fredzia came with me to the competition finals in the Stockholm concert hall. I came second. Though it was a great achievement for me in view of my background, I was very disappointed to have missed winning the championship and aggrieved by the judges' verdict that I sounded too professional. Though Fredzia and I had a few marvellous days together, or perhaps because of it, my return trip was miserable. My parents waited for me at the station. Their first question was "How did it go?" The competition was sponsored by a national newspaper and the results were front-page news. They hadn't even bothered to buy a copy to find out! I lashed out angrily at them. Now I know that it wasn't their apparent lack of interest that caused my anger, but my own frustration.

I now had to find a cogent reason for moving from Gothenburg to Stockholm. Fredzia and I continued to write as often as we had done hitherto and couldn't wait to be together permanently.

It had become obvious that I wouldn't study engineering, as my parents had hoped. At the time the university in Gothenburg didn't have a faculty of political science, but there was one in Stockholm. That was a good enough reason for me to want to study political science. I persuaded my parents that in view of my speaking skills and active involvement in the affairs of the school and the Jewish community, I was destined to be a great statesman. For that I had to have a degree in political science. It was therefore decided that, immediately after my *studentexamen* in May 1955, I'd travel to Stockholm to find a place to live and a job to support myself, all in preparation for my life as a university student.

My marks in the *studentexamen* weren't as spectacular as they had been three years earlier in my *realexamen*, but they were still very good. I remember the garlands of flowers around my neck when we graduated—all dressed up in dinner jackets, mine not rented but bought for the occasion—but I don't remember a party. Since I was due to leave for Stockholm a few days later, Fredzia didn't come. But I have a photograph with the coveted white cap of a student, the sign of someone to be reckoned with in Swedish society, at least in those days. I left for Stockholm seven days later, never to return to live in Gothenburg.

But I didn't enrol in the faculty of political science, because during that week between leaving school and going to Stockholm, my plans to become a rabbi got a new impetus. As a courtesy before leaving town, I was given the honour of welcoming into our youth group the rabbi who'd come to Gothenburg to replace Hermann Loeb the first time he retired. After the meeting, Rabbi Joseph Kalir asked me to see him in his office before I left for Stockholm. In the course of our conversation he suggested that I become a rabbi. Since I had harboured similar thoughts for years, this was the push I needed. He himself had been a graduate of the Liberal Rabbinic Seminary in Berlin and shortly before the war had fled to what was then Palestine. Not being able to find work in his vocation, he had done all kinds of jobs, including selling ice cream. Gothenburg enabled him to return to his real calling. He was now most keen to help me, which indeed he did. Because he didn't stay long in Sweden, we lost contact with each other, but when I came to Toronto, I found him again, now teaching Judaism in a California college. We exchanged a couple of letters and I sent him my first book.

As soon as I arrived in Stockholm, I decided to pursue the plan of going to rabbinical school. With this in mind I went to see the chief rabbi in Stockholm, Kurt Wilhelm. He was supportive but suggested that in view of my interest in the rabbinate, there was little point in my studying political science. Instead, I should enrol in the Department of Religious Studies, which I did. He also recommended me for a job as a teacher in the community's religious school. Once again in the land of the very ignorant, the half-ignorant becomes, if not an expert, then at least a teacher.

The lectures in the Department of Religious Studies were exceedingly boring and the method of teaching archaic, even by the standards of the academic world of the 1950s. Though some of the professors were recognized authorities on so-called primitive religion, a very hot subject at the university at the time, they would turn up for classes, open their notes, which were usually drafts of books they were about to publish, read from them and then leave. We were told that, at the end of the semester, we would be examined on what we had heard. I found it difficult to stay awake and looked for every possible excuse not to be in class.

Fredzia and I were formally engaged in June 1955, a month or so after my arrival in Stockholm. Though we had decided to marry soon after we met, engagements were formal affairs in Sweden, at least in those days, with announcements in the papers and exchange of rings. The event was celebrated with a family dinner and a rather pompous declaration by me. I was in seventh heaven.

A legitimate excuse not to go to classes at the university came a few months later. As a young teacher in the religious school with an alleged rapport with children, I was drafted to tell the story of Hanukkah to a group of young people whom the acting minister at the legation of Israel, Yehuda Yaari, had invited to his residence. After the event Yaari asked me to see him in his office the following day. He was, I found out, a well-known Israeli writer with a special interest in the Hasidism of Nachman of Bratslav. Before his present posting he had been an official of the Jewish National Fund in Jerusalem. He explained that his real role in the legation was to be in charge of press and cultural relations. Because the current minister, Avraham Nissan, was sick and wouldn't return to his post, Yaari was holding the fort until a successor was appointed. To do his job as cultural attaché, Yaari needed a Swedish-speaking assistant with knowledge of English and Hebrew. Would I be interested?

Over the years, when I wasn't thinking about becoming a rabbi I dreamed about being a diplomat. When I had decided to study politics, this was one of the options I considered after getting my degree. Now that dream would become reality! After consulting Fredzia I accepted the offer. I was now the assistant cultural attaché at the legation of Israel in Stockholm with a tax-free salary that would enable us to marry.

My primary duty was to monitor the Swedish press and disseminate information on behalf of Israel. Since my time at the legation was during the Suez crisis, I had a lot of work. I enjoyed all of it: the office, the secretary old enough to be my mother, the card that allowed me to bypass passport control when receiving visitors at the airport, the allowance of duty-free liquor and above all the cause I was serving. I travelled a lot, first only within Sweden to various places where I would give talks about Israel, then to Oslo to mount an exhibition of Israeli postage stamps previously shown in Stockholm. I went there by air—my first experience of flying!

Yehuda Yaari became my mentor. I'd always been looking for a father figure who could be my teacher. And he had much to teach me about literature, about writing, about life. He received many visitors from Israel and he got to know notable members of the Swedish intelligentsia. I was able to meet them too. Though all the relationships were superficial, I still remember warm contacts with the Israeli poet Haim Hefer, the pianist Varda Nishri and the legendary leader of Ulpan Akiva in Netanya, Shulamit Katzenelson. The unlimited duty-free allowances of alcohol, chocolate and other luxury items that the legation had access to made it easy to arrange cocktail parties to which Swedes, during this time of alcohol rationing in the country, were very happy to come.

A significant part of Yaari's agenda in Stockholm was seeing that the Nobel Prize in literature went to Shmuel Yosef Agnon, the Israeli writer. The two knew each other well, and Yaari would tell me of the impatient and vituperative letters he got from Agnon on the subject of the prize. Nothing came of it during the time I was working in the legation, but Agnon won the Nobel in literature ten years later, in 1966, and then he had to share it with Nelly Sachs, one of the great Holocaust poets. In a biography of Agnon, I am mentioned, not in connection with my work at the legation but as a possible translator into Swedish of one of Agnon's books. I was a student in London by then, and according to the biographer, Rabbi Kurt Wilhelm was opposed to the idea. He was right. I hate translating and I wouldn't have been good at it.

Around that time, and in no relation to the Nobel Prize, I got to know Nelly Sachs. Together with Lennart Levi, now a distinguished physician in Stockholm and at that time a friend in whom I confided a lot despite our age difference, I visited Nelly Sachs to arrange a public reading in Swedish of some of her poems. She was shy and frail, but her friend, the Swedish-Jewish composer Moses Pergament, encouraged both her and us; some of his music would also be played, and people familiar with her work would read her poetry. In the end she agreed, but on the condition that she wouldn't sit in the hall where the readings took place. The evening was a tremendous success, and hearing the tumultuous applause, she came out from her hiding place and was overwhelmed by the response. Though Swedish women and men of letters admired her work and had translated some of it—it was said that the intervention of personalities like Selma Lagerlöf made it possible for Sachs and her mother to find refuge in Sweden—this was the first time that a wider public heard of her and from her. She was grateful for what we did, and I'm the proud possessor of all her books, each one with a personal dedication.

Fredzia and I married a few months after I started work at the legation. On May 20, 1956, we stood under the *huppah* in the Stockholm synagogue, Rabbi Kurt Wilhelm officiating. We were dressed in characteristic Swedish style, Fredzia in a beautiful wedding gown she owned, I in a tailcoat rented for the occasion. Looking at our wedding picture now, I realize how young we were, Fredzia twenty, I twenty-one.

Though a lot of people were invited to the ceremony, no refreshments were offered. Only the immediate family went home to Fredzia's parents' for dinner, which wasn't a particularly joyful event. Fredzia herself had been busy most of the day of her wedding preparing the meal. Normally she would have wanted more of a celebration, something we could make up for only when our daughter Elizabeth married in Toronto more than four decades later. But though the celebration was low-key, the fact that our four parents stood under our *huppah* moved us greatly. Most of our generation of Polish Jews, children at the time of the Holocaust, had perished. The few who had survived had usually been hidden by non-Jews and orphaned. I've never ceased to be grateful for my survival and never stopped feeling that I must vindicate the privilege of having survived and having at my side the most magnificent and accomplished human being I've ever known. The family we've been able to build together is a gift for which I thank God daily. My resolve to become a rabbi had found its raison d'être.

Thanks to Fredzia's German reparation money and some help from both sets of parents, we could purchase a little apartment in the south of Stockholm, not far from the city centre. My legation salary was sufficient for our keep, but Fredzia also worked in her mother's millinery shop. Though the mother-and-daughter relationship always complicated things for my wife, particularly at work, we nevertheless led a charmed life.

I was accepted into the circle of Fredzia's friends. With some of them we've remained close to this very day. Salomo Berlinger, the son of an Orthodox rabbi and himself an observant Jew, had always been active in the Jewish community in Stockholm. Many years later he became the chairman of the Jewish day school in the city and subsequently the president of the Jewish community. He remains active even now, until recently mainly representing Sweden in international Jewish organizations. Despite my religious differences with Salomo and notwithstanding his ambiguous role at the time of my efforts to return to Stockholm as a rabbi, Fredzia and I have remained close to him and his delightful wife, Ruth, also a Holocaust survivor from Poland. One of their daughters lives in Jerusalem. She and her family are friends with our son and his family. Ruth and Salomo have a little apartment in Jerusalem, not far from our home there, so we can now see each other not only on our rare visits to Stockholm, but also in Israel. We never cease to marvel how the circle has been closed.

The other couple we were close to was Kim Scharf and his late wife, Gitta. Fredzia had known them long before I came to the city. Kim and his sister, Monica, had been brought to Sweden, without their parents, from their native Germany by their aunt and uncle who had moved to Sweden earlier. Both Kim and Gitta were active in the community and we became something of a foursome. We remained in touch over the years and would meet from time to time, either in Stockholm or in London, where we had moved by then. One of our most poignant visits to Stockholm was some four decades later, shortly before Gitta died. We all knew that she was dying but kept stiff upper lips.

Within days after Gitta's death, Irene Bier lost her husband, Robert. The two couples had been friends. Now Kim and Irene found each other. We remain very fond of them both. Kim retired after a most remarkable career. When we first knew them, Kim had a fairly basic qualification as an engineer. However, despite family obligations—they had three children—he saw himself through university while working full-time. He then advanced in various Swedish firms to end up as an industrialist of note.

In addition to being with friends, Fredzia and I now had the time and the money to go to the movies, the theatre and other places of entertainment as often as we wanted. We also had to attend a lot of receptions in the legation. Though these soon became a chore and a bore, I—more than Fredzia—was nevertheless pleased to mix in these circles. The memory of my family's hovel in Gothenburg was still fresh in my mind. I was astonished and grateful to have come so far in such short a time.

But there was more to come. The staff of the Israeli legation was relatively small. Before being posted to Sweden, the minister, soon to be made ambassador, Dr. Chaim Yahil, had been one of the architects of the relationship between the Federal Republic of Germany and Israel.

Later he became first the director-general of the Foreign Ministry and subsequently the head of the Israel Broadcasting Corporation. His wife, Leni, is a noted historian of the Holocaust. Their two sons were young when I knew them; one of them fell in Jerusalem in the Six-Day War.

Another staff member, working under cover of some diplomatic title, was the Mossad representative in Sweden. I had skills that were useful to him and so he employed me. Ostensibly nobody in the embassy knew that I was working with him, but I've reason to believe that both the ambassador and my immediate boss were fully in the picture. I felt very important, even though I couldn't tell anybody what I was doing.

The Mossad rep was posted to Stockholm because, after the Suez crisis, Sweden had sent a contingent of United Nations Forces into Sinai. My task was to find out as much about the contingent's members as possible to ascertain who could do with some extra money. The task of those chosen was to write seemingly innocuous letters to their non-existent girlfriends. These epistles ultimately arrived on my desk and it was for me to decode the messages and to respond with love and longing. We did similar work with journalists, this time using invisible ink. I now realize that it was very amateurish and highly ineffective, but I found it most exciting.

A second area of my secret concern was helping Jews leave the Soviet Union. Since legal emigration from the Soviet Union was decades away, doctored Swedish passports were needed. Committed individuals would donate their own passports to the cause and then report them as lost to the Swedish authorities. The "lost" passports were then forwarded to Israel by diplomatic pouch, where they were suitably "adjusted." Another diplomatic pouch would take them to Moscow for distribution to those chosen to leave. It was an interesting idea, although I saw no evidence to suggest that people actually availed themselves of the facility.

One day my unofficial second boss, the Mossad rep, asked me to interview a man from Finland who was interested in working with us. I was all of twenty-one and not very experienced in assessing people, yet something about this person made me feel uncomfortable, and so I reported it. Nobody took any notice of my recommendation, and the Mossad rep went ahead and employed the man. It soon became clear that the man also worked for the Egyptians and they were using him to expose the Israelis. The thinly disguised "diplomat" had to be declared *persona non grata* and leave the country immediately. All who had worked with him were now highly exposed; a couple of them even went to prison in Sweden. When one of them was released, he went to Israel expecting a hero's welcome. Of course, he was totally ignored, for that's the way of the intelligence community. The Mossad rep reverted in time to his real name and is now a mover and shaker in the financial world in Israel. Though I've been to Israel countless times and live there now part of the year, I've never made contact with him.

That I, too, might be under suspicion wasn't clear. I did feel rather uncomfortable when I called my father on the phone and he said that he hoped I wasn't mixed up in the messy business he had been reading about in the papers. I knew that my phone was tapped and that my responses would be recorded.

Some time before I had even met the Finn, it was arranged that Fredzia and I would visit Israel in February 1957. We would attend a seminar for Zionist key workers, sponsored by the World Zionist Organization. To make sure that I got out of Sweden without any problems, the ambassador sent his driver to take us to the airport. This meant that we could arrive in the last moment and go directly to the plane. Whatever other considerations were in the ambassador's mind, the formal reason for the courtesy car was that I was travelling with a diplomatic pouch that contained a rare Karaite Bible manuscript. It had been purchased in Sweden from a descendant of one of the early Swedish missionaries whom Selma Lagerlöf wrote about in her book *Jerusalem*. Like other descendants from that group, he had returned to Sweden, brought with him this manuscript that he had acquired legally but now wanted to sell. Yaari arranged for its purchase and entrusted me with the task of taking it to the Ben Zvi Institute in Jerusalem, where I presume it still is.

Flying in those days was an adventure of the highest order. We thought it a miracle that having left Stockholm early in the morning and stopping only in Copenhagen, Vienna and Istanbul, we arrived in Tel Aviv late the same evening. We stayed with friends of Fredzia's family in Tel Aviv before joining the seminar, which took us all over the country. The day after we'd been married, we'd gone to work as usual. Now, ten months later, we had our honeymoon. It was unforgettable.

During our stay in Israel I was contacted by the now expelled Mossad rep and told to return to Stockholm via Paris, where I would get back a number of untouched passports that I was to return to their rightful owners. I'd get a daily allowance and my only task would be to report to the Israeli Embassy in Paris once a day to inquire if my parcel had arrived. Fredzia and I had a marvellous week in Paris doing all the things first-time tourists are expected to do. When the passports arrived we returned to Sweden.

Yehuda Yaari had instructed me to see Walter Eytan, the director-general of the Foreign Ministry, while I was in Israel. I made an appointment and arrived in good time. His secretary told me that he was busy, so I waited an hour or two. When I still wasn't admitted, I left my particulars and asked the secretary to make another appointment while I was in the country. I called once or twice to be told that Dr. Eytan was too busy to see me. When, upon my return to Stockholm, Yaari found out that I hadn't seen Eytan he was furious—with me. He told me that my correct Swedish behaviour made me unfit for Israel. What I should have done was to ignore the secretary and barge right in. Though I was twenty-two by then and good at making speeches, I wasn't confident enough for this kind of action. I'm not sure that I'm able to do it even now.

The reason for Yaari's anger was that he had written to Eytan to let him know that he intended to recommend that when his—Yaari's—term of duty was ended, there would be no need to send another Israeli, for I could do the job and in due course would move to Israel and embark upon a diplomatic career.

But I now know that, even if Walter Eytan had received me, I wouldn't have stayed with the Foreign Ministry. One day I met by chance at Zion Square in Jerusalem my Danish counterpart, Erling (now Ozer) Schild. I had originally got to know him at the youth leadership institute in Kristianstad and had admired him greatly ever since. He was a few years older, Orthodox and very articulate. After having served as the information officer at the Israeli Embassy in Copenhagen, he had decided to emigrate and to continue his career in the Israeli Foreign Ministry. In our chance encounter he told me that nobody took any notice of him now that he had become an immigrant. He said that he saw no prospects there for someone like himself or myself. He was about to become a university student. In time he became a professor of sociology at Haifa University and, for a short spell, its president. We reconnected at some point later when I was the rabbi of a large and allegedly wealthy congregation in Canada and he was in search of donors, but we've no contact now that both of us are out of office, even though we both have homes in Jerusalem. He had exchanged his Orthodoxy for militant right-wing politics; I had remained a Liberal left-winger. I could no longer learn from him as I once had.

The abortive encounter with Eytan and the chance meeting with Schild persuaded me that I, too, should go and study. Having seen the diplomatic life, I realized its limitations and understood that, unless you were an ambassador, the work was basically humdrum and far away from home. The idea, therefore, of becoming a rabbi surfaced again. Though I had heard that there was a Liberal rabbinical seminary in Paris, our week in the French capital persuaded us that it's a terrific city for tourists but not for residents who don't know the language. Rabbi Wilhelm had shown me an article from the London *Jewish Chronicle* about the establishment of a similar institution in London, soon to be named the Leo Baeck College after the legendary leader of German Jewry. Wilhelm recommended that I go there.

About a year earlier, in April 1956, the Liberal group in the Jewish community in Stockholm had invited Rabbi Dr. Werner Van Der Zyl as its guest lecturer. He was at that time establishing the Leo Baeck College. Because in those days an entrant to the college didn't have to have an undergraduate degree, only university entrance qualifications, I was encouraged to apply. Rabbi Kalir in Gothenburg helped me to fill out the application forms for a grant from the Claims Conference, the body that administered some of the reparation funds received from Germany to be used for the rebuilding of Jewish life after the Holocaust. The Jewish community in Stockholm also helped to finance me on the understanding that I would return to serve it once I had been ordained.

I resigned my post at the embassy and, during Hol Hamoed Suk-koth in 1957, Fredzia and I sailed from Gothenburg to a new life in London. The refuge that Sweden had afforded us made us sufficiently at home in the world to face a new life in England.

There was no overriding reason that made me decide to become a rabbi, but there were several factors.

From my early years in Gothenburg, I felt at home in the Jewish community. Though I was very involved in the life of my school, I always saw myself as an alien there. I may have got better marks in tests on Swedish language and literature than others, but like the biblical Abraham, I remained "a stranger and a sojourner" among the Swedes. The rabbinate was a way of celebrating my alien status.

A second reason was my discovery of Jewish learning. When Ove Nordstrandh, my teacher, made me write a paper on Judaism, he opened my eyes to a source of guidance and strength I had not been aware of before. I now began to read whatever was available in Swedish, but I wanted much more. I assumed that rabbinical school would provide it.

Third, Fredzia's encouragement from the moment we met was central to my decision, which now became a joint decision. Though being away from parents and the world we knew would be hard, the opportunity to start afresh was most attractive. We really felt that the destiny that brought the two of us together demanded a fresh start in every sense of the word. Going to London was the challenge we were eager to meet.

A fourth reason was, no doubt, my desire to be somebody. Our intention was to return to Stockholm where I'd serve as the assistant to Rabbi Wilhelm and, hopefully, in time succeed him. Though I had witnessed the bitterness and disappointment of Rabbi Loeb in Gothenburg and now Rabbi Wilhelm in Stockholm, I didn't think it would happen to me. I firmly believed that I could make a difference to the lives of the Jews in my adopted country and at the same time serve as a spokesman for Judaism to the non-Jewish world. Perhaps in the same way as I delighted in excelling in Swedish at school, thus beating the natives at their own game, I now wanted to excel in Judaism and, despite my background, teach the locals what it meant to be Jewish.

Yet another factor was a need, which emerged especially in my time in the Israeli legation, for both of us to vindicate our survival by making a contribution to Jewish life. Fredzia and I were astounded and immensely grateful at our good fortune to have come through the Holocaust. Serving the Jewish people would help us to justify it and endow our lives with purpose.

Though we were more Jewishly observant than the respective homes we'd come from, the decision to go to rabbinical school didn't arise out of a deep religious commitment. At that point in our lives, the Torah of Israel and the people of Israel mattered to us much more than the faith of Israel. I knew that an Orthodox yeshiva that demanded strict adherence to practice and belief wasn't for me, so I sought only Liberal institutions. The Leo Baeck College in London was not only Liberal, it seemed the most accessible. We knew enough English to be able to function, and London was relatively near Sweden, which would make leaving our families less traumatic.

I know now that my reasons for wanting to be a rabbi may have been acceptable as a start, but that much greater commitment was required to remain a rabbi. Such a commitment came with time, as the pages that follow will reveal.

England:
Vocation

*B*efore we arrived in England, Rabbi Werner Van Der Zyl, in sole charge of the Leo Baeck College, had arranged for us to stay in a large house in Hampstead Garden Suburb, a thriving area in northwest London where many of the city's Jews had their homes. The couple who owned the house had both died a short time before and the family was anxious that the house remain intact until the three children finished university. Our task was to act as house-sitters, keeping the place as a haven of happy memories and traditional Jewish observance, a place where the children could stay when in London.

We were impressed by the size and opulence of the house—our first encounter with television—and by its large Jewish library, most useful for a rabbinical student. But we were also overwhelmed by the sadness of the circumstances that brought us there—and the cold. There was no proper heating in the house and our most persistent memory of that first winter in England is one of being perpetually cold, even in bed. I did my preparations for classes wearing an overcoat and gloves. By all accounts the family could have afforded central heating, but in those days conventional wisdom in Britain had it that central heating was bad for your health and definitely not conducive to character building. Whenever I think of George Bernard Shaw's saying that an Englishman thinks he's virtuous when he's merely uncomfortable, I have in mind our sojourn in Hampstead Garden Suburb. We longed for our snug and warm little apartment in Stockholm where comfort and virtue didn't seem to be in conflict.

Our accommodation was only the first of several shocks in the first week of our stay in England. The second was the synagogue. Werner Van Der Zyl was the rabbi of the North-Western Reform Synagogue in Alyth Gardens, a short walk from where we lived. (Being principal of the Leo Baeck College was an unpaid position.) It was, therefore, natural that we should visit Alyth Gardens at the earliest opportunity. We had come from places with very beautiful synagogues, both in Gothenburg and in Stockholm. Services there may have been stilted and remote from the worshipping congregation, but the buildings were solemn and impressive—and that was what we were used to. Now we entered a building that looked more like a car repair shop than a synagogue. And the worship service was largely read, much of it in English, with occasional interventions by a small choir that was neither impressive nor inspiring. We didn't know anybody in the congregation, and in characteristic British fashion, the regulars made sure not to know us. Little did we expect then that some twelve years later I'd be appointed rabbi of that same North-Western Reform Synagogue and spend fourteen very happy years there.

As I was new to London, Van Der Zyl offered to drive me to the Leo Baeck College on the first day of term. We travelled in his little car to the West London Synagogue, the "cathedral" of British Reform, founded in 1842. The college occupied the congregation's old board-room, which was situated over the entrance hall to the sanctuary. Students could also make use of the less than up-to-date library. When Rabbi Van Der Zyl and I arrived that first day, a few men were already there and I was introduced to them: Lionel Blue, Henry Brandt, Edward Gold, Michael Goulston and Michael Leigh. We chatted briefly and then I asked Van Der Zyl if I might meet the other students. "*What other students?*" he said. I had been told before coming that this was a small college, but in my mind a small college was much larger than five students. This, then, was my third shock of the week.

Of the five students, Edward Gold soon left to work in the family insurance business. After a year Michael Goulston decided to continue his studies at the Hebrew Union College in Cincinnati. Lionel Blue, Henry Brandt and Michael Leigh would soon be given the title Reverend, in common use in Anglo-Jewry at the time to describe non-ordained "clergy," and serve respectively the Settlement Synagogue in the East End of London, Sinai Synagogue in Leeds and as an assistant at the West London Synagogue. Within a year of entry, I was left as the sole bona fide student of the Leo Baeck College. Later a few other men joined the program; some stayed the course, others soon went on to other things.

In my panic I would have transferred to another rabbinic school, but I had come with academic qualifications recognized neither in Britain nor in the United States. My Swedish *studentexamen* counted for nothing here. Though I later did acquire the necessary British university entrance qualifications, I didn't have them at the time. In any case I didn't want to prolong my studies more than necessary, which going elsewhere might have done. I was anxious to be ordained as soon as possible and start living. Also, we were too tied to our families in Sweden to consider going to the Hebrew Union College in distant America, and we were not sufficiently observant for me to be accepted by Jews' College, the mainstream Orthodox rabbinic school in London.

Being stuck virtually alone at the Leo Baeck College frustrated me greatly and I didn't make a secret of my desire to leave. This didn't endear me to Van Der Zyl, especially since my being something of a Holocaust survivor made me one—the only?—reason for the college claiming financial support from the Conference on Material Claims against Germany. Van Der Zyl, in turn, didn't endear himself to me. We had a difficult relationship for many years. It was based on mutual need: he needed me to keep the college going, I needed him to be ordained.

In view of what I consider to have been a successful rabbinic career, I've no reason to regret that I stayed the course at the Leo Baeck College. But because it didn't demand or enable me to get academic qualifications, I've always felt constrained in my ability to find a proper setting for my interests in ideas and scholarship. On balance, I'd probably have preferred the work of a university professor to that of a congregational rabbi, but this may be due only to the fact that I couldn't get the former. Throughout my career, the absence of academic qualifications provided reasons for my rabbinic rivals to keep me for many years away as far as they could from teaching at the Leo Baeck College. Some of them, I surmise, thought that as it was, I had advanced in the rabbinate above my station. At times I thought so myself.

The college had only two full-time teachers when I was a student there: Dr. Ellen Littman in Bible and Dr. Arieh Dorfler in Talmud. Littman had studied with Leo Baeck and others at the Hochschule für die Wissenschaft des Judentums, the Liberal seminary in Berlin. When she went to Palestine after the Nazis came to power, her teachers included Martin Buber and other prominent professors at the Hebrew University in Jerusalem. Had she lived a few decades later, she would have been ordained as a rabbi. She was a dedicated teacher. Ordination would have enabled her to have a wider audience and more opportunities to manifest her caring skills. Though she wasn't very *au fait* with so-called higher biblical criticism, she knew, in Buberian fashion, how to get "inside" the original text and make it come to life. This kind of teaching is more acceptable today than it was then. Nevertheless, her influence on most of her students, me included, was considerable. She was the mainstay of the College.

Dorfler's learning came from traditional yeshivas in Eastern Europe, but like Ellen Littman, he had also received a German academic education. He was a very good teacher who opened up for me and others the *terra incognita* of rabbinic literature. But unlike Littman, he was less accessible to students and much less attractive as a human being. His frequent displays of piety in class and outside didn't impress me as genuine.

The college also employed part-time lecturers. The two who made a deep impression on me were Dr. Allan Miller, who taught Midrash, and Dr. Ignaz Maybaum, who taught theology and comparative religion. It was what I learned from them that enabled me to become an enthusiastic teacher and preacher. Miller was the son of an Orthodox rabbi and had himself studied at Jews' College. He also had a doctorate from London University. He was brilliant. His classes were never less than stimulating. If I ever had a role model as a teacher it was Allan Miller, despite the fact that I found him a bit difficult as a human being.

Maybaum was a graduate of the Hochschule. Around the time that the Nazis came to power, Maybaum, after having served two small

German provincial congregations, became one of the spiritual leaders of the Jewish community of Berlin. He and his family came to England only weeks before the outbreak of the war. Like most German Jews (even though he was born in Vienna), the Maybaums didn't care much for *Ostjuden*, Jews from Eastern Europe. Mercifully, however, they made an exception for Fredzia and me. We went often to their home and felt good in their company. I also had the privilege of working with Rabbi Maybaum in the congregation he served, the Edgware and District Reform Synagogue. The Maybaums were our rabbinic role models and I'm proud to be his disciple, albeit a deviant one, as my essays about him indicate.

I had always been a good and conscientious student, but at the Leo Baeck College I found the going tough. To start with, I had to work in a language that wasn't my own. Though I had learned English in my Swedish school and worked with English in the Israeli legation before coming to London, I didn't know the language the way I was expected to know it now. The fact that English was by no means the first language of teachers like Littman, Dorfler and Maybaum further complicated things. I recall, for example, reading the Book of Hosea with Littman and trying to translate the Hebrew *zonah*. The dictionary said, "whore." I pronounced it "war." Dr Littman didn't object. Michael Goulston was still with us at the time and, not being able to tolerate such abuse of his native tongue, offered the correct pronunciation. At that point Littman lit up: *"Ach die Hure,"* she said, suggesting the German equivalent. Swedish has a similar word, but neither she nor I could make the connection without Goulston's help. I dread to think how many other English words I mispronounced in those early days, some of them no doubt from the pulpit.

Though English has now become my first language, the fact that it's not my native tongue is apparent the moment I open my mouth. I was thirteen when I first arrived in Sweden, young enough to learn to speak the language without an accent. People sometimes guess that I come from South Africa or Australia; in any case, I speak English with an accent.

At the college, I was expected to learn a new language, Hebrew, in a language that wasn't my own, English. It was hard work. Though I had learned Hebrew at school during my fewer than two years in post-war Poland, it wasn't the language of rabbinical studies. The Hebrew I used at the Israeli legation in Stockholm was equally basic and colloquial. Now was my first encounter with grammar and a sophisticated vocabulary, biblical and rabbinic. My greatest asset was, strangely enough, my knowledge of Yiddish. Once I learned which of the Yiddish words and idioms I knew were Hebrew in origin, I acquired a vocabulary.

And then there were the practical obstacles, each of them in itself insignificant but together quite formidable: spending a long time on public transport to get from place to place, the cold at home, the loneliness due to absence of family and friends and very little contact with locals. Those first few months were hard. The fact that we didn't give up was largely due to Fredzia's determination, common sense and maturity.

We knew only one couple in London. We had met them originally in Stockholm. The late Saga Friedman came from a Swedish-Jewish family. She married Cyril Chody, a London solicitor. They now lived in Harrow-on-the-Hill and we visited them often. When in the spring of 1958 the three-room apartment opposite theirs became available, we rented it. As she would do often in years to come, Fredzia soon created a beautiful and comfortable home for us. We spent five much better years there. The apartment was centrally heated. By the time we were ready to leave it, the two of us had become four.

Fredzia was pregnant when we moved to Harrow-on-the Hill. I was still overwhelmed by college work and was, therefore, less than enthusiastic about having a child at this stage in our lives. I also felt that we were very young and very poor. The real reason may have been the usual male panic at no longer being numero uno in his mate's life. But mercifully she had her way, for she was definitely sufficiently resourceful and mature to be a mother. We were devastated when the baby was stillborn at seven months. In the two years that followed, Fredzia lost two more babies, even though she spent long periods of pregnancy in the hospital. Each failure was followed by spells of depression and self-blame. Even these ostensibly better years were difficult.

Though there appeared to be no reason why Fredzia couldn't have children, we were beginning to resign ourselves. Lionel Blue, the spiritual leader of the Settlement Synagogue, knew of a couple in the congregation he served that had adopted a child through a obstetrician who owned a private clinic. As soon as we got his name we went to see him. Dr. Immanuel Bierer was born in Vienna, lived on a kibbutz in what was then Palestine and later came to England, where he trained as a doctor. He exuded confidence and power. We were at his mercy and at the interview, he made us feel it. Nevertheless, he soon informed us that there was a baby girl available for adoption. She was born prematurely on April 23, 1960. When we first saw her in July, she was still very small and not very responsive.

Within days of looking after her, she brightened up and has been a source of light and warmth in our lives ever since. We fell in love with her and have remained in love with her to this very day. Feeling still very Swedish and determined to return to Stockholm upon my graduation from the Leo Baeck College, we named her Viveca and waited anxiously for some six months before the court declared her legally ours. Lionel Blue is her godfather. She was blessed at the Edgware and District Reform Synagogue by Rabbi Dr. Ignaz Maybaum.

Her brother, Michael, was born less than two years later, in March 1962. When Fredzia was pregnant with him, it was recommended that we see a doctor in Stockholm. He knew immediately where the problem was and after a very minor operation, she was able to carry the baby full term. Elizabeth, our third child, was born in January 1967.

Whatever other achievements we may have attained in life, nothing compares to being parents to three extraordinary human beings. Our children are the greatest gift that life has bestowed on us, as are Sarah Bernstein, Michael's wife, and their three children—Miriam, Nadav and Gaby—and Anthony Kessel, Elizabeth's husband, and their children, Leone and Ethan.

I entered rabbinical school as a searching Jew. Being a parent turned me into a believing Jew. The change came about thanks to some of my teachers and many books, but it was only when I became a father that I could fathom the true meaning of faith. Viveca's arrival was a miracle, reinforced by the birth of Michael and Elizabeth. I now not only understood the biblical stories that see life as a divine gift, not just a human right, but I also could imagine what God must be like whom our tradition calls *Harachaman*, a variant of the Hebrew for *rechem*, womb. God's love is the same love that a mother feels for her child. Hence Fredzia's deep faith and hence my propensity to describe myself, only half in jest, as a Jewish mother.

In Judaism family isn't only a matter of psychology and sociology but also a theological category. Thanks to it I could experience God, described in Jewish sources as parent and spouse. But it's really thanks to my family that I began to fathom the meaning of love, obligation, trust, grace, forgiveness and hope.

Soon after we moved to Harrow-on-the-Hill, I read in the London *Jewish Chronicle* that Bent Melchior, one of the sons of Marcus Melchior, the chief rabbi of Denmark, was coming to Jews' College to study for the rabbinate. I had met Marcus Melchior at gatherings of the Scandinavian-Jewish Youth Organization and I knew Bent's older brother, Arne. I had heard that Bent was a teacher in the religious school and the day school of the Jewish community in Copenhagen and that he was married to Lilian. They were coming to London with their two young children, Michael and John.

Knowing how difficult our entry into England had been, Fredzia and I immediately got in touch with Bent and Lilian, offering them whatever assistance we could to smooth their path. When we met one evening in early 1958 during a stopover in Copenhagen on our way to Stockholm, it turned out that they would be arriving in London while we were away. We therefore offered them our new apartment for the weeks we weren't going to be there to enable them to look around and find their own place. As our home was consistently kosher, they could cook and eat there.

What started casually blossomed into an intimate friendship that has lasted to this day, even though for the past forty years or so we've lived in different countries, often on different continents. Their third son, Alan, was born a few days before our son, Michael, and their mothers gave birth in the same maternity hospital in London. Lilian and Bent are Michael's godparents, and Fredzia and I are Alan's. Michael's *brit milah* was celebrated in the Melchior home, which was very close to the hospital. The Marmurs have attended several bar mitzvahs and weddings in the Melchior family, and the Melchiors have reciprocated. Both families have always travelled considerable distances to share in each other's joys.

Two of the Melchior sons now live in Israel: Michael—the unorthodox Orthodox rabbi-politician and, justifiably, the darling of the Jewish Diaspora—and Kim, the youngest, born after the family's London sojourn. We don't see a lot of them, even though we now spend much of our time in Israel, but we feel close to the whole family and always see the parents when they come to Jerusalem or we visit Copenhagen. Bent succeeded his father as chief rabbi and retired a few years ago from that position. He remains a leader in European Jewry and continues to play an important part in Danish public life.

If the Maybaums taught us how to be a rabbinical family, the Melchiors taught us how to lead a Jewish life in a Jewish home. Here we found a rich, relaxed and traditional way of life we had never experienced before. It helped to shape us as Jews. Despite our very different views about Judaism, we've quite similar perceptions of what it means to be Jewish, both in personal lifestyle and in commitment to peace and justice in the world. We count Lilian and Bent Melchior not only among our oldest, but also among our closest friends.

In the bed next to Fredzia's in the maternity hospital was a Jewish woman from South Africa who, together with her husband and children, had come to England a few months earlier to escape the intolerable situation in their native country. She was expecting her fourth child this March of 1962. The two mothers-in-waiting got to know each other, and in time our families became very close. Esme and Allan Benjamin, with their children Lee, Larry, Desmond and Michael (born a few days after our Michael), became our other closest friends. As we lived in the same city it was easier to keep the friendship going. When more than two decades later we moved to Canada, Esme's brother, Ivan Samson, and his wife, Toni, as well as Esme's late parents, Rae and Cyril Samson, lived in St. Catharines, less than two hours' drive from Toronto. We grew close to them too.

Allan Benjamin's death in 2000 was not only a devastating blow to his family, but a profound loss to Fredzia and me. For Allan had been an anchor in many people's lives, including ours. I don't think we ever made an important decision without first talking it over with him. He exuded confidence and always showed great wisdom. He knew how to enjoy success and how to overcome failure. I think of him often and always with fondness.

The trials and tribulations of our early years in England were now diminishing. We had a family, a home, exceptional friends and good prospects. With time I had acquired a sufficiently good command of English to be able to function in the pulpit, and I took the studies in my stride, often enjoying what I was learning and usually impressing my teachers. Conscious of my lack of academic status, I enrolled as an occasional student in the Hebrew Department of University College, London. I found the atmosphere there arid. Judaism was largely reduced to philology. I don't think I learned much.

The only exception to a mediocre teaching staff was Joseph Weiss. Born in Hungary, he arrived in what was then Palestine as a young man. He had been an outstanding student of Gershom Scholem, the towering figure of Jewish scholarship at the Hebrew University in Jerusalem and the world's acknowledged expert on Jewish mysticism. Weiss had come to University College as a lecturer some time before my arrival there as a student.

A few years after I finished my studies at the Leo Baeck College and went to serve my first congregation, Lionel Blue sent Weiss to me for counselling, perhaps because he thought I could help the troubled professor, or perhaps because he just wanted to palm him off, for Weiss was very "high maintenance." Sensing that Weiss was suffering from delusions of persecution, especially by Israelis, who presumably were seeking to punish him for having left the country—the guilt of the *yored* (a person who leaves Israel, which at that time was something of a stigma)—Blue had told him that I could help because I had been an Israeli spy. This was, of course, a gross exaggeration of my minor exploits in Sweden, which I must have spoken of to my friend—in strictest confidence, of course.

I saw Weiss often in his large and chaotic apartment. By then he had separated from his second wife, who lived with their son a short distance away. I was mesmerized by Weiss's brilliance, now deployed largely to feed his paranoia. He would invest an innocent note from the milkman with hidden meaning and deep significance in much the way he did an ancient manuscript, which his illustrious teacher Scholem had taught him to do. I've since often wondered if what now goes under the name of *textual reasoning*, a respected academic discipline, isn't touched by the same sickness.

At times Weiss would draw me into his imaginary world in ways that baffled me. Once he told me of people who were after him in Israel. One of his alleged persecutors was, he said, Yehuda Yaari, my former boss in Stockholm. Yaari came from Hasidic stock and had written about Nachman of Bratslav. This founder of an important sect was also one of Weiss's scholarly interests. It seems that at some conference the two had clashed. In his sick state, Weiss now saw the clash as persecution instigated by the government of Israel—had not Yaari been an Israeli diplomat?—and invested the encounter with almost cosmic significance. I didn't tell Weiss that I knew Yaari.

One day Weiss asked me if I could recommend a good psychiatrist. He had to be Jewish and know Israel. I immediately thought of Dr. Joshua Bierer, the brother of our "angel," Dr. Immanuel Bierer, the doctor who brought Viveca into our lives. Mercifully Weiss didn't pursue the matter, for shortly afterwards Yaari came on a visit to London. When I asked him where he was staying, he told me that he was the guest of a good friend from their kibbutz days in Israel—Joshua Bierer. Had Weiss ever gone to Bierer and found out the connection with Yaari, he would have had further "evidence" that Israeli intelligence was out to get him and that I was the agent who had been planted to torment him. The uncanny coincidence made me realize how easy it is to be drawn into the world of paranoia. It was one reason I now decided to learn enough about mental illness to know when *not* to deal with it myself but refer to a qualified person.

After years of inner torment Weiss committed suicide in August 1969. His works, mostly unpublished in his lifetime, have appeared in print over the years, both in Hebrew and in English. He's still considered a scholar of awesome proportions. Some years ago I read a review of a cycle of love poems he had written as a young man to a fellow Hungarian immigrant in Palestine—Hannah Senesh.

I know that Weiss, when still well enough to think rationally, had been disappointed that I didn't acquire the necessary academic qualifications to be taken seriously as a potential scholar. Not long after I left the Leo Baeck College as a student, the late Samuel Sandmel, an expert in the field of Christian-Jewish relations and the history of early Judaism, who served at that time as the provost of the Hebrew Union College in Cincinnati, spent his sabbatical year as acting principal of the Leo Baeck College. He had consulted Weiss, he told me one day, about whom he should groom for the permanent position of principal of the college. Weiss had recommended me—if only I had the academic qualifications. Sandmel talked to me about it, but I wasn't prepared to embark on the project. Neither the Leo Baeck College nor the Hebrew Department at University College had made Jewish *scholarship* very attractive. I thirsted for Jewish *learning* but felt that I could acquire much of it by myself. Moreover, I had by then been sufficiently influenced and inspired by Ignaz Maybaum to want to pursue modern Jewish thought rather than classical text study, and this has indeed remained my interest.

After a couple of years as a student in London, when I had acquired some, albeit rudimentary, rabbinical skills and sufficiently improved my English to speak from the pulpit, I was sent to congregations that needed rabbinical services but for one reason or another didn't have a rabbi. My first regular appointment came in 1959 when I was sent to the Glasgow New Synagogue, which I was to visit monthly for Sabbath services and major Jewish holy days. If my ostensibly academic studies put me off Jewish scholarship, Glasgow nearly put me off the rabbinate as a career.

Like so many Reform congregations, particularly outside London, it was small and something of a pariah in the local Jewish community, subject to unfounded gossip and malicious badmouthing. For example, even many years after the congregation was founded, Jews in the city would tell me that the Reform synagogue was the place where they serve refreshments on Yom Kippur afternoon. The origin of the calumny is telling. The first year that the congregation held High Holiday services, it met in a local labour hall. Yom Kippur fell on a Saturday and a few members of the neighbouring Orthodox congregation, perhaps bored with their own services, decided to walk over to find out what these people who called themselves Reform were up to. Some visitors arrived at the same time as a truck delivering refreshments for the dance that was to be held in the labour hall an hour or so after Yom Kippur was over and the congregation had left the building. But the true reason for the delivery wasn't convenient for the opponents of Reform Judaism. They preferred the myth, which was perpetuated for years thereafter.

Like so many small congregations, the Glasgow New Synagogue was largely run by one individual and his family. Though it did have a German refugee rabbi at some point, only one man really "owned" the services. He had died some time before my arrival, but his widow, two sons and daughter were still the "first family" of the congregation. Others vied for the position, which made for tensions and petty intrigues. One of the consequences was that whatever I may have suggested to the leaders during a visit, usually in an effort to promote consistency and a measure of depth, was immediately cancelled when I left town. It was a most frustrating experience.

At the same time that I visited Glasgow I also worked in the Edgware and District Reform Synagogue, the congregation where my mentor, Ignaz Maybaum, was the rabbi. My primary task there was to run the religious school. As it met on Sundays, I would usually try to catch the last plane out of Glasgow on Saturday night to be in Edgware the following morning. I had no car and therefore spent hours on buses or waiting for buses. I didn't have much knowledge of education and even less of administration, but in the eyes of the blind the one-eyed man is king. There was a lot of blindness about, because Jewish education in British Reform was abysmal in those days, and Edgware was no exception. Perhaps that was why Maybaum called me, less in praise than in irony, the Napoleon of his Hebrew classes.

When Rabbi Maybaum was away I was allowed not only to conduct worship services, which I did from time to time in his presence, but also to preach. All I knew about preaching and much of what I knew about Judaism came from Maybaum. But since neither my thought processes nor my English vocabulary allowed me to express matters in depth, people seemed to understand what I was saying and would often tell me how much better I preached than Maybaum. I was devastated. My cynicism about congreg*ants*—not so about congreg*ations*—has never really left me, even though I've often tried hard to conceal it.

In between all my assignments—the College, Edgware and Glasgow—I was sent to conduct services in other congregations that had no rabbi. At the time I thought that Van Der Zyl was doing what he could to break my morale. In retrospect I believe that though he needed to supply congregations with rabbinical students, he was determined to send me back to Sweden and didn't want me to become too comfortable in Britain. But if that was his aim, he didn't succeed.

When in the fall of 1961 Rabbi Allan Miller left the congregation he had served, the South-West Essex Reform Synagogue in Ilford, northeast London, to be the spiritual leader of the Society for the Advancement of Judaism, the Reconstructionist movement's mother congregation in New York City, Van Der Zyl had to provide students to conduct services while the congregation was looking for a replacement for Miller. I was commandeered a few weeks after Miller's departure. To get there I had to go across London and back on public transport and therefore wasn't happy with this additional assignment. However, the honorary president of the congregation and one of its founders, Bernard Davis, met me at Baker Street station, roughly halfway, and took me there. I promised myself to do my best.

It seems that I did, for this, my first visit to Ilford, changed my life and the life of my family. After I conducted the Friday evening service, which included a sermon, the leaders of the congregation offered me the position. I was dazed. Not that the congregation was impressive. Few of them were there that Friday evening. The worship area was the upstairs of an Edwardian house. It was cold and quite unappealing, especially on this particularly miserable evening. But Allan Miller had served there and would, from time to time, speak in my presence of the splendid people in the congregation. Moreover, as Miller was something of an idol of mine in those days, to succeed him was a great honour, an opportunity of a lifetime.

However, there was a serious snag: I was committed to return to Stockholm and serve there. Therefore, immediately after the offer to succeed Miller I wrote to the Jewish community in Stockholm informing them of the situation and asking what they had in mind for me after ordination. Perhaps suspecting that I was trying to force their hand, they told me that since I wasn't graduating for another few months, there was no need to discuss the matter half a year ahead of time. Things would be sorted out when I got home. I was less than enthusiastic about the prospect, suspecting that, if I returned to Stockholm without a firm job offer, I'd be at the mercy of the congregation's bureaucracy, which was considerable, and its internal divisions, which were even more considerable. So I offered to take the Ilford position for eleven months, from February 1, 1962, until the end of that year, to enable Stockholm to get its act together in the meantime.

The Jewish community of Stockholm was quite relaxed about my return, and there was much to suggest that they didn't really *want* me back. Van Der Zyl, on the other hand, was furious. His dual goal to establish the college as a place that also trained students from abroad and to get rid of me was in danger of being thwarted. He had told me at some point that I shouldn't even think of staying in Britain, because my English wasn't up to it, even though already at that time it was probably better than his. Now his prophecy was about to be annulled.

Van Der Zyl had an additional problem: when it was announced that Allan Miller was leaving, the congregation placed an advertisement in the *Jewish Chronicle* offering an annual salary of "up to 2000 pounds." No rabbi in Britain earned that kind of money in those days. Would I now be getting it? Yes. Because of it most rabbis got considerable salary increases in the congregations they served.

What mattered to me most was that, even before I had finished my rabbinical studies, I had been invited to succeed British Reform's most brilliant rabbi. I felt I had nothing to lose. If things didn't work out, neither the congregation nor I had to endure each other for more than eleven months. But if it worked out, I'd be set up for life.

These eleven months turned out to be difficult, despite the warmth and enthusiasm with which the members of the South-West Essex Reform Synagogue received me. First, I had to complete my two rabbinical theses: one for Dorfler on the laws of *Shekhitah* (ritual slaughter) in the Shulkhan Arukh, the sixteenth-century normative code of Jewish law, compiled by Joseph Caro, by comparing it to the twelfth-century

legal compendium *Mishneh Torah* by Moses Maimonides; the other for
Maybaum about priest and prophet in the Bible and in later literature.
These tracts have in no way contributed to Jewish scholarship. At best
they are indications that I could handle some of the literature.

Second, I had to spend hours commuting across London between
Harrow, where we lived, and Ilford, where the congregation was. It
would be another couple of years before I learned to drive a car. The
members, particularly the men, of my "lower middle class" congregation regarded car ownership as a sign of prosperity and being able to
drive it evidence of manliness. I failed miserably in their eyes, but they
forgave me by suspecting that I was an "intellectual." Kind and generous people that they were, they were always anxious to give rides to
my family and me.

Third, our son, Michael, was born a few weeks after I started working. It was a great joy, but having two children under the age of two in
the small apartment didn't make for serenity and peace of mind, even
though Fredzia was magnificent as usual in protecting me from domestic responsibilities to enable me to complete my studies.

But one final difficulty during these eleven months took the greatest
toll. As soon as I took the position in Ilford, I refused to take money from
the Stockholm Jewish community, but my obligation to it remained of
course. It was quite obvious that I would rather stay in England and that
the leaders of the communities both in Sweden and in England would
rather I didn't return, but neither I nor the Jewish community of Stockholm was in a position to admit it. The peg on which the community
leadership in Stockholm hanged its objection was an address I had given
in Oslo in the spring of 1962 at the annual meeting of the Scandinavian-
Jewish Youth Federation.

The point of that address was that the Jews in Scandinavia should-
n't live their Judaism vicariously through Israel, but had to create their
own style and lead their own lives to ensure a future for themselves and
their children. Being young and careless about the way I used language, and pretending to be self-confident, I must have implied that
the rabbis of the communities, not the *shlikhim*, the emissaries from
Israel sent to the Zionist federations, should be the leaders. In retrospect I realize I was also saying that I wouldn't be marginalized the way

Rabbi Wilhelm had been and that I wouldn't take my orders from the lay leadership, which often looked to the emissaries for guidance. These leaders seemed to consider secular Israelis, sent to them by the Jewish Agency in Jerusalem, more authentically Jewish than those they had chosen as their spiritual leaders in Stockholm. But had I been more experienced and keener to return to Sweden, I would have expressed myself, perhaps, with greater caution. For example, I wouldn't have described Jews in Scandinavia as living as parasites off the Judaism of others. Didn't the Nazis describe Jews as parasites? People were offended. I should have known better.

No adverse reaction reached me in the weeks after my speech, but later, when my return to Stockholm became a distinct possibility, all hell broke loose. The president of the community, Fritz Hollander, was also the president of the Zionist federation. The emissary at the time was Uri Rapp, an academic sociologist. Rapp had been present when I spoke in Oslo and now warned Hollander that I was a danger to Jewish life in Scandinavia. After many meetings and much unpleasant behind-the-scenes work, in the course of which I also learned that the majority of the leaders didn't want a Liberal rabbi in their community, I finally withdrew my application. According to the rules of the Jewish community in Stockholm, rabbis have to be elected by the members. Because I was the only candidate, the electors would have to say *yes* or *no* on the ballot papers. These had already been issued. I've kept copies as souvenirs.

Though Kurt Wilhelm, the chief rabbi, had originally pointed me in the direction of the Leo Baeck College, over the years he realized that he didn't want me as his associate and, perhaps, successor. I don't know if he was under pressure from others. A year or so before I was due to finish he told me that Stockholm would "eat me alive." As an illustration he told me about an "Orthodox" imposter rabbi in the city who was being hailed as a true leader, despite his dubious past and, as it turned out, even more embarrassing future. Wilhelm's letter of recommendation to the congregation prior to the election at which I was to be the only candidate consisted of one sentence: "Dow Marmur preaches without pathos." The electors would, no doubt, get the message.

My supporters in the Jewish community in Stockholm—the members of the Liberal group—were my major embarrassment. Their Jewish

Liberalism was minimalist, while I, on the other hand, under the influence of British Reform and my Eastern European background, never believed in "Judaism lite." I thus learned the meaning of the saying that the Jews I could talk to I couldn't pray with, and the Jews I could pray with I couldn't talk to, or rather, they wouldn't talk to me.

Not only would they not talk to me, they found all kinds of excuses to badmouth me. Hollander let it be known through his henchmen, many of whom were also his employees, that I was denigrating the Swedish *Shekhitah* system. Many years earlier Wilhelm had obtained permission from the then chief rabbi of Jerusalem to declare animals that were stunned prior to slaughtering—as required by Swedish law— as kosher. Subsequently it was realized that the Jerusalem rabbi must have been confused or misinformed when he gave that permission and no Orthodox Jew would eat meat thus slaughtered. One day, over a meatless lunch in a non-Jewish restaurant with Hollander, I remember commenting on this. The conclusions made on my views were his; I don't remember that he objected to what I said at the time, and I know that I didn't take the side of the Orthodox in the dispute. I soon learned that "quoting out of context" was one of his ploys for twisting the truth in his favour.

Some Jews in Stockholm were scandalized by the trial sermon I had preached—according to the rules of the community, every candidate had to preach a sermon in front of the congregation before the election—in which I used ordinary Swedish idioms. As my rich use of the Swedish language and my authentic Swedish accent were much better than those of other rabbis they had heard, it was also comprehensible. It seems that many congregants didn't know how to cope with a sermon they actually understood. I think the definition of a rabbi as "invisible six days of the week and incomprehensible on the seventh" was invented in Stockholm.

One family even "remembered" that I showed disrespect to the customs of the place. When Fredzia and I went to the synagogue in Stockholm a few days before our wedding in May 1956, six years before I became a candidate for the rabbinical position, another couple was rehearsing for their wedding ceremony. I had refused a rehearsal. Prince Rainier of Monaco and Grace Kelly had just been married and I remember saying that ours wouldn't be a show. The parents of the other couple may have overheard my remarks, or perhaps an official of the community fed them my words later. In the controversy over my possible appointment now, they chose to use the incident as evidence that I was "contemptuous of synagogue practice." Telling people that at twenty-one I was immature and arrogant would have been much closer to the truth.

The examples cited above were trivial in comparison to the bombastic resolution that the Swedish Zionist Federation issued, telling the members of the community that in Oslo I had desecrated the memories of the founders of Zionism, starting with Herzl and ending with Hugo Valentin, the latter a distinguished Swedish Jew and an ardent Zionist. When years later I held offices such as the chair of Arzenu, the international movement of Reform Zionists, and the vice-presidency of the Canadian Zionist Federation, and in 2001 was a member of the executive of the World Zionist Organization (WZO), I thought occasionally about that resolution in Stockholm and how petty communal politics can lose all sense of proportion and truth.

For a long time I felt a tinge of unease at having been slighted by the community that I thought of as mine. Though I'm most grateful that we were able to stay in Britain, bring up our children there, serve two magnificent congregations and play a constructive part in the Reform movement, I'm perhaps too much of an only child not to have felt rejected. I know now that I would have served the Stockholm community well and represented it widely in Swedish society, but from what I know of the hardships that Bent Melchior endured in his congregation in Copenhagen—though he is a most talented rabbi and something of a household name in Denmark—I know that I would have had a hard time and unlike Melchior, who stayed, would have left the country at the earliest opportunity.

I've no hard feelings now, only gratitude at having been allowed to stay in England. When in March 2002 I was invited to preach in the synagogue in Stockholm, Rabbi Morton Narrowe, who had taken the position I never got and stayed in the country after his retirement as chief rabbi, told me that he was surprised that he couldn't detect any rancour in my remarks. The truth is that I didn't give the matter any thought, for my sense of rejection has gone long ago. Fredzia's and my parents were probably disappointed that we didn't return to Sweden, but I fear that they would have felt worse had they had to endure the calumnies and criticisms to which I would have been subjected, as are virtually all rabbis in small, smug and remote communities, especially when they have to be all things to all people.

One of my many joys in serving Reform congregations in Britain and Canada has been the freedom to express what I believe in and to practise the kind of Judaism consistent with my views and with the expectations of those to whom I ministered. Serving a so-called *Einheitsgemeinde* (unified community) like Stockholm, a community that embraces all religious streams under one umbrella yet is committed to none, invariably restricts a rabbi, irrespective of his orientation. The few communities outside Sweden that still work under that system, mainly in Germany, are all burdened with similar difficulties. Though most of the members would prefer to have Liberal rabbis as their teachers, the leaders usually want Conservative or Orthodox rabbis to be pious on their behalf.

Before I could take full advantage of the freedom Britain offered me, I had to finish my two rabbinical theses and submit to an oral examination. The former were completed and accepted. Though I'm not particularly proud of either, judging by the intellectual standards of some of the students who came after me, I surmise that my essays were probably better than many others, even though the leadership of the Leo Baeck College, perhaps in its efforts to put me down, would announce at meetings over the many years that followed that "the academic standard of the students had greatly improved since the early days of the college."

The oral examination was a farce. It started badly enough when Ellen Littman gave me as an unseen text the passage in the Book of Ezekiel that rejects the notion of inherited guilt. Like similar passages in Deuteronomy and Jeremiah it asks, "Because the fathers have eaten sour grapes shall the children's teeth be set on edge?" When in the discussion of the text I suggested that this may be a critique of one of the Ten Commandments that asserts that God visits "the iniquity of the parents upon the children unto the third and fourth generations" and

Littman nodded in agreement, Dorfler, who had never been a friend of hers, interjected vehemently and insisted that this is a false and misleading interpretation, borrowed from Gentile critics. The rest of that hour was a heated exchange between the two lecturers.

The liturgy examination was worse. Otto Lehman, one of the part-time lecturers at the Leo Baeck College, who rarely gave the impression that he understood what he was teaching and with whom I had a less than cordial relationship, decided to get even by writing out without vowels a *piyut*, a medieval liturgical poem, from the traditional order of service for Sukkoth. This was to be my unseen text. He himself had in front of him a copy of the Roedelheim Machzor, in use in Orthodox congregations in pre-war Germany. Though Van Der Zyl was normally not on my side, on this occasion he intervened on my behalf and suggested that I should have at least a printed and vocalized copy of the text. "But the only text I have," said Lehman, "has a German translation, and Marmur knows German." To which Van Der Zyl replied, "If you can't trust a candidate for the rabbinate that much, you shouldn't examine him in the first place." Lehman and I now exchanged texts. It no longer mattered how I translated, for I'm convinced that Lehman could hardly read his own writing, let alone understand what it meant.

I'm told that when other students were subjected to oral examinations prior to ordination, some teachers let them know in advance what the unseen texts were going to be, because they couldn't bear the thought of the students doing badly and thus reflecting poorly on themselves. I'm happy to say that none of my teachers seemed to show such concerns about me. I knew already that the lecturers were insecure. None of them had actually taught in rabbinical schools before. They did what they remembered was done at the Hochschule in Berlin and they knew nothing about examinations at British institutions of higher learning. But they wanted to prove to each other, probably more than to the students, that they kept high academic standards. The one who should have guided them, namely the honorary principal, knew less than the others.

I had a learned a lot in my five years at the Leo Baeck College, much of it in spite of the teachers. I longed for vacations, when I could read on my own and deepen my knowledge, especially in areas the college curriculum didn't cover. Bent Melchior and I engaged a private teacher in Talmud, a Litvak (Lithuanian rationalist) of the old school, the late Moshe Vilensky, a serious rabbinical scholar. I felt that being Reform I was obligated to know more, not less, than others. But as hard as I tried I was left with the feeling that I didn't know enough. That feeling has never left me.

According to the records, I was the first student of the Leo Baeck College to go through the course from beginning to end in the five years allotted to it. There had already been a couple of "ordinations" of men who had studied elsewhere. Lionel Blue, Henry Brandt and Michael Leigh began their studies before the college was opened in 1956, and as they now worked in congregations as "reverends," they had not yet completed the requirements for ordination. But Van Der Zyl couldn't bear the thought that I should be ordained before his two disciples, Blue and Leigh, even though he wanted me to leave the country as soon as possible. As a result my formal ceremony was delayed by two years until the others were ready for their own. In the meantime and at my insistence, Van Der Zyl gave me a letter stating that I had completed my studies and was now a rabbi. At the ceremony in 1964, two years after I left the college, each of us received a handwritten document in Hebrew, formulated very much along traditional lines. It still hangs in my study at home. At the ceremony itself, the participating lecturers were very nervous. Some of them read the documents badly.

Years later the Leo Baeck College acquired a proper ordination certificate in English and Hebrew, and I have one that states that I was ordained in 1962. By then at least one of the signatories on the document was dead; the late Sidney Pettle, the sexton at the West London Synagogue, had forged his signature. I keep that certificate behind a cupboard in my office. In the list of graduates that the college now publishes, I'm correctly listed as having been ordained in 1962, but Lionel Blue and the late Michael Leigh are listed as having been ordained in 1958, the year they left the college to become "reverends." Henry Brandt, on the other hand, is listed as having graduated a couple of years after me. Facts are rarely as factual as they seem to be.

But little of that mattered much then and none of it matters now. The South-West Essex Reform Synagogue brought me many joys and soon compensated for all my frustrations of the previous five years. Now with the Stockholm nightmare over, Fredzia and I could look for a house. We didn't want to live in a manse, that is, a house owned by the congregation, as was still the custom at the time. Had we done so, we may never have been able to afford a home of our own, for house prices later skyrocketed in Britain. Our parents helped us with the down-payment and provided some funds for renovations on a splendid four-bedroom house in the centre of the community. We moved early in 1963 into what we considered a palatial home.

My salary, together with the money we made by renting out our apartment in Stockholm and the monthly cheques Fredzia received as German reparations, enabled us to hire the services of a mother's helper. Now Fredzia could have some relief from the very hard work required in looking after two small children and a large house. We decided to take it easy from now on, and we promised ourselves breakfast in bed once a week. The first time the toast, marmalade and coffee were brought in, the phone rang. It was Fredzia's mother, Fela, calling from Las Palmas in Spain, where she and Fredzia's father, Isaac, had gone on holiday. Isaac was seriously ill and would Fredzia come as soon as possible. This is the first and the last time the two of us had breakfast in bed.

Within hours Fredzia was on her way to Las Palmas. Her father was suffering from an obstruction and it seemed obvious that it was cancer. She came back home when her parents returned to Sweden. Her father was operated on, but didn't really recover. Though he managed one more visit to London to see his two grandchildren and our new home, things got worse the following winter. Fredzia, now with Viveca, went to Stockholm for a prolonged stay. Michael, the mother's helper, and I remained in London. No happiness, it seems, is unalloyed.

Isaac Zonabend died early in 1964 at the age of 56. He was a good and intelligent man. His daughter had been much closer to him than she was to her mother. She misses him still, forty years after his death.

It was resilience and instinct, not maturity, that enabled me to cope with the many challenges with which life presented us. Though we had made progress and now had a family, though we had many friends and found time to enjoy the world, my behaviour was superficial and often less than appropriate. It was Fredzia's strength and love that kept us going. One of the earliest entries in the diary I started keeping in Sweden soon after we got married reflects on my need to become mature. In a way I've striven for it all my life. Never having had the opportunity to be a normal child, I tried hard to become a normal adult. It wasn't easy and I'm not convinced that I've succeeded.

The first source of help in my effort to grow up came unexpectedly. While still at the Leo Baeck College, in November 1961, I participated in a seminar intended for Reform rabbis and rabbinical students organized by the National Marriage Guidance Council in Britain. The seminar opened my eyes to a new way of looking at the human condition. Though I had read a lot of books on psychology, they only gave me the theory. They may have helped me to understand ideas and issues, but not human beings, especially not myself. I surmised that marriage guidance was different and that by trying to help others I would get to know myself better. But the rules of the organization at the time demanded that counsellors be at least thirty years old. Therefore I had to wait until 1965 before I could apply. I was delighted when I was accepted and greatly enjoyed the training.

The counselling itself demanded the best part of a day a week: three hour-long sessions with clients; fairly long travelling to the place where I counselled, for I wanted to do it as far away from the congregation as possible; a weekly case conference; sessions with an assigned tutor; and periodic residential retreats. Though I could barely afford the time, I persevered for a decade. It was only after the High Holy Days in 1975, when I would be going to the United States for some six weeks and would have to suspend counselling, that I decided to take a year off. At the end of the year I'd know whether or not to return to counselling. I didn't return, because by then I had not only given the movement the little I had to give, I had received very much from it. I think that the work as a lay therapist changed me for the better. It helped me not only to deal with family and friends in a more mature manner, but also to respond more appropriately to any tensions within the congregation.

I was particularly grateful for the case discussions, even though very often I was under attack, because I was one of the few in the group who had a full-time job and was, therefore, less preoccupied with the question whether marriage guidance counsellors had sufficient professional status. The discussion leader who had the greatest influence on me was the late Dr. Philip Ryder Smith. I think he had been a clergyman before he became a psychiatrist. He was also widely read and knew how to make connections between a particular situation in the counselling room and, for example, a play by Shakespeare or a poem by Auden. We became friends.

Though I remain immensely grateful to the marriage guidance movement, in the intervening more than a quarter-century I've moved away from psychotherapy as a discipline, particularly when it's mixed up with religion, as is often the case nowadays. Though I continue to learn from Martin Buber's stress on the interpersonal and Emmanuel Levinas's emphasis on "the other"—ethics preceding metaphysics—as ways to perceive the presence of God, my interests have shifted from individual to collective concerns. In fact, I've come to distance myself from much of contemporary Reform Judaism and its stress on personal fulfillment instead of collective redemption. But it has given me great pleasure that our daughter Elizabeth worked for a time with Relate, the successor organization to the National Marriage Guidance Council.

On the whole it seemed that I was appreciated at the South-West Essex Reform Synagogue. Though I was compared to Allan Miller, not all the comparisons were invidious. We made many friends, some of whom have remained close to this day. Several have died and we miss them.

In many ways, Miller shaped the congregation into an effective community of caring Jews. But he also left it with a situation that threatened to destroy much of what he had built up. In an effort to enhance the level of Jewish education, he disallowed the celebration of bar mitzvah and bat mitzvah in favour of a corresponding ceremony when the celebrant was sixteen. His argument was that the three years between thirteen and sixteen were vital for the religious development of a person. Since bar mitzvah and bat mitzvah at thirteen meant the end of Jewish education for virtually all children, it was, he felt, for the congregation not to collude in this practice. Families that wanted to celebrate bar mitzvah (bat mitzvah was still very rare) were unhappy and many left the congregation in favour of a synagogue that would allow the celebrations. One of the effects of this was that the South-West Essex Reform Synagogue had virtually no boys beyond the age of eleven in its religious school.

I was determined not to destroy what Miller had built up, yet I also realized the necessity to respond to the needs of the congregation. Within a year or so, therefore, we agreed on a compromise that would make bar mitzvah and bat mitzvah possible on condition that the parents undertook to keep the celebrants in the religious school until they were sixteen. Needless to say, not all families kept their promise and some left as a result, but on the whole the system worked and the congregation was able to grow. It more than doubled its membership during the seven years that I was there and became a major constituent of the Reform Synagogues of Great Britain (RSGB).

Before I arrived the congregation had embarked on a synagogue building program in Newbury Park, in the newer part of the area, close to a subway station and a main road. Many Jewish families lived there. The first phase of the building was ready in 1966 and the congregation moved in. Soon thereafter I attended a conference of the youth section of the World Union for Progressive Judaism (WUPJ) in Arnhem, Holland. There I met a German pastor, Dieter Schoeneich, who had become involved in Jewish-Christian cooperation in Germany. He complained that because of the composition of the Jewish communities in his country, he wasn't able to expose the young people in the parish he served in a Berlin suburb to a congregation of Jews. Many of the Jews in Germany, he told us, were old, often Holocaust survivors, and they were not keen to welcome young Germans into their midst, even though they knew that these youngsters had not been involved in the Holocaust. Schoeneich wondered if he could bring a group to Britain. I thought that the congregation I served would agree to host the visitors now that we had adequate premises. Unlike their counterparts in Germany, these Jews in Britain were prepared to make a contribution to German-Jewish reconciliation. Perhaps it was easier to do so from a distance.

By the time the guests came, many members of the wider Jewish community said they were outraged; one group even threatened to demonstrate outside our synagogue. This, in turn, alerted the press, so that when the group arrived, there were more journalists than hosts to greet them. One journalist told me that his brief was to be the first to report that I had been fired as the rabbi of the South-West Essex Reform Synagogue for associating with Germans. That didn't happen. In fact, because of the publicity at the time and later, including a half-hour program on BBC television, thousands and thousands of people in Britain were made aware of what we were doing, and an overwhelming majority expressed their appreciation. Several Holocaust survivors in the congregation told the cameras that they felt "liberated" to be able to relate to Germans as human beings, not as enemies. The community as a whole felt enriched by the program, and the leaders of the congregation were proud to have been put on the map in the eyes of the public.

Dieter Schoeneich and I continued the cooperation over a number of years, his groups coming to London and mine going to Germany. But what had been revolutionary in 1966 had become commonplace five years later and there was no need for us to do things that scores of others were now doing, including schools and youth groups in Israel. Gradually Schoeneich and I lost contact, and I heard much later that my partner in dialogue had committed suicide. My attempts to reconnect with his family failed. I think of him often and wonder what might have driven him to this desperate act.

Though we were happy in the congregation, I wasn't sufficiently mature to put down roots yet. I began to think about moving on. The first opportunity came when the RSGB, the umbrella organization to which the congregation belonged, was looking for a general secretary. At the end of 1965, some four years after coming to the South-West Essex Reform Synagogue, I applied for the job. Even though I had made controversial statements, particularly at one of the organization's national conferences in Brighton, I commanded some respect and, perhaps, also had a following. But I didn't get the position because, I was told, the RSGB, particularly its Assembly of Rabbis, didn't want a rabbi at the helm lest he became something of a Reform chief rabbi. The other non-Orthodox umbrella organization in the country, the Union of Liberal and Progressive Synagogues (ULPS), had a rabbi as its executive director and it was felt that he wielded too much power and received too much publicity. When some thirty years later Rabbi Tony Bayfield became not just the general secretary but also the chief executive of the RSGB, it seemed that the organization had overcome its original fears—to its great advantage.

In those days I believed that British Reform should style itself as something close to Conservative Judaism in America. Had I become the general secretary of the RSGB I might have pursued this more vigorously. Later, however, I realized that the Conservatives didn't really want us. They pinned their hopes on Rabbi Louis Jacobs, who had been thrown out of the United Synagogue, the mainstream Orthodox movement in Britain, which he served at the time as the spiritual leader of one of its constituents in London. He had also ceased to teach at Jews' College, the principal of which he was destined to become. He now, therefore, established an independent congregation, the New London Synagogue.

Jacobs saw himself more as the authentic heir of mainstream British Orthodoxy, the way it had been before its right wing had "hijacked" it, than an exponent of American Conservative Judaism. Yet in view of his book, *We Have Reason to Believe*, in which he questions the traditional concept of "Torah from Heaven" and which caused his break with the United Synagogue, his theological affinity with Conservative Judaism was obvious. He didn't deny it, even though for some time he eschewed formal affiliation. The Conservative movement, with its propensity to present itself as the rightful embodiment of modern Orthodoxy, preferred to embrace Jacobs than take on the RSGB. Since then, several Conservative congregations have been established in Britain and Louis Jacobs has become their titular head. Most of the rabbis in these congregations are graduates of the Leo Baeck College.

Indirectly, in the early 1980s, I came to the aid of what has turned out to be the most successful Conservative congregation in Britain. Originally the New North London Synagogue—the North-West London offshoot of Jacobs's New London Synagogue, which was located some distance away from where many of its members lived—was meeting in rented premises and private homes. It had no spiritual leader but was looking for a permanent home. One of its members, Leslie Linden, who had attended several of my study groups, called me one day to tell me that his group had found a convent in the area that was up for sale. As the place was too big for the New North London Synagogue and had a school building attached to it, he asked, would I be interested, in view of my having urged the Reform movement for years to have its own day school? I went to see the property and realized that it was too big for us too. So I tried to interest the Reform movement and the Leo Baeck College becoming partners. The result was the Manor House, now the Sternberg Centre, the hub of British Reform in Britain that also houses the Akiva School, the first Reform Jewish day school in Britain, soon to become a state school. Both the centre and the school were made possible by the generosity and commitment of two members of the North-Western Reform Synagogue, the congregation I came to serve in 1969: Peter Levy and Sir Sigmund Sternberg.

Needless to say the New North London Synagogue remained a partner in the enterprise, and the congregation, now led by a gifted graduate of the Leo Baeck College, Jonathan Wittenberg, has grown in numbers and importance. Though that wasn't how I had envisioned the link between British Reform and American Conservative Judaism, that was how it has turned out to be. Only recently, after a Shabbat service in Jerusalem, did a leader of the RSGB tell me how wrong I was in not shedding the New North London Synagogue early on, thus depriving his movement of a headache. He wasn't very impressed by my arguments about integrity.

When I moved to North America my romance with Conservative Judaism came to an end. Now I could see the untenable position in which Conservative Judaism finds itself, trying to balance its commitment to Halakhah, Jewish law, and its desire to be part of the modern world, where it's bound to compete with Reform Judaism for both attention and adherents. I came to understand the polarization within many Conservative congregations, especially in Canada, where near-Orthodox rabbis try to serve largely non-observant Jews. No wonder that many of the Conservative rabbis in Canada seek other affiliations than the ones that the Conservative movement offers them.

When I realized that Reform in Britain and Conservative in America (known in Israel and England as Masorti) would not come together, I began to advocate for the merger of the two Progressive movements in the country, the Reform Synagogues of Great Britain (RSGB) and the Union of Liberal and Progressive Synagogues (ULPS). Though the history of the two organizations was different—RSGB claiming its roots in Liberal Judaism in Germany, ULPS feeling closer to Reform in the United States (so much for terminology)—their aims and practices were remarkably similar. But institutions have a life of their own and a merger hasn't been possible. But the two organizations do cooperate on many projects, including the Leo Baeck College, whose graduates now serve both movements. From the outset, both RSGB and ULPS have been active members of the World Union for Progressive Judaism.

I've often wondered whether the attempt to promote unity in the non-Orthodox camp was cancelled by the establishment of the Sternberg Centre. For the centre, because of the success of the New North London Synagogue, has helped to promote the Masorti movement at the same time as it has greatly raised the profile of the RSGB. By comparison, the ULPS has been pushed onto the margins of Anglo-Jewry and isn't keen to become the junior partner in a merger. The absence of a united non-Orthodox movement in Britain has been beneficial to centrist British Orthodoxy. Though it's constantly being pulled to the right of the religious spectrum, its chief rabbis have had an inordinately prominent position in the country. This is partly due to their personalities, but more so because as long as the organization they represent is the largest in the Jewish community, the non-Jewish public will continue to turn to it in the general cultural debate.

It dawned on me gradually that the elected leadership of British Reform lacked the courage and the imagination to think big. Yet there were many distinguished members of Reform congregations who were resourceful and committed to the cause. I invited some of them to a meeting in our home in the hope of creating a think tank to identify and promote projects that would further our cause. Those invited responded and we would meet regularly. The group continued to exist even after my departure for Canada.

An early topic for discussion was the nature of the Manor House. We knew that it offered great opportunities to make a lasting contribution to the life of Anglo-Jewry, but we weren't sure that the RSGB knew how to respond. As a result of these deliberations and largely thanks to the initiative of Peter Levy, who was a member of our group, Rabbi Tony Bayfield, the spiritual leader of one of our congregations, relinquished his position to become the director of the Manor House. Its subsequent transformation to the Sternberg Centre is largely due to his hard work, intelligence and perseverance. He is today, justifiably, the recognized leader of British Reform.

Another issue that preoccupied the group was the possibility of merging the two Progressive movements in Britain. As indicated previously, our hopes didn't materialize.

Throughout this period and despite not being made the general secretary of the RSGB, I worked quite well with Raymond Goldman, the man who beat me to the job. Though he was very unhappy about not being included in my think tank, which he, for good reason, termed "Marmur's mafia," we did manage to cooperate on issues of mutual interest and have remained friends to this day.

One of my particular interests was the publication program of the organization. The program gave me an opportunity to reach out beyond the congregation that at no time could harness all my energies. I had been a member of the committee that ran the movement's journal, the *Synagogue Review*, and wrote some articles for it. In time I also wrote a pamphlet on intermarriage. When the *Synagogue Review* was replaced by a quarterly magazine, *Living Judaism*, I became its editor and acted in that capacity for some five years.

My aim was to use the journal as a vehicle that would help shape the congregations into a movement with a consistent approach to Judaism, albeit open to different styles of being Jewish and open to other movements in Judaism. I don't think that I had much success. The rank-and-file members of RSGB congregations weren't very interested in ideas, and their leaders were too concerned with budgets and image. But the journal persevered for a number of years even after I ceased to be its editor. Its successor nowadays is the quarterly *Manna*, published by the

Sternberg Centre. Many articles of mine have appeared there. I also edited two volumes of essays on British Reform, *Reform Judaism* and *A Genuine Search*, both published by the RSGB in the 1970s.

Apart from providing an outlet for my excess of energy, my need to write sprang both from a natural propensity, which started at school in Sweden, and a belief, inculcated by Maybaum, that a rabbi should speak also to those who are not there to listen to sermons. The publication program of the RSGB provided me with such a platform. Writing for non-Jewish journals gave me an opportunity to address Christians. To be able to express myself in my adopted language, English, added to the pleasure.

A second opportunity to move from Ilford came when I was approached early in 1969 by leaders of the North-Western Reform Synagogue in Alyth Gardens, the first Reform congregation Fredzia and I attended when we moved to London, with the suggestion that I should become its associate/successor rabbi—or as the British liked to call it in Anglican fashion, minister. When Werner Van Der Zyl left the congregation in 1958 to become the senior rabbi of the "cathedral" West London Synagogue, he was succeeded by Philip Cohen. Cohen trained at Jews' College and started life as an Orthodox minister in the days when his alma mater rarely conferred rabbinical ordination on its graduates. He had been a chaplain in the British armed forces during the Second World War, but upon his return switched allegiances and became the associate minister at the Liberal Jewish Synagogue in London, the "cathedral" of the more radical Liberal movement in Anglo-Jewry. By succeeding Van Der Zyl, Cohen moved back a little closer to the centre.

Philip Cohen was a very gifted and learned man, but he seemed to have lost interest in the rabbinate a long time before he went to Alyth Gardens. His passion was cricket and his addiction was alcohol. As the day progressed, his behaviour became more and more erratic because of the drink. He was always charming and very lovable. I don't think I've ever known a rabbi more popular with a congregation than Philip Cohen.

But he wasn't too popular with its leadership. This large congregation needed more vigorous guidance than he could provide. By inviting me to work with him for the three years leading up to his retirement and then to succeed him, the congregation could treat Cohen with dignity and yet renew itself. I hesitated to accept the offer. I had by then been seven years my own man in a growing and active congregation. Would I now like to play second fiddle? On the other hand, if there was one congregation in Anglo-Jewry that I wanted to serve, it was this one, despite my initial impression a few days after our arrival in the country. I was afraid that if I told the leaders that I'd rather wait until Cohen retired, they'd retire him there and then. This would lead to a lot of unpleasantness that would make it impossible for me to succeed him. There was also the possibility that the post would be offered to someone else and I'd miss my chance.

So I accepted the offer. I had worked with Philip Cohen at the Assembly of Rabbis, when he was the chairman and I the secretary. We had a nice and easy relationship. He wanted me to join him at Alyth Gardens, for he realized that this was his best chance of staying in office until retirement. He gave me carte blanche and told me I could do what I wanted in the congregation—on condition that I'd always tell him what was happening so that he could look good and be supportive. He didn't want me to put him to work on any of my projects. He asked me not to come to his little isolated office uninvited. He taught many would-be converts to Judaism there and he didn't want me to know much about them. They paid cash, which enabled him to buy all the whisky he wanted. Without that source of income, things would have been difficult, for it was quite obvious that his wife disapproved of his drinking and probably controlled the domestic cash flow.

Though Cohen kept his word and I did my best to be loyal to him, the three years were not easy. For despite my great affection for him, I couldn't muster much respect. At meetings of the synagogue board, for example, held in the evenings when he was palpably hazy, he would at times say outrageous things. If people suspected what was happening, they colluded with it. This was most noticeable at weddings, bar mitzvahs and similar events, which Cohen attended "religiously," partly because he was trained to believe, as he told me, that being there was the secret of a successful ministry, but largely because these functions usually provided unlimited access to alcohol. While his wife tried to keep him away from the bar, members of the congregation would bring him drinks, whether he asked for them or not. My only explanation for it is that they may have derived some perverse pleasure in being able to look down on their rabbi by exploiting his weakness. Strange as it may seem, it may have also contributed to his enormous popularity, for people like to feel superior to their spiritual leaders. The skepticism about congregants that I'd acquired in Glasgow was reinforced here.

Congregants would encourage Cohen by telling stories about his alleged wit. As was customary in Anglo-Jewry, the minister would recite grace after meals at functions. If he felt like it, Cohen might tell the assembled party that, as this was a small meal, he would only do a short version. Or he would interrupt himself and say, for example, "The next paragraph is for the smoked salmon" or "for the excellent chicken we had." If guests realized that he had lost his sense of propriety and judgment under the influence of alcohol, they didn't let on. Instead, Cohen was regarded as "a regular guy" and "one of the boys."

Cohen and I preached on alternate Sabbaths and shared the duties on festivals and High Holy Days. His sermon preparation consisted of thinking about what he was going to say during the fifteen- to twenty-minute bus ride from his home to the synagogue. Some of the openings were quite brilliant, often inspired by what he had read in the newspaper that day, for he was neither a fool nor an ignoramus.

As correct as he was in his behaviour toward me when sober, things could get out of hand when he wasn't quite in control of himself. A particular instance comes to mind. He would normally rehearse *bnai mitzvah* (there were few, if any, *bnot mitzvah* in his time) on a Friday afternoon before services. I would be teaching a class in another part of the building at the same time. One particularly hot Friday the bar mitzvah boy came running through the building screaming, "Reverend Cohen has collapsed!" Though I suspected what must have happened, I rushed down and saw him in a sorry drunken state. When I offered to help him, he muttered something about not going to be pushed around by me so that I could take over before my time. Recognizing that the situation was too difficult for me to handle, I asked the synagogue's administrator, who happened to be in the building, to take over. He called the chairman, who got Cohen home. I dismissed my class, finished the rehearsal and conducted the Friday evening service.

It never occurred to the bar mitzvah family what was really the matter. When Cohen turned up for services the following morning and people asked about his health, he gave some vague response and things proceeded as usual. But my level of frustration had increased further. Still, I did my three years and upon the retirement of the Reverend Philip Cohen in the summer of 1972, I became the sole spiritual leader of the North-Western Reform Synagogue. I didn't see much of Cohen thereafter. He died after we left for Canada.

Once the congregation was "mine," I was able to enjoy a happy and productive ministry. The congregation flourished and our children were growing up nicely. At one point all three went to the same Jewish day school at the other end of the road on which we lived. We enjoyed the house into which we moved when we left Ilford in 1969 and had turned it into a place where we spent happy times with friends and congregants. We celebrated Viveca's bat mitzvah at home during Pesach of 1973 with several parties and much fun. Fredzia catered them all. She did the same for Michael's bar mitzvah in 1975 and Elizabeth's bat mitzvah in 1980.

Viveca's bat mitzvah was the last time my father was with us. Both he and my mother had retired a few years earlier and, though physically strong, he was deteriorating mentally. The fact that my mother continued to push him around didn't help. Between Rosh Hashanah and Yom Kippur that year he had a massive heart attack and died within a couple of days. He was seventy-one. After the funeral I took my mother home with me to London and arrived a day before *Kol Nidre*, in time to conduct services on the Day of Atonement.

A day or so after my mother and I returned from Sweden, the Yom Kippur War broke out. Elizabeth, six at the time, was overheard telling a friend that since her grandmother came to stay and everybody is listening to the radio, the family hasn't been the same.

I considered my involvement in communal life to be an important part of my work. It also suited my temperament and ambition. What I had to say was often reported in the *Jewish Chronicle*. Sometimes I also wrote for it. Occasionally I would do radio broadcasts and be interviewed on television. We arranged interesting events in the congregation and invited prominent speakers to address the members. All this enhanced both my own profile and the profile of the congregation. But some of its leaders were ambivalent about it. On the one hand they wanted to be identified with a congregation people talked about, but on the other they resented that I was so up front. They argued that I promoted myself on synagogue time. Though I refused to lie low, I did my best to tell my congregation as little as possible about my outside activities. Unlike many of my rabbinical colleagues, I didn't publicize them in the synagogue bulletin and only rarely did I make the pieces I wrote for other publications available to members.

I didn't even say much to the congregation when I got involved with the Leo Baeck College. First, I was invited to present a comprehensive report about its academic work. When it appeared it was, at least implicitly, critical of Rabbi Albert Friedlander, who was in charge at the time; it fractured our friendship forever. Professor J. B. Segal now became the principal of the college. He was the honorary president of the congregation I served, succeeding such luminaries as Leo Baeck and Norman Bentwich. He had by then retired as a professor at the School of Oriental and African Studies in London. He served as principal for a number of years, giving the college greater visibility and much academic respectability. I happened to be in London when he died in 2003 and I was honoured to officiate at his funeral. He was one of the finest human beings it has been my privilege to know.

And I didn't say much to the congregation when I taught homiletics at the college and supervised students' fieldwork. Despite my formal academic deficiencies, I had now become more acceptable, perhaps as a reward for having helped to bring some order into college affairs.

Of all the criticisms I've faced as a rabbi over the years, none was as persistent as the accusation that I was an intellectual. My work at the college would have come under that rubric, as did of course my serious preaching. The ideal clergy model in Britain at the time was the Protestant pastor who's "a nice chap" and easily accessible—and decidedly not an intellectual. But my role model was Ignaz Maybaum, not Philip Cohen. Maybaum's humanity was for all to see, but his pastoral skills were not. Though I tried to acquire counselling skills, I was happiest in intellectual circles.

Michael Goulston, upon his return from Cincinnati to serve first the Middlesex New Synagogue and then the West London Synagogue, created many opportunities. He was a prime mover in the creation of *European Judaism*, the serious journal that still exists and provides a forum for debate. Within its framework we tried to attract Jewish intellectuals. Lionel Blue had persuaded a Dutch publishing firm to sponsor the publication. Michael Goulston sought to vindicate their investment by bringing together under their auspices significant Jewish thinkers.

I particularly remember a meeting in Amsterdam with George Steiner of Cambridge and Jacob Taubes of Berlin. We rabbis tried to prove ourselves their philosophic equals as much as possible until Taubes told us something to the effect that what he wanted rabbis to be was first-class exponents of Judaism, not second-class philosophers. The admonition made a great impression on me. I have since always tried to speak and write as an exponent of Judaism, not as an amateur theologian, philosopher, psychologist or historian.

At the same time I tried to temper my intellectual ambitions with community activism. Hence my involvement in the Soviet Jewry campaign. For a number of years, our congregation conducted High Holy Day services at a local cinema, close to the synagogue itself. One day in the early 1970s we were informed that the Red Army Choir was to give a series of concerts there. It was at the height of the Soviet regime's punitive measures against Jews. The Red Army was the regime's pride and joy. Together with the chairman of the congregation, I sent a letter to all our members suggesting that to make a statement, they not attend any of the concerts. As we also sent copies to the press, our gesture received a lot of publicity, virtually all of it positive. I don't know how effective our plea was, but it had symbolic significance, and henceforth both the congregation and I were actively involved in the Soviet Jewry campaign. My activism brought back memories from the mid 1950s and my feeble, abortive attempt to help Jews leave the Soviet Union by collecting Swedish passports for "treatment."

I don't know whether the campaign abroad did much good for the Jews in the Soviet Union, but I'm sure that it did much good for our communities and for the individuals who, thanks to the campaign, were now identified as Jewish leaders. That the Jews from the former Soviet Union were able to leave and settle in Israel and elsewhere is one of the miracles of our time. In the struggle for their freedom they imbued in us in the free world a greater sense of peoplehood and collective responsibility. This was particularly important for Reform Jews, who too often relate to their tradition in terms of personal needs, not collective obligations. My own preaching and writing was very much along the collectivist lines, which is yet another reason it wasn't always well received. Instead of telling worshippers about the plight of fellow Jews and our responsibility to them, many wanted to hear things that, according to their expressed wishes, made them feel good about themselves.

The stress on collective obligations over the individual wishes also brought me into Zionist activism. I had been involved with the World Union for Progressive Judaism since my arrival in Britain in 1957. In those days Sweden was still considered one of its constituents and I became the Swedish representative at many WUPJ gatherings. As I became more established in Britain, I was invited to represent British Reform. And so when Leonard Montefiore, one of the patricians in the West London Synagogue and a staunch supporter of the Leo Baeck College, died, I was appointed by the RSGB to replace him on the WUPJ governing body. At my first meeting I could hear the WUPJ president, Rabbi Solomon Freehof, a patrician of American Reform, audibly express his outrage that the great Montefiore should have been replaced by a nobody like "What's-his-name Marmur." This spurred me to vindicate my presence and I volunteered for many thankless tasks. Thus I chaired the youth section for a few years and was very involved in trying to keep together the European board of WUPJ, despite the lack of any significant budgetary support.

That was how I got to know Rabbi Richard Hirsch. He had been an official of the Union of American Hebrew Congregations (UAHC) for a number of years, first as a regional director and then as the founder-director of its Religious Action Center in Washington, D.C. Hirsch had always been a Zionist, his Russian-born wife was Israeli, they spoke Hebrew at home and brought up their four children to have close ties with Israel. His aim was to live in Israel and, when the post of executive director of WUPJ became vacant, he was prepared to accept it on condition that its headquarters move to Jerusalem. His argument was persuasively ideological, enhanced by his personal commitment.

To start with I was among those who were opposed to the move, for I have always been suspicious when personal ambition tries to determine ideology, but I was won over by Hirsch's great charm and power of persuasion and I continued to be active in the organization. I came to believe in his cause. After WUPJ joined the World Zionist Organization, Hirsch wanted an even broader Reform representation. That was when the Association of Reform Zionists of America (ARZA) was created. In order to have full status in the WZO, five countries had to have ARZA-equivalent organizations. That was how I became involved in the British one and, in time, the first chairman of the international body, Arzenu. When I moved to Canada I took my Zionist activities with me and in time also served as the chairman of the Canadian branch.

In that period of my life I was impressed by being in what seemed the centre of Zionist activity, meeting with important leaders of Israel's Labor Party, our allies in the WZO. But once I understood what was going on, I also realized that the WZO is a depository for Israeli politicians who don't make it to government. Participation of the Reform movement in the WZO may be useful because of the allocation of funds, but I don't think that it does anything for us intellectually or ideologically. The year I spent on the WZO executive, 2001, when I was the interim executive director of WUPJ, confirmed my worst suspicions. But that in no way diminishes my commitment to Zionism, Israel and the relationship of both to Reform Judaism. I firmly believe that though the Zionist organizational apparatus may be defunct, Zionism is alive and well, whether or not we believe that it must manifest itself in aliyah.

Though I was brought into the Zionist movement as a child in postwar Poland, I had distanced myself from it during my years in Sweden. The speech I gave in Oslo that may have cost me my job in Stockholm reflected this. I became even more remote from Zionist ideology in my early years in Britain, largely under the influence of Ignaz Maybaum. My work in WUPJ and Arzenu brought me back to the fold, not only practically but also intellectually. At one of the WUPJ conventions in Jerusalem I delivered an address on the relationship between Reform

Judaism and Zionism, sharing the platform with the best-known exponent of that relationship, the late Rabbi David Polish.

Though my first book, *Beyond Survival* (1982), still belongs to my non-Zionist era, my book *The Star of Return* (1991) tries to place Liberal Judaism within the Zionist tradition. I remain a convinced and committed Zionist to this very day and much of my speaking and writing is of that ilk. Living part of the year in Israel, as Fredzia and I now do, is the consummation of the process.

My links with Richard Hirsch were very strong for many years. He gave the principal address at my installation as the senior rabbi of Holy Blossom Temple in Toronto in 1983. But when I became the interim executive director of WUPJ at the end of the year 2000, our relationship soured. I take my share of the blame for it and regret it deeply. Both of us have made efforts to restore at least some of the openness and cordiality that once characterized our encounters, but we haven't yet come much beyond civility.

My Zionist activism brought me often to Israel. Fredzia and I went there for the first time in 1957. Our finances and our young children made it impossible for us to travel together for many years thereafter, but I did attend the first WUPJ convention in Israel in 1968, a year after the Six-Day War, and spent time after the convention comparing what we could see in 1957 to what there was to visit in 1968. I joined an Israeli group of tourists going to the Golan Heights and was caught up in the euphoria that came with Israel's victory in the Six-Day War. Since the early 1970s we have travelled to Israel frequently, once even exchanging homes with a family in Jerusalem. By the 1980s I travelled to Israel for one reason or another at least once every year.

In the course of one of my visits I spent a memorable afternoon with the late Professor Yeshayahu Leibovich and his wife in their home in Jerusalem. A few years earlier Mrs. Leibovich's brother and his wife had joined the North-Western Reform Synagogue in London. When I visited them at the time they told me that their only son had been killed in Israel's War of Independence in 1948, which seems to be the major reason they no longer could live in the Jewish state and decided to settle in England. They told me about their connection to Yeshayahu Leibovich, who by that time had achieved both fame and notoriety as a staunch advocate of rationalist strict Orthodoxy and was an out-spoken critic of Zionist politics in general, including the politics of the religious parties and the political stance of the government of Israel in particular. I had read some of Leibovich's incisive writings, mainly on subjects of Jewish thought and tradition.

When his sister-in-law died in London, I officiated at the funeral. Her husband now became even more withdrawn and was not amen-able to the pastoral care I could offer. One day he was found dead in the street. He had left clear instructions that he wanted to be cremat-ed. Like all my Reform colleagues in Britain I often officiated at cre-mations of members of the congregation and had no difficulty doing it this time. But as the deceased had no family other than Mrs. Leibovich in Jerusalem, I decided to speak to her before making arrangements. When I telephoned, Yeshayahu Leibovich answered and I broke the sad news. I then told him about the instructions that his brother-in-law had left. He consulted his wife and then told me to go ahead. As much as he himself was opposed to cremation, he felt that, in this instance, the wishes of the deceased should be honoured. He thanked me for having called him and invited me to visit them next time I was in Jer-usalem, which I did not long thereafter.

Their home was similar to the homes of many Jews from Germany I had seen: heavy furniture obviously brought from the old country, books everywhere, delicate china and interesting art. We talked about life and Judaism. Though he knew where I stood he made no attempt to chal-lenge me. There was nothing of the fiery polemicist the papers wrote about. Afterwards, Mrs. Leibovich drove me to my next destination.

On an earlier occasion I went on a "mission" (as such visits were called, using quasi-religious terminology) at the end of 1974, organized by what was then known in Britain as the Joint Israel Appeal. Though we saw many interesting things not otherwise available to tourists, such as the Sinai and the Suez Canal in Israeli hands after the 1973 Yom Kippur War, I promised myself not to do it again. I couldn't take the attempts to coerce people to give more than they were prepared to and I resented the distortion of Israeli life in an effort to generate "emotion." For example, to illustrate poverty in Israel, which was considerable then and is, alas, no less now, we were taken to a slum area in Tel Aviv. I hated the voyeurism and identified with the hapless children staring back at the strangers who stared at them. When one of my fellow "missionaries" told me that he couldn't imagine how anybody could live in such circumstances, I let it slip that I had lived under much worse conditions for many years during the Second World War. This was reported to the organizers as criticism and, to make their point, they took us to another area, allegedly even more derelict. I was viewed with suspicion during the rest of the trip.

I broke my resolve and went on another mission. Days after Israel's invasion of Lebanon in 1982 I joined a large group of Anglo-Jewish leaders on a thirty-six-hour mission to Tel Aviv, where we heard the Defence Minister Ariel Sharon; to Jerusalem, where Prime Minister Menachem Begin was the speaker; and to the outskirts of Beirut where we were briefed by high-ranking officers. On the way back to the airport we were taken to a park where captured weapons and ammunition were on display. We accepted uncritically the story as told and in the plane going home signed a prepared "resolution" in support of the Israeli action in Lebanon.

With my usual fear of being manipulated I was uncomfortable being a signatory, but I had no evidence to the contrary and not enough courage to be the odd man out. Because I was the chair of Arzenu at the time and we were in coalition with the Labor Party in Israel, I was pleased that its international chairman, General Chaim Bar Lev, happened to be in London when we returned. I invited him to dinner in our home, along with some friends of ours, in an effort to check out what I had heard in Israel. By and large Bar Lev confirmed what we were told. He even implied that had he been at the helm, he would have acted as the current Israeli government had. I now felt comfortable to offer the party line to my congregation and to other audiences. I was wrong and am embarrassed about it to this very day. I know that I shouldn't have broken my resolve not to go on another mission, however prestigious it seemed at the time. I've made sure that I haven't been on any since, despite many invitations.

I was considered a "Jewish leader" and included in important events in Anglo-Jewry because I served a high-profile congregation, chaired for a couple of years the Assembly of Rabbis of the RSGB and subsequently chaired the Council of Reform and Liberal Rabbis. The council was created as a way of making the presence felt of the non-Orthodox religious movements in Anglo-Jewry as a kind of counterpart to the chief rabbinate. To stress the democratic nature of our movement, our chairs were elected only for two-year periods. In addition to meeting regularly in the home of the then Orthodox Chief Rabbi Immanuel (later Lord) Jakobovits to discuss matters of mutual concern, the chair would also represent his constituents at public events. Thus, for example, when the president of Israel came on an official visit and attended services in an Orthodox synagogue on a Saturday morning, I made sure that he came to the West London (Reform) Synagogue on the Friday night. President Katzir responded graciously and said something to the effect that he regarded himself as an emissary on behalf of the Jewish state to the entire Jewish community, not only to a section of it.

On another occasion I attended a reception in honour of the then Ashkenazi Chief Rabbi of Israel, Shlomo Goren. We got talking and presumably in an effort to pay me a compliment, he asked me the question I've heard many times from Orthodox Jews: "What's a Polish Jew like you doing in the Reform movement?" I said in response, "Why is a wise and learned rabbi like yourself so prejudiced?" Jakobovits, who was present at the exchange and was afraid that things would get out of hand, came to my defense by telling Goren that I had been a child in the Soviet Union during the war. That was his way of describing me as a *tinnok shenishba* (literally, imprisoned as a child), a technical term in Jewish law that absolves non-observant Jews from being labelled sinners or apostates. I didn't appreciate the gesture, though I'm sure it was well meant, for I was always under the impression that Jakobovits rather liked me—and I liked him very much—though the religious barrier between us prevented friendship. He did invite my wife and myself, though, to two weddings of his children, both more state occasions than private events.

At another time and unintentionally Jakobovits did me a great favour. Many years after I'd been a rabbi he went on a visit to Gothenburg, my hometown. When my mother was introduced to him he was most complimentary, referred to me as "Rabbi Marmur" and "a dear colleague." My mother, who never really believed that I was an authentic rabbi, for my world was so totally alien to her, now accepted it and told people about it. I therefore wrote a note to Jakobovits thanking him for giving me *semicha* (ordination) in the eyes of my mother.

In April 1977 he even came to my congregation to lecture to its doctors and lawyers on medical ethics, his area of expertise. Afterwards he couldn't conceal his prejudices. He told me how overwhelmed he was by the numbers who came to listen, the quality of the questions and comments, and the audience's obvious commitment to Judaism. Needless to say, it didn't change his attitude to Reform Judaism. In the fashion of the prejudiced, he made an exception for me and the congregation I served, perhaps even sharing Goren's view that I was in the wrong camp.

My invitation to lunch with Queen Elizabeth and Prince Philip at Buckingham Palace in October 1978, however, had nothing to do with my position of leadership in British Reform. In the latter capacity I was indeed part of a delegation on behalf of Anglo-Jewry a year earlier to present a "loyal address" to the Queen, apparently a relic from ages past when Jews were a tolerated minority in the country. This time the invitation was personal.

Some time in the early 1970s I was invited to an interfaith dialogue at St. George's House at Windsor Castle, the conference centre run by the dean of the chapel under the patronage of Prince Philip. I must have impressed the dean, Michael Mann, and the warden, Charles Handy, for they invited me back on several occasions to participate in conferences and give papers. It was because of Michael Mann that I was included in the Commission on the Family that set out to take a fresh look at the role of the family in British society. Though my contribution to its work was minimal, I got to know many interesting men and women in the country. Perhaps it was my membership in the commission that prompted the RSGB to appoint me to chair a similar working party for the Reform movement. I worked closely there with Sheila King-Lassman and Wendy Greengross, both good friends to this day.

I surmise that when Buckingham Palace asked Michael Mann to suggest someone who could be invited to one of the informal lunches held by the Queen for "interesting" people she would normally not come across, he mentioned my name. Seven other such individuals were included on that occasion, among them a bishop and an actress. The Queen and the Duke of Edinburgh were of course briefed about each guest. When I was introduced to Prince Philip, he asked me if I was about to become chief rabbi. I mumbled something to the effect that it was quite unlikely. The duke said that as the Poles are occupying centre stage—Pope John Paul in Rome and Prime Minister Menachem Begin in Jerusalem, both born in Poland—perhaps my turn, also born in Poland, was next.

The whole event was so brilliantly orchestrated that it seemed informal, almost spontaneous. I was suitably nervous, but relaxed when the very senior civil servant sitting next to me was told by the footman that he had put the salad cream on the wrong part of his plate. After the meal when the corgis joined us, we each had an opportunity to converse with Her Majesty. The subject she raised with me was hunting at Balmoral. I didn't contribute much to the conversation. What I wanted to say to her when I saw the dogs was that coming from the ghetto, I was afraid of them. But I held my peace, which is just as well.

Neil Benson, who has a flair for events of this kind, had arranged for himself and his wife, Ann, together with Fredzia and our mutual friend, the journalist and author June Rose, to meet me for tea afterwards at the Ritz in Piccadilly. When I told them that I was less than impressed by the Queen, June gave me some good advice: be enthusiastic about the encounter when asked by the press, unless I wanted to be sensationalized by the media and crucified by the public. I did as I was told and was quoted accordingly.

Not having any family in England made us very dependent on friends. Partly out of rabbinical duty and partly as a way of binding people we liked closer to ourselves, we entertained a lot, Fredzia invariably doing all the work. The children probably resented the constant stream of guests, especially on Shabbat, though I hope that they got something out of it too.

Soon after we came to Alyth Gardens, we became friends with Ann and Neil Benson and have remained so. This was a new departure for us, for by and large, we avoided close friendships with people active in the synagogue I served, especially after one bitter experience with a past president who was also our next-door neighbour in Ilford and who committed suicide. But our friendship with the Bensons has only grown over the years, even though Neil was the chairman of the congregation at the time that I left it and he and I disagreed about who should succeed me.

Several of our friends died as young men and left us bereft. I've already mentioned Allan Benjamin. Rabbi Michael Goulston had been a trailblazer in many enterprises within British Reform. His sudden death in February 1972 was a great blow to me. I keep his picture in my office. So was the death of Michael Flower, whom we met when we first arrived in England; we later renewed the friendship when he and his wife, Vivien, joined the congregation I served. Our friendship with the Maybaum family extended to their children, Alisa and Michael. Alisa's husband, Eric Jaffa, died shortly before we left Britain, and her brother, Michael, not long thereafter.

The tragedies of friends who died before their time made us feel very vulnerable. The memory of Fredzia's father dying at only fifty-six was often with us. We could accept it more easily when friends died in old age, among them Stanislaw Brunstein, an artist we got to know in Ilford and whose paintings we displayed for the congregation. He and his wife, Ester, were, like ourselves, born in Poland and we had much in common. His art evoked the now lost world of Polish Jewry. We think of him every day because several of his paintings hang in our home in Toronto and one in our home in Jerusalem. I'm grateful to have been asked to write an introduction to the charming book about his paintings, *The Vanished Shtetl*, published in Britain in 1999. We've remained close with Ester.

I no longer remember how I met Lily Pincus, but in the last years of her life she was a source of much joy and love for Fredzia and me. Her writings on death were very helpful to us, and her determination to die with dignity and acceptance was a source of great inspiration. Gerhard Adler was the leading Jungian psychoanalyst in Britain at the time. He was a member of the congregation and we became friends. We once invited to dinner him and his wife, together with Lily Pincus. When Lily asked him if he was related to *the* Adler, meaning Alfred Adler of Vienna, he replied half in jest, "What do you mean? I *am* the Adler!" Adler and other Jungians would tell me that I preached like one of them.

Susan Bach was also a Jungian but of a different ilk. I never quite understood what she was doing, but it seemed important, for she tried to help sick children to die in peace. Her husband, Hans, had been the editor of the *Synagogue Review* when I joined its editorial committee. As the Bachs were members of the North-Western Reform Synagogue, we renewed our friendship when I served the congregation. One day at dinner in our home, to encourage them to start eating the soup while it was hot, even though Fredzia had not yet come to the table, I began to eat with the explanation, not necessarily untrue, that I was a food addict and couldn't bear seeing food in front of me that I wasn't consuming. Nothing more was said about that, but not long afterwards, when Hans died and I did my best to be a helpful rabbi, his widow told me that she wanted to give me a present for being good to her. "When we were in your house," she reminded me, "you said that you were a food addict. I would like to give you ten sessions to cure you." I assumed that this unprofessional gesture was well meant but would soon be forgotten once the shock of Hans's death had given way to sober reflection. I was wrong. She persevered and I went.

That was my only experience of being a patient in the consulting room of a psychotherapist. She told me, and she might have been accurate, that my mother gave me food instead of love; she rejected my more socialist idea that it was the years of starvation during the war that made food so important to me. When I continued to insist on my idea, she told me that I was denying the truth. After a couple of sessions I couldn't take the manipulation anymore and told her that my discomfort at being treated was greater than my discomfort at being overweight. She accepted that and we remained friends. She had left instructions that, wherever I was in the world, I had to officiate at her funeral. I happened to be in London when she died and so could do my duty.

Fourteen years is a long time to serve the same congregation and as time went by my work became more and more routine. As there was no other congregation to which I could go, I did my best to engage in new activities and keep myself alert and fresh. Writing was a welcome diversion and the publication, in 1982, of my book *Beyond Survival* became a source of great joy and pride. The *Times Literary Supplement* printed a lengthy review by Geza Vermes of Oxford and the *Jewish Chronicle* carried an extract. Louis Jacobs, the most learned Jew I've ever known and one of the great rabbis of Anglo-Jewry, spoke at the launching of the book, even though I'm not at all sure that he cared much for it.

As engaged as I've always been in my work and in the Jewish world in general, I'd like to think that concern for my family came first—though its success has always been thanks to Fredzia's talent as a caring mother, indispensable partner in my work and a consummate homemaker. It was her love that illumined our lives and brought to us much happiness. Whether the children and I were sufficiently responsive to her needs is less certain. I've always felt that she deserves more than I'm able to give.

Our children brought us boundless happiness and continue to do so to this very day. Though schoolwork was never Viveca's strong point and her early adolescence created tensions in the home, the stay with her school—JFS, the Jewish secondary school in London—at Givat Washington in Israel when she was fourteen matured her considerably. We've known since she was a child that she would make a wonderful nurse, but because we said it so often, it was enough of a reason for her to try other careers. But once we left Britain in 1983 she enrolled in a nursing school and has done tremendous work ever since. For many years she worked out of the North London Hospice, looking after terminally ill patients in their homes. Many are the men and women who directly or through friends told us how much Sister Viv has meant to them and their families when a loved one was dying. But the strain has taken its toll on her and she recently left nursing for a less demanding occupation. However, it's impossible to imagine that Viveca will not find her way back to a caring profession.

Unlike her siblings, Viveca has chosen a less bourgeois existence. Though she had many opportunities to marry she chose to remain single. Her three dogs are her trusted companions and her horse the focus for her free time and energy. She has many friends and is herself capable of great friendship and boundless generosity.

Having a bright and effervescent brother, Michael, born less than two years later, complicated Viveca's early childhood. The relationship between the two has always been difficult. As adults they get on well but aren't close. Michael is blessed with a good mind and, more important, his mother's nature. Though he never shone academically, he always sparkled as a person and did well enough to get into Haberdashers' Aske's School and from there to Mansfield College, Oxford. Between school and university he spent some time in Israel and decided to settle there as soon as he could. Had he not got a place at Oxford, he would have done his undergraduate work in Jerusalem. But as soon as he finished university in 1984 he made aliyah and has lived in Israel ever since. He got his M.A. from the Hebrew University and his rabbinic diploma from the Hebrew Union College in Jerusalem. After a few years at the Leo Baeck High School in Haifa, where he also acted as the spiritual leader of the synagogue on the campus, he was appointed in 1998 as the dean of the Jerusalem school of the Hebrew Union College. He is loved by his students, respected by his colleagues and adored by the support staff. He's currently completing a doctorate on an aspect of the writings of Abraham Joshua Heschel.

Michael met Sarah Bernstein at a gathering of Zionist youth when he was in his last year at Oxford and she a student at London University. She, too, wanted to live in Israel. She finished her degree a year after Michael, but instead of following in her mother's footsteps and studying medicine, she chose her father's career and studied law in Jerusalem. After working as a lawyer for a few years in Haifa, Sarah is now engaged in interfaith dialogue in Israel, but her real interest is mediation. During their sabbatical year in Britain, Sarah has been able to pursue reconciliation studies in an academic setting. In time these will bring her to many innovative and exciting projects.

Sarah and Michael were married in 1986 in London. Miriam, their first child, was born in 1989, followed by Nadav in 1991 and Gaby in 1994. All five are a true blessing to Fredzia and me, and nowadays a major reason we spend a part of the year in Jerusalem.

Elizabeth was the only one of our children to come with us to Canada. It's less than prudent to move a sixteen-year-old to a new environment far away from friends, but Elizabeth's resilience was such that she got over the two less than happy years of high school in Toronto to enjoy three good years at McGill University in Montreal. After graduation she enrolled in the London School of Speech and Drama; from the age of twelve she knew that she wanted to be an actress. Having completed her studies there, she returned to Toronto and began to make a name for herself in the theatre. All the while, she stayed in touch with a childhood friend, Anthony Kessel, and in time the relationship blossomed into romance. We had known Anthony's family for many years, for we were patients in his father's medical practice, close to where we lived. Elizabeth returned to England, where Anthony's career as a doctor, specializing in community medicine and medical ethics, was anchored. She has been able to pursue her acting career there. She and Anthony were married in Toronto in 1998. Some one hundred guests came from abroad to join an even larger number of local friends, and we did our utmost to make the event memorable and enjoyable. Elizabeth and Anthony's daughter, Leone, was born in 2000 and their son, Ethan, three years later. Both have become great sources of joy, happiness and gratitude to their grandparents.

Though, despite the onset of congregational fatigue, I wasn't looking for a job and had no intention of moving from Britain, I was flattered when in the course of the Zionist Congress in 1982 in Jerusalem, I was asked if I wanted to be the senior rabbi of Holy Blossom Temple in Toronto, one of the largest and best-known congregations in North America. I had known Arthur Grant for a number of years as the director of the Canadian Region of the Union of American Hebrew Congregations as well as of Kadima (later ARZA Canada). He had just been elected a vice-president of the Holy Blossom Temple. The congregation had been looking for a senior rabbi ever since Harvey Fields, who had succeeded Gunther Plaut, had left earlier that year. Its search committee had been through the proper procedure for interviewing candidates and was now able to headhunt. Hence Arthur's approach. I have been grateful for it ever since. His untimely death on a flight from Jerusalem to New York in early 2003 was a blow to his family and many friends.

I told Arthur that I wasn't an applicant, not even a member of the Central Conference of American Rabbis, and thus not entitled to be in the running. I also reminded him that I was a maverick with deviant views. As an illustration I gave him a copy of *Beyond Survival* and suggested that he and his colleagues read it carefully before pursuing the matter further. If, after careful reflection, they were still interested, I'd be pleased to come and give some talks as the chairman of Arzenu, but I wouldn't be a formal applicant. Neither Fredzia nor I had ever been to Toronto and we would need to find out what kind of city it was and what kind of congregation Holy Blossom Temple was before we could even consider it.

The congregation remained interested and early in 1983 the president of Holy Blossom, Myer Brody, and his late wife, Faigie, came to London and we talked. As a result, I was invited to give lectures and sermons in the congregation. Fredzia and I flew to Toronto in February 1983. When before our trip a friend asked what the chances were that I would accept the post if offered, I replied five percent. Fredzia said fifty. She has always known me better than I know myself. She sensed that I was ready for a change and a new challenge.

February isn't Toronto's best month. The grey sky and the cold air depressed us, but the congregation and the community intrigued us. When I was offered the job, I asked for a month to think things over. On our way back we travelled via New York in order to find out if I'd be acceptable to the Reform movement. As we were so much of two minds about moving, had there been any opposition to my coming, I would have dropped the matter. Though there wasn't much enthusiasm, there wasn't any opposition either. Rabbi Stanley Dreyfus, the director of the rabbinic placement office, told me that he was sorry that he couldn't provide an American candidate for Holy Blossom, but that he wouldn't oppose me even though I was an outsider. The late Rabbi Joseph Glaser, the executive director of the rabbinic body, thought that a job change was a good way of dealing with a midlife crisis. As he put it in his inimitable way and with his vast experience of rabbinic antics in midlife, "It's better than an affair."

Upon our return Fredzia and I talked things over with our children and with close friends—and decided to accept the offer. If our time in England was a period of hope and fulfillment that turned my profession into a vocation, Canada constituted a new challenge and held the promise of achievement. We parted on very good terms with the North-Western Reform Synagogue. It has remained our home away from home whenever we are in London.

(*above*) Shortly before the outbreak of the Second World War, age 4.
(FAMILY PHOTO)

(*below*) Back in Sosnowiec after the war with my parents, 1947. (FAMILY
PHOTO)

My school in Katowice, early 1948. I am sitting to the right of the male teacher. (FAMILY PHOTO)

High school graduation portrait, May 1955.
(FAMILY PHOTO)

High school graduation class photo, May 1955. Would-be graduates were expected to appear on the last day of the university entrance examinations in black tie. Those who passed were greeted by cheering relatives and friends, who then bedecked the new graduates with flowers and balloons. I am fourth from the left in the front row.
(ARNEBORG FOTO, GOTHENBURG)

After the national public speaking competition in Stockholm, with Fredzia, March 1955. (FAMILY PHOTO)

Our wedding, May 20, 1956. (FAMILY PHOTO)

(*above*) On vacation with Fredzia's parents and Viveca, summer 1961.
(FAMILY PHOTO)

(*below*) Teachers and graduates of the Leo Baeck College, early 1970s.
Dr. Ignaz Maybaum is seated third from left; next to him are Dr. Ellen
Littmann and Dr. Werner Van der Zyl with his wife. I am seated second
from right with Rabbi John Rayner on my right and Rabbi Lionel Blue
on my left. (HAY WRIGHTSON, LONDON)

With Marek Edelman (second from right), the last surviving leader of the Warsaw ghetto uprising, and the late Louis Lenkinski (far left) and Dr. Frank Bialystok, leaders of the Polish-Jewish Heritage Foundation of Canada. (FAMILY PHOTO)

With our children and grandchildren, Fredzia and I visiting my mother in Gothenburg in 1999. (FAMILY PHOTO)

Trying to look like a rabbi. (FRANK LENNON)

Canada:
Challenge

*I*n August 1, 1983, I became the senior rabbi of Holy Blossom Temple in Toronto. I spent seventeen years there, meeting the challenges without too much loss of nerve on my part or loss of patience on the part of the congregation, despite their periodic complaints, usually voiced to me by the leaders but no doubt spoken of widely in the congregation. Even if Harvey Fields, my immediate predecessor, wasn't long enough the senior rabbi to have made much of an impact in Toronto, his work made mine easier, if for no other reason than, being his successor, I was compared more to him than to Rabbi Gunther Plaut, who had served the congregation with great distinction for most of the 1960s and 1970s.

Plaut was in no way involved in my coming to Toronto. He wasn't even in the city during my first visit. But I had known him for many years, mainly through the World Union for Progressive Judaism and, of course, I had read his writings. When we reconnected we soon established a warm and relatively uncomplicated relationship that has lasted to this day. I believe that Gunther Plaut is one of the most talented persons that the Reform rabbinate has ever seen and I know that he has made a lasting contribution to our movement. Holy Blossom Temple is truly fortunate to have had him as its spiritual leader.

His accomplishments include being a highly respected congregational rabbi in two important congregations, first in the United States and then in Toronto. He has been a highly effective social activist, as well as an accomplished writer and exponent of Judaism in general and Reform Judaism in particular. He is known for many lasting achievements, but perhaps best as the editor of the *Torah Commentary*, which has opened the eyes of many Reform Jews to the truths of Judaism. Through this and in many other ways W. Gunther Plaut has helped to bring the Reform movement, which he has served with such distinction, into the mainstream of Jewish life. As I wrote in a tribute volume published by Holy Blossom Temple to mark his ninetieth birthday in November 2002, "our admiration for him is only surpassed by our gratitude." I deem it a unique privilege to have been his colleague.

Not being blind to his need to shine, however, I made it clear at the outset that I'm not a gentleman and would confront him if he tried to invade my space. As he couldn't cope with confrontation, he learned to live with the limitations, especially as he has been given much scope in the congregation and much deserved respect from us all. Sensitive to his reputation among his colleagues, aggravated by the premature departure of Harvey Fields, Gunther Plaut has gone out of his way to tell people how well he and I get along. I hope he has always believed it, for I've done my best to give him his due without letting him interfere in the way I led the congregation.

Plaut's presence both in the general and in the Jewish community was towering and well deserved. I had no intention of competing. Even though Holy Blossom Temple, by the very nature of the congregation's history and reputation, provides a platform for the senior rabbi and, whether he likes it or not, turns him into a political figure in the Jewish community, my priority was the congregation itself, not my image to the outside world. Though in later years I did indeed become something of a public person in my own right, my initial chosen path was to attend to matters in the congregation. This path had its own obstacles and stumbling blocks.

The first, though by no means the most formidable, was the late Margaret Davidson. Since the days of Abraham Feinberg, Gunther Plaut's predecessor, the senior rabbi's executive assistant, as she described herself, wielded enormous power by making herself indispensable to those who mattered, especially her boss. Margaret Davidson was a highly intelligent and very capable woman. I'm sure that, had she not been attached to Feinberg, she would have found a job more challenging and more commensurate with her talents. When after his retirement Feinberg was widowed and married someone else, a Jew by choice, I surmise that she must have been devastated. Though a loyal Presbyterian until the day she died, I'm sure she would have converted to Judaism had marriage to Feinberg been an option. But she remained loyal to him. Whenever he came to Toronto to perform mixed marriages, she made all the arrangements. After her death a special register, in which she recorded such marriages, was found in her apartment. Plaut seems to have tolerated the system, perhaps because he had become so dependent on her that he didn't want to alienate her, but more likely because he'd rather see Feinberg officiate at mixed marriages than one of the rogue rabbis who plague the Toronto Jewish community.

My impression upon arrival was that Margaret Davidson was running the congregation. She would cite decisions in the name of the senior rabbi on all kinds of problem issues, including religious matters, often without informing him of the problem, let alone the solution. She intimidated the other members of the staff, even the executive director. She had given instructions to the office receptionist that no phone calls were to be put through to me directly, but had to go through her. In this way she was in a position to decide who could speak to me. The door to my office had to be closed so that when people wanted to see me without an appointment, she would determine whether I was available. I felt like the proverbial Soviet ambassador who, though the titular head of mission, in reality must report to the KGB colonel acting as his chauffeur. I had little doubt that Davidson reported my every move to selected members of the congregation and to one or two of my rabbinic colleagues.

Her declared reason for acting in this manner was to protect me, just as she had protected my predecessors. Not only did she apportion honours, especially on the High Holy Days, in the name of the senior rabbi, but she even offered to arrange catering in his home. Angry at not being consulted about the neighbourhood in which Fredzia and I had bought a house, she mounted something of a campaign to persuade us to forfeit the deposit and find a more chic home. Though Scottish, she had all the earmarks of a snobbish English butler. Ostensibly to help me in my work, she was most eager to tell me who was important in the congregation, for she believed in cultivating people of rank and influence. Apart from the rich, these included presidents and past presidents of Holy Blossom. As a result, many movers and shakers she lionized considered her essential to the well-being of the Temple.

From the very outset it was clear to me that Miss Davidson and I had to part company as soon as possible. As I had just arrived and she was long past retirement age, it would be she who'd have to go. It took several months and much unpleasantness before I got a new secretary.

The first of many reasons for the delay was my installation. According to the leaders of the congregation, only Miss Davidson would be able to arrange it. The event turned out to be a show of enormous proportions at which more Christian clergy, including the cardinal, than rabbis were in attendance. I realized that after the less than solemn parting with Harvey Fields and the hiatus that followed, the congregation needed to make a statement that it was back in business, but I'm not sure that its message was addressed to the relevant public. In retrospect, the event was something of an epitaph for a bygone era.

I've little doubt that there were those who hoped that with time I, too, would become dependent on the ubiquitous Miss Davidson and ask her to stay. One or two of her friends even gave me lunch to tell me how indispensable she was. It seems that she knew how to exploit the insecurities of the Jewish children of immigrants who wanted to make it in the general community and act as WASPs, but didn't know how. Some of them may even have joined Holy Blossom Temple to mix with "the right people." Davidson was considered an expert on etiquette and proper behaviour, and they needed her in order to look good in the eyes of non-Jews. The fact that I took no notice of her instructions and admonitions infuriated her and worried many others. When I once told her that she was no longer the senior rabbi of Holy Blossom Temple, she stormed out of my office in a rage. In the end, therefore, she submitted to the inevitable and retired. But she never forgave me.

The second immediate obstacle that made my work at the Temple difficult was the senior staff, the team of professionals who, in the absence of a senior rabbi, had run the Temple during the previous year. All of us seem to have replaced people who had left the Temple under less than happy circumstances. It made for a lot of insecurity. The most secure person was James Prosnit. He, too, had replaced a rabbi who had spent a very unhappy year in the congregation. However, though he came to Holy Blossom immediately after ordination from the Hebrew Union College in New York, he was a few years older than others when he entered rabbinic school and was a mature person with many skills, boundless charm and a lot of common sense. He was the mainstay in the congregation during the hiatus. I think that had he had a few more years' experience, he would have succeeded Harvey Fields. When during my first visit to Toronto I asked him how he felt about my possibly becoming his senior, he was honest enough to tell me that he had mixed feelings: regret at not being in charge and relief at not being in charge. We worked very well together until he left some three years later to further his career. We have remained good friends.

Friendship with the others was more difficult. As they had been running the congregation without senior supervision, I must have appeared to them something of an imposter. My coming from abroad added to their unease. In the early days they tried their best to marshal the support of their cronies in the congregation to thwart my efforts. I had to be tough and blunt in my endeavour to turn rebels into colleagues. Thus when a member of that group did some clumsy plotting, I had to remind him that the congregation had taken a great risk by bringing me from England and giving me a five-year contract. If they were forced to choose between him and me, they'd have to keep me even if they wanted it otherwise. He didn't believe me and had to learn the lesson the hard way.

That after some time we learned to work together was in no small measure due to the Reverend Stanford Lucyk, at the time the senior minister of the neighbouring Timothy Eaton Memorial Church, the most significant Toronto congregation in the United Church of Canada. Lucyk and Fields had been friends. Soon after my arrival Lucyk got in touch and offered whatever assistance I needed. He had a sizable team at Timothy Eaton. Together they did great things for their congregation. As I had until now been largely a one-man band, I had much to learn and Stan Lucyk was a patient teacher. We've been close ever since.

There were other obstacles. Though each was relatively minor, their cumulative effect made my life difficult. At times I wasn't even sure that I'd work out my initial contract. I had periodic confrontations with congregants over one thing or another. In an effort to put me in my place many insisted that they were founder members, even though the congregation had started 125 years earlier. When I questioned their assertions they thought me uncouth. Many weren't shy about voicing their complaints to me: I was too cold and remote; I didn't smile enough; I was arrogant and standoffish; I irritated them when I fiddled with my tallith; I couldn't speak English properly and needed elocution lessons; I didn't know how to use the microphone; I didn't understand Canada; I didn't understand Reform Judaism; I didn't flatter them enough. One woman actually told me that she had been instrumental in getting rid of Harvey Fields and if I didn't behave myself she'd do the same to me. Had I not had a successful career as a rabbi in Britain for more than two decades, I'd have been beside myself.

The main line of attack was that I was incomprehensible, not an easy challenge to meet when your main tool is speaking. A particular incident may illustrate my plight. One day a dentist who had treated me soon after my coming to Toronto came to see me. Though I was no longer his patient and he had never been a member of the congregation, he had continued to take an interest in my progress. He was therefore concerned about a conversation he overheard in the locker room of his tennis club between two members of Holy Blossom Temple. Both agreed that they didn't understand a word of what I said. He now wondered whether this was because of the work he had done in my mouth and felt badly about it. I assured him that the problem wasn't dental but mental.

Nowadays I could also tell him that members of the congregation speak of the lucidity and clarity of my teaching and preaching. If I'd let them, they'd love to tell me that they don't understand my successor. Most Jews tend to agree that the best rabbi they've ever had was the one who just left.

The leaders of the congregation berated me periodically for the above-mentioned and other misdemeanours. Even those who wished to describe themselves as friends told me how they had to defend me against attacks by other members of the congregation. When I asked them why they reported this to me, they insisted that it was out of love and a desire for me to succeed. Perhaps I should have believed them, but I didn't. It was probably my "otherness" that was the reason for many of my problems. Gregory Baum, the distinguished Canadian Catholic theologian, told me once that, in his view, had the leaders of the congregation really read my book, *Beyond Survival*, a copy of which I gave to Arthur Grant when he first approached me in Jerusalem, they would never have hired me. Other prominent Canadians also told me that Holy Blossom Temple didn't really know what they had let themselves in for when they invited me to be their rabbi.

Thus there were many reasons I should have been depressed, but there was too much for me to do to have time for introspection. Realizing that I was usually attacked when I wanted to change things helped me to forge forward despite the obstacles. But I was painfully aware how difficult it was for Fredzia to start all over again, with me continually under stress and with no friends of her own to offer support. I also felt guilty for having brought Elizabeth to Canada. To transplant a sixteen-year-old from a safe and comfortable environment to another culture, again with no friends close by, was almost irresponsible. And that I did it to further my own career made me feel ashamed of myself. There were times in the course of those early years when I felt that the opposition within the congregation might provide us with a cogent reason for returning to Britain. I wouldn't have been the first rabbi who left for North America only to return somewhat depleted. At the same time, however, I knew how difficult it would have been to go back. I felt trapped. After all, Britain wasn't home either.

The only way forward, therefore, was to respond as best I could to the many challenges and to try to make this congregation my own. Apart from the personal tensions, the primary religious challenge had to do with the way worship services were conducted at Holy Blossom Temple. The congregation, the first in this part of Canada, was founded in 1856 as a traditional Jewish place of worship. As more Jews moved into the city, they established their own congregations, many of them with names of the places in Eastern Europe where they came from. Holy Blossom, which seems to have acquired its peculiar and largely inexplicable name soon after its inception, remained the congregation of the acculturated Jewish families, some of whom had originally come from German-speaking lands. Whereas the Eastern European newcomers stayed with the Orthodox ways they brought with them, Holy Blossom was considered more liberal, even when it was still nominally Orthodox. By 1920 it had become an affiliated Reform congregation.

The rabbi who shaped Holy Blossom Temple religiously was Maurice Eisendrath, the third incumbent after the congregation became Reform. He served from 1929 until 1943, when he became the president of the Union of American Hebrew Congregations. The present Temple building on Bathurst Street was erected in 1938. Both in form and content it was shaped by Eisendrath's classical Reform theology. Thus, whereas synagogues are usually built with the ark that contains the Torah scrolls in the east, Holy Blossom has the ark in the west, making the deliberately anti-Zionist point that the worshippers in this place won't be facing Jerusalem; and whereas in synagogues the ark usually dominates, at Holy Blossom the enormous marble pulpit stands out. The stress is on preaching and the man doing it, not on Holy Writ. Altogether, the interior and exterior of the building gives an impression of a church, and not surprisingly it was known in the Jewish community as "the church on the hill." Time, however, has bestowed on the building an aura of beauty, sanctity and even Jewish authenticity. Nowadays friends and foes alike are impressed by it and many feel very good in it.

I was told that as the Temple was being built, a refugee Jewish artist living in New York submitted an outline for a fresco that depicted the biblical Jacob's dream. It would go over the cupola above the *bimah*. However, the project was abandoned because it was considered too expensive. The name of the artist was Marc Chagall. I've often speculated about what would have happened if Chagall's fresco had been accepted and as a result he had been asked to do the stained-glass windows. The Temple wouldn't have been just a minor landmark in the city, as it is today, but Toronto's major tourist attraction.

Not that those who built the Temple on Bathurst Street were small-minded. The congregation numbered at most 250 families at the time, yet the sanctuary seated 1400 people. For Eisendrath's purpose was to speak to the entire community, Jewish and non-Jewish. His Sunday sermons attracted crowds and his words had an impact, albeit not always for the good. For in those days he was a fierce opponent of Zionism. Some members even resigned from the congregation in protest.

Eisendrath's successors, Feinberg and Plaut, tried to make the service warmer, the mood more traditional and the interior of the sanctuary more reflective of Jewish practice. And so Feinberg brought in a second pulpit when a cantor was hired, and Plaut made the congregation build a platform for a third pulpit from which the Torah would be read. But the ambience remained "classical Reform." Even Plaut didn't wear headgear at services, and in place of the traditional tallith he wore a stole of the kind clergy don in church. However, when in 1975 the Reform movement produced a more traditional prayer book, Holy Blossom was among the first to adopt it. It also acquired an adequate number of copies of the Plaut Torah commentary, when it appeared in 1981, in an endeavour to bring worshippers closer to the text.

Harvey Fields worked hard at making the services more traditional. He was the first Reform rabbi at Holy Blossom to wear a *kippa* and a tallith on the *bimah*. Though many of his innovations were met with much opposition, he made my endeavour to continue in the same vein easier. Inadvertently I gave notice of things to come in the course of my first visit to the congregation in early 1983, before I was offered the position. When I spoke from the pulpit on that occasion I wore not only a *kippa* but also a large woollen tallith. Packing before leaving for Toronto, I grabbed the first tallith I laid my hands on and that was the one I wore. I was told later that it caused something of a stir. Some said that it was chutzpah to so openly flaunt Holy Blossom practice, while others insisted that it showed courage and independence. In reality, of course, neither was my intention.

But I did intend to change the ambience of the liturgy once I became the senior rabbi. Though I've never been enamoured of *Gates of Prayer*, the *Siddur* of the American Reform movement, I don't think that it's the words on the printed page that ultimately determine the quality of the service. The continuous liturgical reform in Reform Judaism, in North America and elsewhere, has, alas, not brought the Jews to the synagogue, whereas worship services using ostensibly archaic Orthodox prayer books seem to be doing better. I believe I could conduct a Reform service from an Orthodox prayer book, for what matters is participation, music, energy and devotion.

I found the services at Holy Blossom Temple to be cold and the music intended for performance, not for participation. I could discern neither energy nor devotion. As in so many classical Reform synagogues, at Holy Blossom worshippers were "beprayed, besung and bepreached." Congregational passivity was the order of the day and the essence of decorum. Even though the congregation has a most gifted and knowledgeable cantor, Benjamin Z. Maissner, he wasn't as yet showing his strength as an accomplished leader of worshipping congregations but rather as a soloist of liturgical music. The congregation listened to moving renditions interrupted by prayers, mainly in English, that were occasionally impressive but more often banal.

I've since experienced the same tedium in many Reform congregations all over the world. They're living illustrations of the truth that no amount of liturgical reform and politically correct language brings Jews to the synagogue. I was determined to get Jews to Holy Blossom by reducing the tedium and increasing the intensity. Yet despite considerable progress, it would be presumptuous of me to claim great success. It has taken a long time to create what tradition calls an *oylem* (Hebrew *olam*: universe), that is, a critical mass of regular worshippers who shape the liturgical culture of the congregation.

Our first High Holy Day services in the congregation were the most depressing I had ever experienced. It seemed that worthy members, among them many past presidents, were given sections to read, irrespective of their ability to do it well. The coordination between readers, choir and cantor was poor, and that made the services unduly long, at times even incoherent. The readings of the biblical texts were often inaccurate. If the emphasis, like in so many Reform congregations, was to be on aesthetics, the result was disappointing. I found the services neither beautiful nor authentic, neither artistically accomplished nor participatory.

The choir, consisting exclusively of non-Jewish professional musicians, dominated. It was led by a well-known church organist who did his best to impose the mood and tempo of his church onto the synagogue service. When I told him that the rhythm of Jewish worship was different, I think he considered me a vulgar philistine. Like everybody else who worked in the Temple, he had his own coterie, usually consisting of those who resisted change and believed that traditional Jewish music wasn't good enough for the Temple.

Though members of the congregation would be asked to open the ark at certain points in the service, carry the Torah scrolls and read the blessings before and after the readings, those so honoured were usually men whom Margaret Davidson considered to be important, for it is she who assigned the honours—in the name of the senior rabbi of course. As High Holy Day services had to be held in more than one location and most members wanted to be seated in the sanctuary, Davidson had an opportunity to accommodate those whom she thought worthy of it. I caused some consternation when I insisted that in the future a committee would distribute honours, not the senior rabbi and not his secretary.

I was determined to change things in as many ways as I deemed necessary. Not prone to diplomacy, I confronted the relevant committees, as well as the members of the senior staff, urging them to change direction and giving reasons for it. Services would be led by those who knew how to lead them, be they laypersons or professionals. Texts would be read accurately, for I've always insisted that Hebrew, being a holy tongue, had to be read with utmost respect and accuracy. Traditional themes were brought into the liturgy and several new English prayers were pruned. Nothing of this happened within a short time, but even by the following year, the High Holy Day services had a different feel. The modifications continued for many years, usually after lengthy discussions, some unpleasantness and the occasional battle. On the whole, however, the congregation seemed to appreciate the opportunities to actively participate in worship and the resulting much warmer atmosphere.

Unlike many members of long standing, the families that had joined the Temple in recent years didn't have a need to be radically different from the Orthodox and Conservative congregations in which they grew up. They were attracted to Reform Judaism, not as an act of defiance, but out of a genuine search to belong to a community that met their religious needs, however feeble these may have been at times. Those who thought that their rabbi from London would be an English gentleman found out that they got a Polish Jew instead. Despite the periodic tongue-lashings I received from the leaders, not every rank-and-file member was upset by what I tried to do.

The turning point for me was probably the introduction of a worship service on the second day of Rosh Hashanah. Reform Judaism has prided itself on being rooted in biblical and therefore allegedly authentic practice. As the Bible prescribes one day for every festival, including the New Year, there would be no services on the second day. Since nothing was happening in the Temple on the second day, the new assistant rabbi of the congregation, Elyse Goldstein, interested in providing services for the hearing-impaired and herself a signer, wanted to conduct a service for that group. Being present at that service, I discovered that among the sizable congregation there were only a few hearing-impaired worshippers. Most of those who came were members of the Temple who were in search of a service on the second day of Rosh Hashanah.

I had introduced such a service in the congregation I served prior to coming to Toronto and I now proceeded to try to bring it to Holy Blossom. The aim was to make it very much a Reform Rosh Hashanah service, but using traditional and modern prayers and readings that the existing Reform *Machzor, Gates of Repentance*, omitted. The service would be on the theme of Rosh Hashanah, yet different from the service on the first day. My argument was partly that, despite the biblical institution of one day, rabbinic Judaism described Rosh Hashanah, unlike the other festivals, as *yoma arikhta*, an extended day, that is, two days, and partly that there were obviously members of the congregation who wanted it. Those who didn't needn't attend.

The opposition was formidable. Many established members who in their youth would have been taunted by other Jews for celebrating only on one day, now felt that their opponents would be vindicated and that what they had been taught by their rabbis was wrong; Feinberg had even urged parents to send their children to school on the second day of all festivals. Members were also fearful that Conservative, perhaps even Orthodox, Judaism was being smuggled in by the Polish Jew and that this could lead to the disintegration of Reform Judaism. Several members of the congregation told me that what they perceived to be the largely secular nature of the Temple was being invalidated. A neighbour told my wife that she had heard rumours that "your husband is religious."

Around that time I also got a letter from the late Rabbi Alexander Schindler, the president of the Union of American Hebrew Congregations, the organization of which the Temple was a constituent member. His message seemed to have been prompted by a complaint from a member of the much more "classical" Reform congregation in Montreal and spoke of my alleged heretic views and actions, some of which now began to appear in the *Canadian Jewish News*. Schindler's letter was, of course, couched in liberal euphemistic language. I replied by citing the school principal who offered the parents of his students a deal: "If you promise not to believe what the children say about your teachers, I promise not to believe what they tell us about you." It's the last I heard from him on the subject, but when we met thereafter, as we often did, he always called me Dave.

Incidentally it seems that not only Jews steeped in the classical Reform tradition were troubled by my connection to the *Canadian Jewish News*. The late Ray Wolfe, who had created the publication some years earlier and was the most influential member of the Jewish community until his death, told me that a delegation of Orthodox rabbis in Toronto had come to see him to protest my frequent appearances in the paper and the views I was expressing. I had learned a long time ago that exponents of Orthodox Judaism are often irritated by Reform Jews who affirm traditional positions. They prefer their opponents to be as far removed from their stance as possible, thus making them easier targets for attacks. Being now criticized by both sides made me realize that I was on the right track.

In the end, however, common sense prevailed at Holy Blossom. I was given permission to organize an *experimental* service for one year only. It was a tremendous success. Since then, every year the sanctuary at Holy Blossom Temple is filled to capacity on the second day of Rosh

Hashanah. Many of those who attend say that for them it's the high point of the liturgical year. The congregation is still very much Reform, but its members came to realize that the mode of worship and observance was changing.

While keen to add the second day of Rosh Hashanah to our calendar, I was determined to remove from it the late Friday evening services that were held during the winter months. These services had once been the main activity of every Reform temple, including this one. As late as the 1970s a substantial part of the congregation attended them. When Plaut was the senior rabbi, he would periodically give public affairs lectures that attracted large audiences—audiences, more than congregations. Fields tried to continue the tradition, but by then the Jewish public had long ceased to need the pulpit to inform it as to what was going on in the Jewish world. Now, therefore, the Temple would put on special programs, usually musical events, to bolster attendance. On at least one occasion, I'm told, both the senior rabbi and the cantor appeared in tuxedos as befits performers at galas.

By the time I came to Toronto, attendance at late Friday evening services was low. The original need to hold such services was no longer there. In the first century of Reform Judaism, from the middle of the nineteenth century, many members of Reform congregations were shopkeepers. Saturday sales were essential for their businesses. Attendance at Sabbath morning worship didn't seem possible. Hence the late Friday evening service, which included the reading from the Torah and was followed by a reception where members met and mingled. Hence also the Sunday morning services in many Reform congregations, including Holy Blossom Temple. These services also had a second purpose: to enable non-members, including non-Jews, to attend and to give the impression that the only thing that divided Jews from other Canadians was the way they worshipped. When Christians went to church, Jews would go to synagogue.

But things began to change in the 1950s and 1960s. Few, if any, members of Reform congregations were shopkeepers. As professionals they had long weekends for themselves. And after the establishment of the State of Israel in 1948, most of them no longer believed that the only difference between Gentiles and Jews was their place of worship.

Also, more and more members seemed to celebrate Shabbat with their families and were not prepared to rush out in time for the late service. Because I objected to the creation of artificial congregations by providing programs put on at considerable expense for those who didn't celebrate Shabbat and didn't want to pray, Friday night congregations grew consistently smaller. The trend was recognized already in Plaut's time when an early pre-dinner *Kabbalat Shabbat* service was introduced. It was informal and attracted a small number of worshippers, but I thought it had potential. When attendance at the late services was smaller than at the earlier services, I realized that it was time to close down the former. At the end of his term of office as the president of the Central Conference of American Rabbis, Rabbi Plaut had suggested in his presidential address at the annual convention that the time of the late Friday evening service had passed. Though his words created something of a furor among his colleagues, I knew that I could refer to them when my turn came to struggle with the conservative forces in the congregation that almost on principle resisted every change, but for whom Plaut had been the undisputed authority.

The battle this time was even fiercer than over second-day Rosh Hashanah and entailed many tactical retreats and regroupings. In the end a sufficient number of people saw the merit of the proposals. We discontinued the late service and, to provide room for new regular worshippers, moved the early one to the so-called youth chapel on the third floor of the religious-school building. It has retained its informal "user-friendly" style and has become a focal point for many Temple families. Whereas the Shabbat morning services in the sanctuary attract many visitors who come only for bar mitzvahs or bat mitzvahs, not for God, the congregation at the Friday evening services consists of members of all ages who *want* to be there. Their very presence has been another factor in shaping the new culture that now prevails at Holy Blossom.

One of the characteristics of these informal services is that many worshippers, men and to a lesser extent women, wear headgear. This is the result of yet another struggle in the congregation.

Being bareheaded at prayer was considered a hallmark of classical Reform. It was yet another sign of acculturation to Christian mores.

Though nobody who wore a *kippa* at Holy Blossom was ever asked to remove it, this happened in many congregations in the United States. Some of them even have it in their bylaws that officiating rabbis and cantors are forbidden to wear headgear. Until Harvey Fields came, this practice, though not enshrined in law, was followed at Holy Blossom. I decided to pose the question in as many ways as I could why members of the congregation would rather present themselves in the Christian than in the Jewish mode of prayer at services.

I went further. Normally the *Kol Nidre* service in our congregation, as in many other congregations, would be interrupted by an appeal made by the officiating rabbi on behalf of Israel Bonds. The appeal was preceded by a letter sent to members of the congregation and signed by the president and me urging them to buy bonds. After the appeal from the pulpit, ushers would go down the aisles to collect the pledges. There were cards and pencils in the pews. (This has now been modified: the appeal is made by a layperson and the ticket that admits members to the High Holy Day services and has their name on it includes a pledge card, thus eliminating the need to write.) I've always found the procedure disruptive and saw it as a manifestation of the secularization of worship in general and the Day of Atonement in particular. The fact that Conservative and Orthodox synagogues also did it in no way made it more acceptable; it only showed that no movement in Judaism is free from secularization, often with Israel as the pretext. I knew, therefore, that because of pressure from the community at large, I wouldn't be able to stop the bonds appeal, once it had become a fixture of the *Kol Nidre* service.

But at the 1988 *Kol Nidre* service, when I had been the senior rabbi of the congregation for five years, I asked rhetorically in my address from the pulpit how those present would react if a couple of weeks earlier, I had sent them a letter urging them to cover their heads in worship in the Jewish way, then had appealed from the pulpit for members to put on a *kippa* provided in the pews. Perhaps, in conclusion, the ushers might go down the aisles to collect unused *kippot*. Even before I could answer my question, I heard hissing from the pews.

Those most offended, however, had a problem. They were proud that Holy Blossom had a free pulpit and rabbis had the right to say what they deemed appropriate, so how would they now censure me? They went for the usual compromise: of course I had the right to say what I said, but I said it at the wrong time, in the wrong place and in the wrong way. As so often before and since, when people couldn't respond to the matter in hand, they attacked the manner in which it was said. In the end I didn't act on the strictures. Today, men who've remained bareheaded at services are probably in the minority and their number is decreasing. It's not unusual to see nowadays on the *bimah* a bareheaded grandfather, a son wearing a *kippa* and the grandson celebrating his bar mitzvah, or a granddaughter celebrating her bat mitzvah, wearing both *kippa* and tallith. And the congregation is still very much Reform.

For Reform Judaism isn't social custom, as many of its adherents may think, and it's not rigid law, as many of its opponents assert, but an understanding of the Torah as God's word that women and men in every generation try to hear in ways they can understand to enable them to live authentic Jewish lives. Developing and promoting the Temple's extensive and varied adult education program is evidence of its adherence to the tenets of Reform Judaism. Holding on to mores that belong to a bygone age, when conformity took precedence over authenticity, negates fundamental assumptions of Reform Judaism. I saw it as one of my tasks to liberate the congregation from this particular straitjacket.

The reasons for those nowadays holding out against changes are rarely assimilationist. They reflect the conservative trend in every religious community, even in one that wants to be progressive. Reform Judaism, especially in its earlier years, attracted staunchly anti-Orthodox women and men who in Orthodox fashion made a point of showing disdain for the practices of others, especially if they were traditional. Their offspring were brought up in this atmosphere and saw no reason to change. But unlike the case of the second day of Rosh Hashanah when they could stay away, when it came to headgear, they had to mingle with those who wore it. They didn't like it. Some will admit that even if they wanted to, they wouldn't know how to make the switch without losing face. Those who have been mature enough to change the way they present themselves in the Temple haven't lost face at all.

Part of the secular nature of Holy Blossom Temple was that its religious school met on Saturdays. This gave the message that the Sabbath isn't the Lord's day but the Jews' day. Students would come dressed not to honour the day but to be informal. On the rare occasions when parents were asked to join their children in the sanctuary at Shabbat services, the former came dressed as if for golf. The religious-school office was always busy on Saturdays. There was no *neshama yitera* in sight, the additional soul that according to our mystical tradition, enters a Jew on the Sabbath. In my effort to make Holy Blossom Temple a truly Jewish place, I began to explore the possibility of changing religious school from Saturday to Sunday. Once again, the same conservative forces, fearful of making the place Orthodox or Conservative, came to the fore.

The religious school at Holy Blossom Temple had a tremendous reputation in the city, especially at the time when there were few Jewish day schools and non-Reform congregations didn't provide much instruction for girls. The director of education at Holy Blossom, Heinz Warschauer, was a towering figure who despite his allegedly autocratic manner and brisk attitude, was highly respected in the congregation, in the Toronto Jewish community and in the Reform movement in North America. He had attracted many gifted young people, usually university students, as teachers. Some of them were now active members of the congregation. Though Warschauer died a year or so before my arrival and had retired a few years before that, I heard his name all the time. If Saturday school was good enough for him, it had to be good enough for me too.

Warschauer ran the school as his fiefdom with very little, if any, input by the rabbis. The fact that I was determined to be involved was sufficient cause for the then director of education to try to undermine my effort. So I had to wait until Robert Tornberg became the director. He is a committed and observant Jew and felt very much the way I did. Together we accomplished our goal and for many years now our religious school has functioned most satisfactorily on Sundays. The change has also made it possible for us to create a very successful family service on Saturday mornings. Now as soon as one enters the building one feels the ambience of Shabbat. No Jew has reason to feel that s/he is a stranger there.

Tornberg's real ambition had always been to be in charge of a Jewish day school. He was, therefore, most receptive to the proposal to open one on our premises. Though traditionally Reform Judaism, in its commitment to integration and its disdain for Jewish separatism, has been opposed to parochial schools, Reform congregations in Toronto were among the first to break with that tradition. In 1974 the Leo Baeck School was established. It was first housed on the premises of sister congregations, then in a rented school building until it got its own magnificent campus in the north of the city, where the majority of Toronto's Jews, particularly families with young children, now live. But parents living in the vicinity of the Temple wanted something closer to their homes. For many years, the Temple ran a very successful pre-school for some 120 children. A campus on Temple premises would enable many of these children to continue their Jewish education.

Originally both Bob Tornberg and I had hoped that the new school would be under the direct authority of the Temple itself. Neither he nor I were greatly enamoured of the way the Leo Baeck School was run in those days. We were particularly disturbed by what we regarded as inadequate instruction in Judaism. We were defeated. Our opponents included those who didn't like Jewish schools in general, but the arguments that won the day had to do with money. It was felt that the Temple shouldn't assume financial responsibility for the enterprise. The compromise, therefore, was to let Leo Baeck be responsible and run the school at Holy Blossom as its branch. It has turned out to be a most successful effort, both educationally and financially, and since Zita Gardner, a respected member of the Temple, became the director of the Leo Baeck School, I've had no difficulty having full confidence in all its undertakings. As she retires in 2004, I hope that her successor will follow in her footsteps.

Bob Tornberg wasn't allowed to lead the campus at Holy Blossom on the grounds that it might impede his work in the religious school. This was the principal reason, I believe, that he left us to be the head of a very successful Jewish day school in Marblehead, Massachusetts. In the years he was at Holy Blossom he understood and supported my desire to make the place more rooted in Jewish fundamentals. I miss him.

It's this desire that was also behind my campaign to make catering at the Temple adhere to acceptable standards of *kashruth*. For reasons that have always baffled me, perhaps because of my own childhood diet of pork and ham, Jews in North America regard pork products as abhorrent but shellfish as totally acceptable. Thus the kitchen at Holy Blossom not only served non-kosher meat, apart from pork, and mixed it with milk products, but one also found shellfish there. Though the caterers were always ready to provide prepared packages of kosher food for those who wanted it, many member families felt that they had to go elsewhere to celebrate. Instead of citing Jewish dietary laws, I argued my case from a liberal standpoint, suggesting that it was *un*liberal to make the Temple inaccessible to any of its members. Though even those who didn't care for *kashruth* could enjoy kosher food, those who did couldn't partake of the current menu at the Temple.

Like the opponents to *kashruth* in the Temple I didn't want a supervisor from the Kashruth Division of the Canadian Jewish Congress to dictate what we could and couldn't do. But I saw no reason we should not decide on our own standards and follow them. All our members, like the majority of Jews who call themselves observant, would eat from plates in non-kosher restaurants as long as what they ate was not tref. These are the standards I proposed: no forbidden foods, always kosher meat, no mixing of milk and meat products and access to vegetarian dishes for those who wanted it. Once again the opposition was formidable. Some even said in public that kosher food was inedible. But in the end, common sense prevailed and the standards of dietary observance outlined here are being observed. When the Temple decided to remove the sole concession from one caterer, meticulous adherence to the regulations was taken for granted, because non-compliance may sever the caterer's relationship with the congregation.

My involvement with catering surprised members of the board. The Temple was administratively divided into six departments. Five of these were worship, education, finance, administration and membership. The sixth one was called the department of Jewish living and dealt with social action programming, interfaith activities, festival celebrations and so on. It was assumed that the senior rabbi was in charge of only the department of worship. Catering belonged to administration and was the province of the executive director. I was utterly amazed when early in 1984, a few months after my arrival, I was expected to present a budget for "my" department. I refused, not only because I didn't know how to do it, but also as a matter of principle. I saw my role as being concerned with all aspects of the congregation, not just with prayer. For me, what happened in the religious school and in the catering hall was no less a part of the religious life of the congregation than the worship services.

At the same time I maintained that others, both professionals and lay leaders, had not only a right but a duty to be involved in all aspects of Temple life, worship services no less than finances or social action programs. It took a good few years before this new way of looking at things was accepted. I believe that it has greatly benefited the Temple.

I'm most anxious not to give the false impression that my ministry at Holy Blossom Temple has been a series of spectacular successes. Reality was much more complicated and it's only now, in retrospect, that I can identify the elements that turned the congregation into what it has become. Previously, when members and visitors were pointing to the changes I had brought in, I genuinely couldn't see them because I was invariably in the midst of yet another struggle, yet another frustration that made people challenge my competence, my judgment, my integrity as a person and my authenticity as a Reform Jew. And they made much of my many deficiencies as a human being.

It was only thanks to Fredzia's love and unfailing support that I could continue. She and our children reminded me constantly of what's really important in life and that I only worked at Holy Blossom, I didn't own it. Though I had often contemplated leaving, I also decided to carry on as long as I was there and as long as the congregation would put up with me. I wanted to continue the struggle, because I was imbued with a sense of mission, even though many of my proposals were rejected or ignored. I really felt that I was part of a trend in Reform Judaism that tried to bring it into the mainstream of Jewish life, save it from becoming a sect on the margin by turning it into an authentic manifestation of living Judaism.

My aim was to articulate that trend through preaching and teaching. I came to the conclusion, not only in self-defence, that many of those who said they couldn't hear or couldn't understand what I said didn't want to hear or understand, because what they heard was very different from what they had been told before. Though the congregation had been urged to be part of *k'lal Yisrael*, the Jewish people, over many years, its participation was primarily expected in political and philanthropic actions, such as the Soviet Jewry campaign and financial support for Israel. I had been involved in these activities throughout my rabbinate, but in addition, I also believe that Reform Judaism as such must rid itself of its internal sectarian tendencies. Many of my challenges in the congregation, as described above, stem from this conviction. I saw my activities in Toronto as a continuation of my work in London, albeit under different circumstances and in a different key.

The prevailing mood in American Reform was, at least two decades ago, that "Reform is a verb," that is, it's a constantly changing "dynamic" movement. That which was new was almost invariably deemed preferable to that which had been before. If strict Orthodoxy laboured under the formula that "everything new is forbidden by the Torah," Reform would point in the opposite direction. Hence the search for new heights to scale, irrespective of the consequences for the Jewish people as a whole. Ironically, of course, yesterday's innovation had become today's established practice that nobody was allowed to tamper with. Thus the commitment to "Reform is a verb" was often manifest in the unwritten assumption that Reform is *reformed*, that is, changes once made must now be carved in stone. It may have allowed innovations, but not return to tradition. My intention to facilitate such a return was, I believe, a major cause for the opposition to me.

The decision to change the criteria for Jewish status is a case in point. With the laudable aim of trying to attract unaffiliated Jews, the Reform movement decided to accept as Jewish a person who had at least one Jewish parent, mother or father, whereas traditionally only the offspring of a Jewish mother was considered Jewish. Even now, in retrospect, it's difficult to determine if unaffiliated Jews flocked to Reform synagogues as a result of this approach, but it's obvious that at least some women who otherwise might have converted to Judaism before marrying a Jew had no reason to do so, as their children would be considered Jewish, whether or not both their parents were Jews. The proviso that children of such marriages had to have a Jewish up-bringing was so vague that nobody has ever determined what it means.

A corollary of this decision served as encouragement to Reform rabbis to perform marriages between Jews and non-Jews as long as "they promised to bring up their children as Jews," another vague stipulation with no possibility of follow-up. Though the Central Conference of American Rabbis (CCAR), the organization to which Reform rabbis belong, doesn't officially condone mixed marriages, it in no way censures those who perform them.

My first visit to the mother campus in Cincinnati of the Hebrew Union College-Jewish Institute of Religion was in April 1983, days after the CCAR adopted the resolution that bestowed on the offspring of a Jewish father the same rights as on a child of a Jewish mother. The pleas that other Jewish organizations in North America—particularly the Conservative movement, which in so many ways is close to Reform—made to the Reform rabbis that the Reform resolution would deepen the rift in the Jewish world fell on deaf ears. *K'lal Yisrael* wasn't that important, after all, for American Reform considers itself by definition to be normative.

The purpose of my Cincinnati visit, a few months before I formally assumed my office in Toronto, was to interview potential candidates for the post of assistant rabbi at Holy Blossom Temple. As I entered the building, the late Jakob Petuchowski, a professor at the College and long-time critic of the "Reform is a verb" school, whom I had met before in Britain, greeted me by saying, "Welcome to American Reform just as it's about to leave *k'lal Yisrael*." Instead of making me reconsider my decision to become part of American Reform, Petuchowski's remark encouraged me to struggle within it. Though in many ways Toronto made such struggle easier—its Reform rabbis would, for example, decide not to act on this latest decision by their American colleagues—my determination to spell things out in sermons and lectures made for a lot of unrest.

My basic approach is that "Reform is an adjective." Whereas I feared that the "Reform is a verb" approach was prepared to compromise with the noun "Judaism," my stance was that the noun was the essential, and Reform was only a way of understanding it. Like so many of my teachers, I've viewed Reform Judaism as the latest but by no means the last link in a long chain of ways of making Judaism speak to the needs of the times. So Reform had to be dynamic and changing, but always in a dialectic relationship to the vast body of Jewish teachings that have come before us. I knew that it was possible, for I had practised it for more than two decades in Britain, to conduct worship services in the Reform tradition and yet make them consistently and recognizably Jewish. The religious school didn't have to meet on Saturdays to teach Judaism to its students. The integrity and sovereignty of Holy Blossom Temple would remain intact, even when its kitchen was kosher.

I stressed the distinction between private and congregational practice. As a liberal congregation, it wasn't for it or its rabbis to tell members what to do in their own homes or how to conduct their own lives, though they should be given maximum opportunities to study Judaism in order to be able to make up their minds. But a liberal congregation that respects democracy must have the right to determine democratically how it wants to conduct itself in its own home, that is, in the Temple. I always stressed my role as the professional who informs the lay "jury" about what tradition has to teach and alerts it to the consequences of the actions it may take. But the final decision must always rest with the members or their elected leaders. That was how all changes came into effect at Holy Blossom and that was also why many other proposals of mine fell by the wayside. However, those that have been adopted have remained part of congregational practice, even though I'm no longer responsible for the direction of the Temple.

I saw my primary role as a teacher. Although I taught children for much of my rabbinate, even as the senior rabbi at Holy Blossom, my first aim was to teach adults. I'm a passionate advocate of education for children, but I realize that within the framework of supplementary education that the religious school is, at best children can be taught only a few skills and, even more important, a general respect for Judaism and Jewish life. In Reform households, where observance is often sporadic and attitudes confused and confusing, only by attracting adults to serious learning would we be able to move from mild indifference to commitment.

I advocated what I called incremental Judaism, urging members to add one mitzvah at a time to their lives as Jews.

It would be too much to suggest that I've succeeded, but it would be fair to say that over the past two decades, adult learning at Holy Blossom Temple has become more central. In small groups and in large gatherings, studying ancient texts and listening to modern exponents of Judaism, members of the congregation have been exposed to ideas and stimulated by them. I think that it has come to shape much of the culture of the Temple. My predecessors, notably Gunther Plaut, advocated and practised the same approach, but I'd like to think that I built on it and in so doing helped to instill respect and understanding for all dimensions of Judaism. With it came a greater commitment to be part of the mainstream, not only in matters of politics and philanthropy but also in questions of philosophy and practice. I surprised Temple members by talking a lot about God.

I believe that it's my skills as a teacher that saved me from being booted out of Holy Blossom. Even my fiercest critics, including those who said that I couldn't speak English, had to concede that I'm a good teacher and that I had something to say. How they knew it, since they insisted that they didn't understand what I said, continues to baffle me, unless I assume—in self-defence, perhaps—that they understood more than they let on and much more than they were willing to accept. With time they may even have accepted it more, albeit grudgingly. Thus many of the fiercest opponents to the changes in the way we conducted services have become regulars, some of them wearing *kippa* and tallith. They can even be seen in the sanctuary on the second day of Rosh Hashanah. And they turned up at the study groups and courses I conducted. For the last dozen or so years of my ministry at Holy Blossom, I was often praised for the same things I had been blamed for in the first five.

In fact, after my first five years with the congregation, I refused a contract and preferred to work only with a customary proviso for notice of dismissal or resignation. When the officers at the time wanted to know how I'd deal with salary negotiations, I told them that I'd accept whatever they'd offer. The offer I received was paltry, but I stood by my word. A few months later a small delegation came to see me to tell me that the earlier offer was unfair. Would I accept an increase? My stance had been vindicated. I believe that the frequent contract negotiations between rabbis and congregations contribute much to the bad feelings between them. I didn't choose to be a rabbi in order to get rich.

I was much more concerned about being accepted by my peers. This did happen in Britain, despite my personal shortcomings. If I didn't know how accepted I was when I worked there, I certainly found out through the tributes that appeared in the general and Jewish press when we decided to leave for Toronto.

My acceptance in North America has been less successful. The Reform rabbis in Toronto have always had mixed feelings about their colleagues at Holy Blossom. Being the "mother synagogue," it attracted a certain amount of resentment and jealousy. I did not experience much open hostility, but there was a fair amount of passive aggression, often directed against me personally. Thus, for example, when my turn came to represent the Canadian region on the executive of the CCAR, someone else was appointed. I didn't react at the time because it didn't matter to me. I raised it with my colleagues much later—for the record, not for restitution.

The decision to omit me may have been coordinated with the leaders of the CCAR, for there, too, I was never more than tolerated. In fact, I hadn't been a member of the CCAR while in Britain, but when I came to Holy Blossom, the leaders of the congregation felt that I should join. My membership was processed quickly, even though the CCAR has been less than hospitable to graduates of the Leo Baeck College. My swift passage may have been due to the late Rabbi Herbert Drooze, who helped out during the hiatus at Holy Blossom and was the chair of the relevant committee at the time of my application. Since my previous twenty-one years in the British rabbinate didn't count, I started as a novice and have remained a junior to this very day.

Yet in some ways I came to reflect the new trend in Reform Judaism in North America, a trend that had never left British Reform. This may have been one reason that it took so long for the Americans to adopt it, for any idea that wasn't theirs to start with was by definition suspect. I've rarely come across such provincialism, particularly among ostensibly educated Jews. Thus when in 1979, four years before I arrived in Toronto, I went as an invited guest to a convention of the CCAR to report on how British Reform was dealing with personal status that allowed for both liberalism and tradition, I was met with enormous hostility from the rabbis of my generation. Nothing a colleague from abroad had to tell them could be worthy of their attention. The fact that some two decades later the CCAR adopted similar proposals suggests that by then, what had once been outrageous had now become commonplace.

Though still a junior in the eyes of my American colleagues, I've grown old in the meantime. And while I have attended most CCAR conventions since coming to North America, I have always been on the margin. At times, when walking in the corridors of a convention centre, I have had the distinct feeling that many people view me the way Woody Allen in *Annie Hall* imagined his non-Jewish girlfriend's family in the Midwest saw him—as a Hasid with *peyot* and a *kapote*. On the few occasions that I've been asked to sit on a panel or write something for the CCAR journal, it has been as an advocate of the "right wing."

I brought the isolation upon myself. After my first visit to the United States in 1975 I wrote an article in *European Judaism* that described the secular nature of American Reform. Years later, when I was already living in Canada, speaking at a session at a convention of the World Union for Progressive Judaism in London, I was critical of the tendency in American Reform to see itself as the only legitimate exponent of the liberal Jewish way. On another occasion, addressing an ARZA board meeting as president of Arzenu, the international organization of Reform Zionists, I was critical of similar trends in our American constituent, for which the ARZA president, Rabbi Charles Kroloff, rebuked me. He later became president of the CCAR. My stance didn't win me friends in the United States. When Canadian Jews liked what I had to say on the subject, it may have been due to their generic anti-Americanism. One who didn't like what I had to say, as I mentioned previously, complained to Rabbi Schindler.

When I became the chair of the Canadian constituent of Arzenu, which is an affiliate of the Union of American Hebrew Congregations (UAHC), the lay body of Reform Judaism, I had automatically a seat both on the UAHC board and its executive. I even sat on the *bimah* at several of its conventions. One occasion gave me cause for considerable embarrassment. As is my custom I listen to speeches with eyes closed. On occasion I may even doze off. In this particular instance, the president himself, Rabbi Alexander Schindler, was speaking, and the vast gathering could see my state of semi-consciousness on the vast screens in the convention hall. An organizer rushed up to ask me to move out of sight, but the videotape exists and I saw it not long ago. I didn't feel good about it. Perhaps this was yet another factor for putting me in the bad books of those who mattered. But as Holy Blossom Temple was among the top dues payers to the UAHC, I couldn't be disregarded altogether and was never criticized head on.

Critical views by individual rabbis were at times more open. Thus on my aforementioned first visit to Cincinnati to interview a potential assistant rabbi, one of the candidates started off our encounter by telling me that he wasn't sure he wanted to join me, because my coming from abroad meant that there wouldn't be much he could learn from me. His tactics, I found out later, were to put me on the defensive. When instead I told him that our interview was over, he was shocked. A few years later, when a very well-connected potential candidate to fill the vacancy left by Prosnit came for an interview, he told me that many of our colleagues were waiting for me to fall on my face. Since that hadn't happened yet, he decided to apply. It wasn't clear whether his aim was to trip me up or prop me up, but this wasn't the only reason he didn't get the job.

To this very day American colleagues who assume that I must have some skills, as I was the senior rabbi of a congregation as large as theirs or larger, nevertheless go out of their way to make some patronizing remark to indicate that I'm really an outsider. I agree with them.

My standing in the Jewish community in Canada was also ambiguous. On the one hand, I was the senior rabbi of Toronto's most noticed congregation. On the other, I didn't conform to expected patterns. Past mavericks, notably Rabbi Reuben Slonim, who had expressed critical views about Israel, had been shunned. It was a little more difficult to demonize me, even though I was obviously not of the same ilk as Gunther Plaut, who had been in the centre of the Canadian Jewish establishment. I was therefore tolerated and occasionally invited to speak. An early assignment was to address a gathering paying tribute to Scandinavian rescuers of Jews. Some of those present seemed surprised that I expressed views they couldn't disagree with.

The reason for their surprise was that I had allied myself with Peace Now and similar organizations expressing reservations about Israeli government policy. Though my commitment to Israel and active involvement in Zionist affairs couldn't be ignored, I often felt marginalized. It was only toward the end of my tenure at Holy Blossom that I was made chair of a committee of the Ontario region of the Canadian Jewish Congress. I found that a very unsatisfactory experience, partly because of attempts by right-wingers to disrupt activities. Various efforts were being made to discredit me among the fundraisers in the community, but since I was probably the one to make the largest contribution of all rabbis to the annual campaign, that too proved difficult.

In the spring of 1988, the then Canadian Minister of Foreign Affairs, Joe Clark, invited a number of Canadian Jews and Canadian Palestinians for a consultation on how we could work together to help ease the tension in the Middle East. It was a useful encounter, but obviously not much was achieved, and other meetings were planned. But some Jews who had not been invited, perhaps because of their known views, were outraged that others should speak to Palestinians. As a result, pressure was put on the government ministry and no further meetings were held.

But I did meet again with Canadian Palestinians, occasionally before the Oslo Accord and more often thereafter. In fact, the first meeting took place in our home in Toronto as early as December 1988. Our aim was to pool our experience of peaceful and peace-loving Canada for the good of all. In the same spirit I attended two meetings with the late Feisal Husseini, one in 1995 as a representative of the Canadian Jewish Congress, a second privately three years later. Again not much has happened and no meetings are held nowadays in the shadow of the *intifada*.

The members of the Toronto Board of Rabbis, an organization consisting of Reform, Conservative and a few Orthodox rabbis who work for communal institutions, were generous enough to elect me as their president for the customary two-year term. Though the impact of the Board of Rabbis is limited, I like to think that I served it well and enhanced its status in the community.

As President of Kadima (now ARZA Canada) I did get involved in the Canadian Zionist Federation, one of the most moribund organizations in the community. I was even elected a vice-president. The only election for delegates to the 1990 Zionist Congress resulted in several of our representatives attending the Congress. It left our opponents amazed and angry. But my attempts to bring democracy into the federation and to propose its realistic restructuring failed. Though I have a very high regard for the organization's almost perennial president, Kurt Rothschild, I couldn't live with his paternalistic style of leadership and I resigned in 1998. The decline of the Canadian Zionist Federation mirrors, of course, the decline of the World Zionist Organization. I have more to say about that in the next chapter.

To compensate for some of the frustrations of the pulpit rabbinate, as I now experienced them, and to make up for my constant sense of not being sufficiently educated, I tried to publish as much as I could. The quarterly journal *Viewpoints*, edited from Montreal by the late Bill Abrams, provided a congenial forum and printed many serious articles of mine. Some of them started as lectures or papers at conferences in Canada and elsewhere; others were written especially for the journal.

In 1988 a publisher in Burlington who specialized in books of sermons published a collection of mine dealing with the festivals of the Jewish year under the title *Walking Toward Elijah*. David Azen, at that time the assistant rabbi at Holy Blossom, selected and edited the sermons and wrote an introduction. At the same time, I was also speaking with Malcolm Lester about a book. Together with Louise Dennys, he ran Lester & Orpen Dennys, a leading Canadian publisher at the time. Though he encouraged me to complete the manuscript, he was not able to publish it. Thanks to Carol Rittner, the editor of a book on Elie

Wiesel, to which I contributed a chapter, I got in touch with the Greenwood Press in Connecticut. In 1991 they published *The Star of Return*. This book is a serious attempt to integrate Zionism into Reform Judaism. The starting point for much of my teaching and writing ever since, it's the only book of mine published in hardcover. Though more impressive to look at than the paperbacks I've written, it's very expensive and nowadays is usually only found in libraries.

When I had served the congregation for ten years, some members contributed money to a volume I called *On Being a Jew*. It contains a number of essays I had published in *Viewpoints* and in the journal of British Reform, *Manna*, together with some unpublished material. Though the aim was to make the book available to all members of the congregation, the finances didn't allow for distribution. As a result, thousands of copies linger in the storerooms of the Temple.

Thanks to an unsolicited donation to my discretionary fund, I was able to edit the many sermons I had preached in conjunction with memorial services at the Temple. The result is a little book called *Choose Life*, intended for mourners who seek other perspectives on death and grieving than are usually available. As far as I know, it's still being sent to newly bereaved members of the congregation. I reread it during the week after my mother's death in January 2003.

In addition to the psychological reasons for wanting to write, I've also always had an inordinate respect for the printed word. One of my joys in retirement is being able to continue to write and to see my words appear in Jewish and non-Jewish publications. Though none of my books have had much of a readership, and even less of an impact, I write out of a need to express myself, coupled with the vain hope that perhaps one day in the future my writings will come to matter more.

My vanity has been fuelled by the approach on behalf of the Canadian Archives to keep my papers for posterity. I've already deposited manuscripts of all the sermons I've ever preached, the typescripts of my books and some correspondence. Soon I hope to hand over the many volumes of diaries I've kept since 1956, all published articles and essays, as well as the many scripts of lectures and papers I've delivered over the years.

Though my writing has had a very limited impact in the Jewish community, it seems to have enhanced my standing outside it. For I also wrote in many non-Jewish publications, including *The Toronto Journal of Theology* and *Catholic New Times*, as well as occasional articles in the general press.

I've always taken an interest in Christian-Jewish relations and so while still in London, when I read that Pope John Paul II would visit Toronto in 1984, I approached the organizers and invited the Pope to come to Holy Blossom Temple for a public community-wide event, where he could address the Jewish community. In view of the large number of Holocaust survivors living in Toronto, many from the Pope's native Poland, I thought that this would be widely appropriate. I was given all kinds of "logistical" reasons why such an event wasn't possible. It took a few more years before John Paul II did visit a synagogue, and another decade or so before he met with Holocaust survivors.

Though I had received an invitation to attend the planned interfaith service during the Pope's visit to Toronto in 1984, I accepted the offer of the Canadian Broadcasting Corporation to remain outside and be one of the commentators. Before the service started we received the text of the Pope's homily. It began with the words "Dear brothers and sisters in Christ." I reacted on air and pointed out the distinction that many Christians seem to ignore between Christian ecumenism and interfaith. The other two commentators agreed. The Very Reverend Lois Wilson, a past moderator of the United Church of Canada and a leader of the World Council of Churches, later a member of the Canadian Senate, spoke out strongly. Even Dr. Mary Jo Leddy, a prominent Catholic thinker and at that time still a member of the order of the Sisters of Sion, though more cautious in her pronouncements, shared my concern. It seems that the Church took no notice, for a similar phrase appeared in the papal homily at the ostensibly interfaith service in Edmonton.

But my links with the Catholic community, particularly its liberal wing, were strong. Not long after my coming to Toronto the Jewish Chautauqua Society, dedicated to interfaith understanding, asked me to lecture at the Faculty of Theology at the University of Toronto's St. Michael's College. I've been teaching a semester course there on aspects of contemporary Jewish thought ever since. The faculty even bestowed on me the title of senior lecturer. Professor Michael Fahey, the dean when I started teaching, has become a friend, as have his successors. The current dean, Dr. Anne Anderson, teaches at the college on Jewish worship and has been the prime mover in organizing an annual inter-session course in Jerusalem. A retired member of the faculty, Maureena Fritz, now runs the Bat Kol Institute in Jerusalem, dedicated to Christian-Jewish understanding. She and I often meet at services in our local Liberal congregation.

I've had several opportunities to meet with Hans Küng, the distinguished Catholic theologian, during his visits to Toronto when he lectured at Holy Blossom Temple. It has also been my privilege to be close to the late Professor William Dunphy, principal of St. Michael's College School and a tireless worker for Israel and the Jewish people. I was honoured by his family to be invited to speak at his memorial service. I had met Professor Gregory Baum in London many years earlier when I chaired a public meeting at which he was the principal speaker. We reconnected in Toronto and, though he soon moved to Montreal, we've remained in touch. I've contributed articles to the *Ecumenist*, the journal he edited. I even wrote an article in the *Canadian Jewish News* explaining why, though born of Jewish parents in his native Germany, he was brought up as a Protestant and became a Catholic only when he came to Canada. The Jewish disdain for those who leave the fold is totally misplaced in the case of this leading exponent of Catholic thought.

The links between the Timothy Eaton Memorial Church and Holy Blossom Temple, to which I referred earlier, were symptomatic of the connection between liberal Christians and liberal Jews. Even when that relationship was greatly soured by the anti-Israel stance of the *United Church Observer* in the 1970s and the many, to my mind, unbalanced pronouncements about Israel that the United Church has made since, contacts with individuals and groups continued. Stan Lucyk and I have continued to work together; I've been the "Jewish resource person" on several trips to Israel he has organized. I was also honoured to be invited by another former moderator, Bruce McLeod, to co-chair with him the Canadian campaign against the reintroduction of capital punishment.

When Bill Phipps was moderator we appeared on platforms together; I was very impressed by the contribution he made to the United Church's statement on Christian-Jewish relations. I had the great honour of being invited in the summer of 2003 to the 38th General Council of the United Church in Canada where the statement on the Church's relationship to Jews and Judaism, *Bearing Faithful Witness*, was adopted.

Earlier in 2003 Bill Phipps and his wife, Carolyn Pogue, together with Alexa McDonough, then leader of the New Democratic Party of Canada, and other members of her delegation, spent a happy Sabbath Eve in our home in Jerusalem. Even before they visited us, I urged them to allow Israeli realities speak for themselves rather than be influenced by preconceived left-wing ideology. I tried to persuade them to leave Israel less certain and more confused, albeit on a higher level. In the course of our dinner together, I suggested to Alexa McDonough that, when she reports to her party, she should go beyond the cliché of most critics affirming Israel's right to exist and express more even-handed compassion.

The Anglican archbishop of Toronto, Terrence Finlay, has participated in many interfaith events. Once he invited me to address his bishops about what it's like to be part of a minority community of faith. I first got to know the former primate of the Anglican Church, Edward Scott, after he retired from that position. We worked together on a project to affirm Canadian unity at a time when the country was in serious danger of breaking up. Since then, through our close and dear mutual friend Hope Sealy, a prominent member of the Anglican Church, we've met socially on several occasions. When I think of the quintessential ideal prince of the Anglican Church, I think of Ted Scott. John Fraser, another prominent Anglican, has been extraordinarily generous in welcoming me as a fellow of Massey College in Toronto, of which he is Master. The provost of Trinity College was a gracious host when I delivered the 2000 Larkin-Stuart Lectures there. Together with Holy Blossom, both colleges made sure that what I had to say was published as an attractive monograph.

When the Interfaith Social Action Reform Coalition (ISARC) was formed in Ontario, I was delighted to be actively involved in its work. There I've learned to greatly admire men like David Pfrimmer, ordained minister and official of the Lutheran Church, Brice Balmer, representing the Mennonite community, and Gerald Vanderzande of the Citizens for Public Justice whose passion for what's right and his commitment to advocacy on behalf of justice has been an inspiration to me.

When the Ontario government of Mike Harris launched its so-called common sense revolution in 1995, I was asked to write a theological critique of it for ISARC. The response my paper received was tremendous and for a long time it was quoted in many circles, including the Ontario legislature. Four years later I followed it up with an open letter to Harris, published in the *Globe and Mail*. In 2002 I had an opportunity to write another paper on the theme of social justice, this time on the ethics of inclusion, sponsored by the Laidlaw Foundation.

Though Christians, secularists and Jews work well together on social issues, our respective attitudes toward Israel continue to divide us. Despite my personal friendships and institutional contacts, I find it increasingly difficult to cooperate with those whose criticism of Israel is so unbalanced that it shows traces, or worse, of the age-old anti-Judaism of the church. Though I sympathize with Christians' commitment to the underdog and though I realize that Palestinian Arabs, not Israeli Jews, qualify for that category, I'm disturbed by the fact that the Jews' quest for survival in the decades after the Holocaust often only gets a perfunctory acknowledgment. I'm distressed to read in many of the church pronouncements a lack of concern for the Arabs' refusal, since before the creation of the state, to accept a two-state solution. The way the churches usually present the case to their adherents is as if the conflict started in 1967 when Israel unilaterally invaded Palestine. But the fact was that between 1948, when Israel was established, and 1967, when the so-called Six-Day War took place, the Arab states kept the Palestinians in refugee camps and offered them no prospect of independence under the pretext that Israel would soon vanish and then the Palestinians could have it all to themselves. I've expressed these views in print in general and Christian publications.

I'm aware of course of Christian Zionism in evangelical circles. But as a liberal I find it difficult to associate with them, even though I, at least in part, appreciate their commitment to the Jewish state. In the back of my mind is always the comment I once heard made by Yehuda Bauer, the distinguished Israeli historian, that these Zionists may like Jews but they hate Judaism. The End of Days theology that motivates many of them seems to imply that, once all the Jews live safely in Israel, they'll "see the light" and accept Christ. On the other hand, there are Christian groups whose commitment to Israel and the Jewish people has no hidden agenda, but I haven't yet been able to find congenial dialogue partners in those circles.

Because my name appeared in print in non-Jewish publications and periodically my face was seen on television, the Jewish community learned, in this roundabout way, to take me more seriously than it would have otherwise. The fact that I didn't fall on my face and the congregation was flourishing also helped. Thus, after the first few years of struggle and uncertainty, things settled down nicely and I was able to show members of the congregation paths to greater depth and commitment. Many of them came to the various classes I gave. As I encouraged my rabbinic colleagues at Holy Blossom to teach, the network of adult study activities grew. Though the Temple often hosted lecturers with international reputations, in recent years a gift from the philanthropic couple Gerry Schwartz and Heather Reisman made it possible for us to invite stars on the Jewish firmament, including Elie Wiesel, the late Abba Eban and Amos Oz.

Holy Blossom Temple has among its members distinguished academics. We've been anxious to involve them in our work and they've invariably responded generously. For example, Michael Marrus, the respected Holocaust historian, gives every year a much appreciated lecture at the Temple during the Toronto Jewish community's Holocaust Education Week. The philosophy professor Howard Adelman has spoken during the study period on Yom Kippur afternoon. His combination of religious commitment and philosophic analysis is a source of inspiration and stimulation. David Dewitt, a professor of political science, has been involved in helping the Temple to plan its Israel programming and has often been one of the participants. My associate and now successor as senior rabbi, John Moscowitz, was very much involved in making these and many other events happen.

When I approached Joseph Rotman, another Toronto philanthropist and personal friend, for help in our educational work, he wished to combine his commitment to the Temple with his interest in the University of Toronto. The result was a cooperative effort between ourselves and the university's Department of Philosophy that enabled us to run several conferences about the nature of the city, a subject that has since become significant in many circles. The project brought me together with Frank Cunningham, at that time the head of the Philosophy Department and now the principal of the university's Innis College. Fredzia and I and he and his wife, Merike Omatsu, have been friends ever since. Rose Wolfe, at that time chancellor of the University of Toronto and a highly respected member of the Temple and the Jewish community in general, also worked with us on the project. Fredzia and I have always valued her friendship and the friendship of her late husband, Ray.

Our adult educational program also saw as its aim the provision of a platform for "left of centre" opinions on many aspects of contemporary Jewish life, particularly those concerning Israel and its quest for peace. At a time when other synagogues were satisfied with the narrow approach of the Jewish establishment, Holy Blossom Temple was prepared to widen the perspective. Though this gave rise to periodic criticism in the community and I was often the primary target, the quality of our presentations and the integrity of our approach earned us widespread respect in the community and beyond. We were also the synagogue that was prepared to be involved in social issues in general. The then coordinator of our Department for Jewish Living, Sandy Wise, was a driving force in this endeavour. Thus a few years after my arrival in Toronto we staged a Third Seder that drew attention to the plight of refugees and our responsibility for them. The event had a great impact. So did the encounter, still in the days of apartheid, with Bishop Desmond Tutu when he addressed a packed sanctuary on our mutual responsibility to fight discrimination. Forces in the Jewish community put great pressure on the lay leadership of the Temple to cancel the event. We didn't. When afterwards the Temple board expressed its delight with the successful evening, I tried to persuade our leaders that it would have been worth doing even if it hadn't been successful in terms of attendance and press reports.

An ever-growing number of members of the Temple learned to judge programs not by the opinions of others but on their intrinsic merits. Thus the leaders were prepared to participate in the Out of the Cold project, started by a Toronto nun and taken up by many local churches. Each church would provide, once a week during the cold winter months, hot meals, shelter for the night, breakfast in the morning and a packed lunch to as many homeless people as it could house. Other places would do the same thing the following evening so that the whole week would be covered. Holy Blossom Temple was the first congregation of Jews to be a partner. This was mainly due to the initiative and effort of one of the members, Freda Ariella Muscovitch. Before it happened, there were fierce debates within the congregation and with its neighbours at which individuals gave vent to every fear and prejudice in the book about the nature of the homeless. Once again, however, common sense prevailed, and today the Out of the Cold project is one of the jewels in the impressive crown of social action activities in the congregation.

In my early days at Holy Blossom, social action was often seen by many as an alternative to prayer and study. I recall an early encounter with two leaders of the congregation who came to complain that I opposed the desire of a group of our young people to participate in a worthy activity at a time on Saturday when Jews are expected to pray in the synagogue. I stood my ground and in time could show that it's possible to be both socially conscious and Jewishly sensitive without bringing them into conflict. Jews didn't have to jump on every bandwagon that ran for the convenience of those for whom Saturday was not Shabbat.

Because of the larger register of activities in terms of study opportunities, worship and social action, a growing number of women and men came forward as leaders of the congregation. Their presence has enriched it and helped it grow. Since we've not only preached gender equality but also practised it, many of our leaders have been women. Because we did our best to make Jews feel at home in the congregation by choice, a good proportion of them have continued to study Judaism and live by its precepts; some have become leaders. And most of the people I saw at board and committee meetings during the week I also saw at services on Sabbaths and festivals.

Unlike many other congregations, where it's often difficult to find suitable women and men to provide leadership, Holy Blossom Temple seems to have had a surplus of capable people willing to engage in communal activities. I cannot think of any Jewish organization in Toronto that has not had among its activists members of our congregation, many of them having first served, or continuing to serve, in the Temple. Being aware of this reservoir of talent, I was among the founders of at least four community organizations, two, perhaps three, of which relied heavily on Holy Blossom members.

In our efforts to attract young people to Jewish life, we were conscious that those who wanted to deepen their knowledge of Judaism often joined groups outside of Reform Judaism, notably Aish Hatorah, a successful largely Orthodox outreach group. Judging by its publicity, many of the funds of Aish Hatorah came from members of Reform congregations. Some of the children of these members, occasionally also their parents, became fervent adherents. It became obvious to us that we had to create something similar. Together with Rabbi Arthur Bielfeld of Temple Emanuel in Toronto and Stephen Morrison, a respected lay leader of Temple Sinai also in Toronto, we went to work on a project that ultimately became Kolel—The Centre for Liberal Jewish Learning.

Characteristically, in order to involve other Reform rabbis, I agreed to have a low profile in the enterprise, for Bielfeld and especially Morrison felt that had one of my colleagues, the rabbi of a large congregation, discerned a strong presence of Holy Blossom Temple, he'd stay away. As I didn't seek recognition, only favourable results, I was quite happy to operate behind the scenes.

Rabbi Elyse Goldstein, who between 1983 and 1986 had been the assistant rabbi at Holy Blossom Temple, where she contributed much as a teacher and a leader, was enticed to come back a few years later to lead the institution. We had secured enough money to guarantee her a three-year appointment. She was very successful, and in time the original promoters of the program, myself included, withdrew and others took over. Thanks to Elyse, Kolel is today a major centre in Toronto for outreach among largely unaffiliated Jews. But because of her personality and religious inclination, the bonds with the Reform movement have been loosened and the relationship between the original parent body and the developed "child" is strained. Though the presenting problem seems to be the lack of commensurate financial support from the Reform congregations in the city, the real reasons may have to do with the eclectic religious direction of Kolel that alienates it from Reform. In retrospect I believe that the founders, including myself, should have stayed around longer to make sure that what we set out to do was achieved without the risk of Kolel being hijacked by the highest bidder. As things turned out, the Reform movement in Toronto has lost a most valuable constituent.

At several conventions of the Union of American Hebrew Congregations, the Temple's parent body, I had heard about healing services and even a Jewish healing centre in San Francisco. I had also been a member in the 1980s of the Union's commission on religious living, which set out to find ways to revive religious life in Reform congregations. I had been aware of the secular nature of many Reform congregations in the United States from the time of my first visit in 1975. A decade later, it seems, Americans themselves had become aware of the malaise and in typical American fashion, tried to do something about it. One of the recurring themes at our meetings was spirituality. Healing seems to have been a manifestation of it.

Though I'm not enamoured by the touchy-feely sort of religion, so prevalent in contemporary Jewish life, I recognized that many women and men, often unaffiliated with any congregation, felt frustrated by what conventional synagogues offered. They needed their pains and fears expressed and addressed in the context of Judaism. I therefore brought together in 1994 a number of people, many of them members of Holy Blossom Temple, to explore the project further. The result is the Toronto Healing Project, now part of a network of such endeavours in North America.

Despite lack of funds and continued suspicion on the part of many Jews, the project has had a real impact on the Jewish community. This is largely due to one woman: Etta McEwan Ginsberg. She had recently retired as the chief social worker at Baycrest, the preeminent geriatric centre that comprises a home for the aged, a retirement home, a hospital and a research department. Though confined to a wheelchair, she is a bundle of energy and a force in every sense of the word. Though many of us offer whatever help we can, she runs the project almost single-handedly. Significantly, through her involvement in it she has become a regular worshipper at Holy Blossom, attends lectures and classes and participates in the leadership of the congregation. Officiating at her bat mitzvah around her seventieth birthday was one of the most moving memories of my ministry.

Though many members of Holy Blossom are involved in the Healing Project, it has, unlike many others, managed to appeal across the denominational spectrum in Toronto. Conservative, Orthodox and Reform rabbis and members of their congregations are involved in the work. A similar transdenominational approach was adopted when, again following an America initiative, Mazon Canada was created. Despite humble beginnings in the 1980s, it has grown to an important organization in Canadian Jewry determined to provide a Jewish response to hunger by raising funds and supporting organizations engaged in the work. Though the lion's share of the work was Arthur Bielfeld's, I was privileged once again to work with him in the initial stages of the project.

I did my best to alert the members of Holy Blossom to the enterprise and many responded with characteristic generosity and enthusiasm. Other congregations were more reluctant. One argument we heard from many Jews was that they would be interested in cooperating in a project that would be a response to *Jewish* hunger, but they were less keen to be part of a Jewish response to hunger in the general community.

I'm happy to record that I never heard that kind of argument at Holy Blossom Temple. The Temple has a distinguished tradition of social action that reaches out to the community at large. Hence its early involvement in Mazon. Hence also its pioneering work as the first congregation of Jews to engage in the Out of the Cold Project.

My fourth special project—the Polish-Jewish Heritage Foundation— had less involvement of members of Holy Blossom Temple, although in its earlier years many of its programs were held on Temple premises. When we lived in London I was acquainted with Anthony Polonsky, an expert on Polish history and at the time a professor at the London School of Economics. As a specialist in the history of Jews in Poland,

Polonsky was very keen to stimulate interest in his subject in the Jewish community and beyond. Knowing full well that most Polish Jews shunned everything Polish, for they associated it with their tragic experiences during the Holocaust, Polonsky wanted to alert us to the fact that Polish Jewry has an almost thousand-year history, much of it distinguished and only some of it tragic. As a native of Poland and a Polish speaker, I shared his views and so responded with enthusiasm to his suggestion that we try to create an organization in Canada, where many Polish-born Jews and their descendants live and where many non-Jewish Poles have their home.

Originally, we thought that one body would serve the two major communities of Montreal and Toronto, especially as another expert on Polish Jewry, Professor Gershon Hundert, teaches in the Jewish Studies Department at McGill University. It didn't happen. The two groups have gone their separate ways. The one in Toronto has persevered by putting on programs and promoting events that seek to stress the long history of Polish Jewry, but it has been very difficult to move beyond the Holocaust. At every opportunity, Jews on one side and Poles on the other stress the uniqueness of their victimhood with little understanding for the other. But we haven't given up hope.

One of the most memorable programs our foundation sponsored at Holy Blossom was an evening in October 1989 with Marek Edelman, the last surviving leader of the Warsaw Ghetto Uprising. I had heard of him through Hanna Krall, the Polish-Jewish writer whom I had met in Toronto, where her daughter lives. Her book on Edelman is one of the few of her writings to be translated into English. Her genre is a mixture of reportage and imagination and quite popular in other countries. I figure in one of her stories.

Edelman didn't speak much about the Warsaw Ghetto, more about Poland and our duty to support Solidarnosc (the Solidarity Movement), the movement that helped to bring down the Communist regime. He fought Communism, he said, for the same reason that he fought the Nazis, became a cardiologist and remained an atheist: to fight evil. Strident and bitter as he was, he didn't differentiate between God and Satan. When asked how difficult it was to be a ghetto fighter, he replied, "Easier than going to the gas chambers."

Even before my family and I first went to Poland, I had been interested in the roots I knew so little about, even though I was thirteen
when I left the country. I've now been there several times and, for a
couple of weeks, even lectured to theology students at various univer-
sities under the auspices of the American Jewish Committee. There are
times when I feel that I should spend more time in Poland to help the
emerging Liberal group in the community that has come to challenge
the majority who engage in a kind of non-observant Orthodoxy. Fredzia, on the other hand, who has travelled with me in Poland, is considerably less enthusiastic.

By the late 1980s our personal situation in Toronto had stabilized. When
my aunt Renia died, her husband, Abe, having predeceased her, she
bequeathed her money to me. This eased our financial situation considerably. We were able to repay the mortgage on the house and to have
money for other things. We've always tried to support our children as
much as possible. Now we could also travel with them. In 1988 we
decided to take Viveca, Michael and his wife, Sarah, and Elizabeth to
our native Poland to show them the places where we were born and to
visit the landmarks of Jewish martyrdom in the country. It was a very
important excursion, for it helped our children to sense what it was like
when their parents were children. To ease the pressure of the Poland visit
we spent a few very happy days in Prague afterwards. I still have it in
mind to take the family, now blessed with six more members—Anthony,
Elizabeth's husband, and Leone and Ethan, their children, as well as
Sarah's and Michael's three children, Miriam, Nadav and Gaby—to
Uzbekistan and the places where I spent five years of my life.

Our children with their spouses and our grandchildren have always
been our main source of pride and joy. The relationship to our mothers
was more complicated. Mine came for a month every summer to
Toronto, as she had come to London when we lived there. Being a person who didn't enjoy life, she did her best to make sure that we didn't
either, at least while she was with us. The only way I could cope with
the situation was to distance myself emotionally from her as much as
possible, which didn't make for a happy atmosphere at home. Members
of the congregation, many of whom spoke Yiddish, were wonderful to

her and entertained her regally. Unfortunately Fredzia had to accompany her on these outings while I escaped into work.

Fela, Fredzia's mother, was much more independent. Her visits to us were less regular, but we would always see her when we went to Israel. Soon after the death of Fredzia's father in 1965, she spent much of each year in Tel Aviv, returning to Stockholm—first to their old home, then to our little apartment, which she took over—during the hot summer months. After a few years she met David Hirschberg, a widower who had come to Palestine as a pioneer in 1935 yet still spoke good Polish, which mattered a lot to Fela. After a time they went to live together in her Tel Aviv apartment. For the sake of what they perceived to be propriety, they told us that they got married quietly by a rabbi. We knew that wasn't true but decided there was no point in challenging them. Though Fredzia and I could never warm to Hirschberg, we were happy that she had found him and that they had a good life together. We were on good terms with his two daughters and their families. At one point the daughters stayed with us when we still lived in London.

On a visit to Israel, this time without Fredzia, to attend a conference on hate that Elie Wiesel had called in 1990, I realized that Fela wasn't well enough to travel to Stockholm and stay on her own there as was her custom. As a result, I suggested that she and Hirschberg come stay with us in Toronto. Though Hirschberg described her condition as the onset of Parkinson's, we should have known that the problem was bigger than that, at least from the moment they arrived at the airport and Fela said to Fredzia, "I've a daughter here, do you know her?" We didn't realize that Fela was suffering from Alzheimer's. Instead, we assumed that the fatigue of the long flight had confused her momentarily. Even when she couldn't seem to find her way back to their bedroom at night, we denied the obvious. One night she fell and broke her hip. What followed was emergency surgery and months in hospital in Toronto. Though Hirschberg was an insurance agent by profession, it was by no means obvious that her insurance would cover the costs.

The situation was tense. It was clear that Hirschberg wanted to get out of Toronto as soon as possible and leave Fela behind. His younger daughter, Nira, arrived and helped him to return home, ostensibly to look for a nursing home for Fela when she was ready to fly to Israel. There's much to suggest that he had no intention to do so, but even in her present state, Fela was adamant that she wanted to go back to Israel. With the help of a friend in Tel Aviv, Bruriah Barish, whose mother lived in a good nursing home in Kfar Saba, and the efforts of Fredzia, a place was found for Fela. Hirschberg was livid, though he played the good husband and visited Fela frequently. Fredzia spent long spells in Israel to be with her mother, whose physical and mental state was steadily deteriorating. She died early in 1992 at eighty-four.

Hirschberg insisted that he had been badly treated by us. We didn't pay much attention to it. These were hard times and I'm sure we didn't accord him the honour he expected from his children, who, for example, would all turn up at the airport each time he departed from or returned to Israel. After Fela's death we realized that there was more to his complaints. He found out where she kept her money and one day took with him to the nursing home a less than scrupulous lawyer who witnessed Fela's by then very laboured signature on a number of blank air letters. Hirschberg filled in the rest, sent it to the relevant banks and transferred the money to his account. We had to resort to a lawyer, who managed to retrieve some of Hirschberg's booty.

Fredzia was deeply hurt that the money her father had left for her mother should now go to a stranger. And then the questions: had her mother promised Hirschberg the money? If not, why was she so adamant about not making a will? It was a period of much anguish.

Whether or not the aggravation was a contributory factor, a few months after her mother's death, Fredzia was diagnosed with breast cancer. Our good friend Dr. Saul Sidlofsky, a specialist in breast surgery, operated and has kept an eye on her ever since. The experience only deepened my love for Fredzia, and we've tried to live life as fully and as prudently as possible in the shadow of the greater insecurity that her illness has cast on us.

Though I often escaped into work, partly because it's my nature and partly because it has always been a source of comfort and consolation to me, I did my utmost not to turn myself into a one-man band. In the same way that I've insisted that as senior rabbi every aspect of synagogue life was my concern, I also made sure that colleagues and lay leaders alike were involved in everything that was going on in the congregation. My prime collaborator since 1987, when he became the associate rabbi of the congregation, has been John Moscowitz.

Rabbi David Katz, who had worked in the Leo Baeck School in Toronto a few years before moving to the New York area and who knew that the position of associate rabbi was vacant after James Prosnit left Holy Blossom, suggested to his friend John Moscowitz that he apply. David warned John that I was "an acquired taste," but he thought that so was John. Though he had been ordained five years earlier, Moscowitz had had relatively little experience in the active rabbinate. He had embarked on an academic career and only did part-time work in a congregation in Los Angeles. But despite his intellectual interests, he seemed to have found the academic life less than satisfactory, and Los Angeles, the city where he'd grown up, less than congenial. These may have been part of the reason that prompted him to come to Toronto.

I'm vague about his motives, for John Moscowitz is a very private person and it's very difficult to know what he really thinks and feels. Though he and I, after an initial period of adjustment, have worked extremely well together and I've learned to rely on him and to trust him completely, I don't really know him. For example, though he has had a home of his own for most of the time he has been in Toronto, I've never been inside it

My initial criticism of John Moscowitz has been that he wouldn't commit himself easily. With time, however, his attitude changed and he began to hint at his readiness to take over when I retired. I was delighted. To ease the prospective transition, I decided in the fall of 1997 to arrange a celebration to mark ten years of his service to the congregation. We sought out such events and had, for example, celebrated several of Gunther Plaut's birthdays, because they helped us to instill a sense of community, which is very difficult in a congregation of some six to seven thousand individuals. The Moscowitz celebration was a great success. Many older leaders of the Temple were impressed by his large following and by the affection and respect with which he was held.

Not long thereafter I met with the officers to confirm that it was my intention to retire as the senior rabbi when I was sixty-five, in the year 2000. I suggested to them that they make up their minds about John Moscowitz. I knew, and told them so, that he wouldn't apply for the position like any other candidate. If that was all they were prepared to offer him, they should tell him so and thus give him time to find another commensurate position before my retirement was announced. I also told the officers that I thought this would be a wrong move on their part, for they wouldn't find a more suitable incumbent, and should therefore begin negotiations with him to arrange for him to succeed me. Ultimately they acted on my advice and the congregation was told of the arrangements in good time.

I was very pleased. After what would be seventeen years I knew that I should retire. I had seen too many rabbis cling to their office past retirement age. I also knew that if Moscowitz were not allowed to succeed me, I'd have to wait until he left and a new associate rabbi was in place, probably a person who would be told at the outset that he wasn't going to be the successor. Only then would I be able to retire. This would be a long and unsatisfactory process. In recent years, American rabbis have been reluctant to accept positions in Canada. The disparity between the value of the Canadian and American dollar and the difficulty in getting work permits for spouses were cited as the main reasons. But I also suspect that American provincialism plays a role.

If John Moscowitz were not to succeed me, then, I might have to stay on for several years beyond retirement age, and I didn't want that. For I, too, had become tired of what I less than generously described as customer service, the pressure to be always on, always at the disposal of others—and always having opinions on a whole range of subjects, whether I knew something about them or not. Though I love preaching and teaching I felt that I might have said all that I had to say. I needed time for reflection and renewal, away from the pressures of being the senior rabbi of a large and very active congregation.

In anticipation of the smooth takeover following the Temple board's decision to appoint John Moscowitz without a formal search for my successor, we could now engage a new assistant rabbi with the view that the person hired would succeed John as associate. Thanks to the efforts of Michelle Lynn, who at the time was the director of education at the Temple, we obtained the services of her good friend Yael Splansky when she graduated from Hebrew Union College in Cincinnati in 1998. She is a gifted rabbi, the daughter and granddaughter of rabbis, and together with her husband, Adam Sol, has fitted very well into the life of Holy Blossom Temple. I now felt that I was leaving the congregation in good hands.

The warmth and joy was well reflected in the way Fredzia and I parted from the congregation. In addition to providing me with office space and access to secretarial help, I was also given a stipend on the understanding that I would teach courses in the congregation. (In the year I had other employment, I made sure that the Temple was adequately reimbursed.) The farewell party was unforgettable, with our whole family present and some five hundred members of the congregation and friends in attendance. I really felt that the congregation and I were parting without unfinished business between us. The feeling has persisted to this very day. Fredzia and I attend services when we are in the city and are very happy to sit together in a pew, trying to be as inconspicuous as circumstances permit. We see our personal friends, both in Canada and when they come to Israel, and we continue to feel part of the community.

I have total confidence in John Moscowitz, even though I don't always share his views, particularly on Israel. Holy Blossom Temple has always provided a platform for left-of-centre opinions, not all of them popular, in a community that automatically tends to lean to the right. But his stance has created a healthy climate of cooperation between the senior rabbis of the principal synagogues of the two other movements— the Conservative Beth Tzedec and the modern Orthodox Shaare Shamayim. At the same time, however, Holy Blossom Temple has continued to provide a platform for all opinions

I've also been impressed by John Moscowitz's ambitious plans to remodel the Temple facility. The building most decidedly is in need of repairs and alterations. Though Holy Blossom Temple has been a large congregation for a long time, it has avoided becoming an American-style mega-synagogue. I hope that it will retain its character even after the changes.

A mega-synagogue requires mega-fundraising. I'm not sure that those who belong to Holy Blossom Temple are prepared to make major contributions. My experience of the congregation is that its members, especially the wealthy ones, have often complained that the dues are too high. It's with this in mind that a few years before I left, we started the Holy Blossom Foundation, which with relatively modest sums, would enable us to do things that dues have not been able to accomplish. We had a good start. However, in anticipation of the big push, the earlier relatively modest yet cumulatively significant efforts seem to have ground to a halt—only temporarily, I hope.

I'm delighted, though—and have told John so repeatedly—that he has found his own style and his own projects, which on the one hand, assure the members of continuity and, on the other, indicate that their new senior rabbi is very different from his predecessor. That he has chosen to move into the mainstream of the community, rather than being a maverick as I had been, speaks well of him and gives me great joy.

Israel:
Homecoming

Being able to spend much time in Israel, as Fredzia and I now do, has been the fulfillment of a cherished long-held dream. But before I can say more about it, I need to explain the circumstances that brought us to Israel as soon as I retired from Holy Blossom Temple. My aim is not only to provide a context for my work there, but also to give an eye-witness account of developments in one of the most significant institutions of Reform Judaism.

One of the guests at my farewell party in June 2000 was Austin Beutel. Though not a member of the congregation, he had been invited by his friends and ours, Esther and Marvin Tile; Esther chaired the committee that organized this most splendid event. In the course of the celebration, Beutel told me that he needed to speak to me soon. I assumed that he wanted to engage me in some project, for I had worked with him on various things over the years, especially when he was president of the Canadian Region of the Union of American Hebrew Congregations (now the Union for Reform Judaism) and, later, as president of the World Union for Progressive Judaism. I've the highest respect for his integrity and generosity. Deservedly he's held in the highest esteem by all who have worked with him.

Austin Beutel, as president of the World Union, and Ruth Cohen, as senior vice-president and chair of its search committee, had invited me in 1998 to be a member of the group that would find a new executive director. For it had been determined that Rabbi Richard (Dick) Hirsch would now retire. I didn't think that he was keen to do so, even though he told me from time to time that his wife, Bella, urged him to step down. In fact, a few years earlier, when his retirement was first mooted, he made it clear that he didn't want to go and agreed that I should convey this to the then president of the World Union, Donald Day. Day and I had a long-standing warm relationship and I didn't find it difficult to tell him what Dick had said to me. I don't know if it was my talk that delayed the retirement, but it may have contributed to it. Now, however, after the successes of the Reform Zionist organizations in elections to the Zionist Congress, particularly in the United States, resulting in a much larger share of the pie of the World Zionist Organization, Hirsch had become the head of a department in the Jewish Agency and so found it easier to give up the World Union job.

The search committee was unanimous and enthusiastic in recommending that Rick Block, at that time a very successful congregational rabbi in the San Francisco area, succeed Hirsch. Block had trained as a lawyer before entering the rabbinate. His intelligence, experience and maturity made him a worthy successor. Unfortunately things didn't turn out well and within the first year of Block's taking up the position, the post of executive director was vacant. I knew nothing of that at the time of my conversation with Austin Beutel at the party.

It's tempting to apportion blame for the failure, and different people have different versions of events. My impression is that what happened in the World Union happens in many organizations where one individual has held the reins for a long time and as a result, the successor is very likely to stumble and fall. To what extent the predecessor contributes to it is never quite clear. That's what happened, I believe, at Holy Blossom Temple when Harvey Fields, the successor to Gunther Plaut, left and, and that's what happened, it seems, now in the World Union.

Whatever the reasons, Block and the World Union were to part company, and several weeks after the party, Austin Beutel came to see me to offer me the post of interim executive director until a permanent replacement was found. In view of my involvement with the World Union over more than four decades, I accepted. Having just retired from Holy Blossom Temple, I had time on my hands, and the prospect of working and living in Israel, where the office of the World Union is located, was most appealing. Once again, it seemed, I'd be cast in the role of a successor's successor.

But I had my reservations. Knowing much about the World Union, I quoted to Beutel the Yiddish saying that with a healthy head one shouldn't lie down in a sick bed. And I did feel that the World Union was far from healthy. Yet I was also keen to do the job. One of several attractions was the opportunity to work with Ruth Cohen. She and her husband, Harvey, had been involved members of the North-Western Reform Synagogue in London, the congregation I served between 1969 and 1983. Fredzia and I considered ourselves to be their friends and kept in touch with them while in Canada. Though Ruth became chair of the congregation and subsequently chair of the Reform Synagogues of Great Britain after we left London, I was well aware of her commitment to whatever her task at hand may have been and of her outstanding leadership skills. Her work in the World Union was of the same quality. She and Harvey had moved to Israel some time earlier, and she was now the officer most directly involved with day-to-day activities. I knew I'd work well with Ruth when I assumed my responsibilities on November 1, 2000. I wasn't wrong.

Dick Hirsch had dominated the World Union for more than a quarter century and made it his own. Before he came on the scene, it was a small organization. It came into being in 1926 with the modest purpose of bringing constituents together (Reform and Liberal groups under the generic name of Progressive) to conventions every couple of years and to encourage groups in countries where there was no organized movement to form themselves into congregations and to affiliate with the World Union. In the decades after the Second World War resourceful rabbis and lay leaders created networks of Progressive-Reform-Liberal congregations in Australia, South Africa, Holland and many other places. And, of course, there was the large Reform movement in North America and a growing one, albeit split into two organizations, in the United Kingdom. By seeking to combine his commitment to Zionism and to Israel with his position as the executive director of the World Union, and moving the head office of the union to Jerusalem, Rabbi Richard Hirsch had put it on the map as a world movement that, perhaps for the first time in its history, looked larger than its constituent parts.

With his enormous talents, great charm and experience as a leader in American Reform, Hirsch had developed a network of resourceful members of congregations in the United States who were willing to support his work. He now enrolled many of them in World Union activities, with special emphasis on developing Progressive Judaism in Israel. Being a strong believer in buildings that identify and define institutions, Hirsch, with the help of his supporters, created Beit Shmuel and Mercaz Shimshon, Jerusalem landmarks that contributed to making Progressive Judaism better known in Israel. The existence of these buildings, the two Reform kibbutzim that had been established, again with Hirsch as a driving force, and the creation of other centres made it possible to raise money for programs and projects in the Jewish state.

With the revival of Jewish life in the former Soviet Union in the early 1990s, Hirsch recognized the opportunities of Progressive Judaism and helped to establish the movement there. Despite limited resources and the lack of trained leaders, rabbinic and lay, Progressive Judaism in Russia, Ukraine and Belarus has, in a relatively short time, come to play an important part in the lives of individuals and in the structure of Jewish communities there.

At the time of Hirsch's retirement, however, things had changed. The Israel Movement had grown and now depended on much more money than individuals from abroad could provide. Though the Jewish Agency for Israel, thanks to the affiliation of the World Union and Arzenu to the World Zionist Organization—again, Hirsch initiatives— provided funds, more were needed. The congregational rabbis in Israel, many of them now trained by the Jerusalem school of the Hebrew Union College–Jewish Institute of Religion, would raise money for their own buildings at times in competition with the World Union, as they resented the patrician manner in which the Union was run. The Leo Baeck School in Haifa, in existence long before Hirsch came on the scene and greatly developed by its then head, Rabbi Robert Samuels, had its own ambitious fundraising and building program, almost totally outside the World Union framework. I recall from the days I served in Toronto receiving annually a long line of emissaries on behalf of one or another branch of our movement seeking funds from reluctant donors. Our attempt in Canada to create a combined appeal on behalf of all Progressive causes failed, partly because the various components, including the World Union itself, worked as much against one another as they worked together. Hirsch's creativity didn't extend to team-building.

The World Union buildings in Jerusalem, instead of being sources of revenue as projected, became liabilities: tourism had virtually disappeared with the second *intifada*. This meant that Beit Shmuel, built primarily as a youth hostel for visitors from abroad, stood empty most of the time, especially once the youth branch of American Reform suspended its operations in Israel. The building was also in great need of repair and upgrading. Much of the money set aside for that purpose had been spent on plugging holes in the financing of the new building, Mercaz Shimshon. Though perhaps never as profitable as it had been assumed, Beit Shmuel now became something of a drain on the World Union's very strained finances. The institution continued its educational programs, but not much of them showed a clear link to Progressive Judaism. Making ends meet in order to survive now became much more important than making Progressive Judaism known in Israel.

The new building, Mercaz Shimshon, inaugurated in 2000, wasn't completed even two years later. Its major sponsor, the Schusterman family of Tulsa, Oklahoma, became disillusioned with, perhaps even hostile to, the World Union, especially after the father of the family, Charles, died. Mercaz Shimshon was to become the world centre of Progressive Judaism, but again the delay in completing the building, coupled with diminished tourism, has resulted in its being empty most of the time. Its theatre, properly named for Bella and Dick Hirsch, is used occasionally for local groups and its great hall more frequently for weddings and bar mitzvahs, but there's little sign of its being a world centre of anything. The offices of the World Union, also planned for the new building, have proven to be most inadequate. As a result, a couple of rooms in the proposed conference facility have now been taken over. It's not at all certain that the original intention of those who created Mercaz Shimshon will be revived, even when conditions improve.

It became obvious that the World Union now needed more than an impressive façade. The buildings, once viewed as part of a solution to the World Union's political and financial needs, may now have become a major part of the problem. More money was needed and the new executive director—who, presumably to enhance his status, wished to be known as president—was supposed to provide it. Despite Rick Block's excellent record as a fundraiser in the congregation he served and the high hopes attached to his appointment, not enough money came into the kitty. And as in less than perfect families, when money becomes an issue, all kinds of other problems emerge.

Many of these can be put under one rubric: the danger of running a world organization as a one-man-band, which is precisely what Dick Hirsch had done. There was little structure in place that a successor could go on with. Only a Hirsch clone could have carried on reasonably successfully. In the absence of such a being, whoever now was to assume the role of the father of the family would find herself/himself at sea, because many frustrated stakeholders wanted a part of the action.

When Block left, the management of this dysfunctional family became my task. In view of my interim status, I saw myself as a kind of foster parent. I got on well with Rick Block, who together with his wife remained in Jerusalem until his appointment to a prestigious pulpit in Cleveland, but my relationship to his predecessor, Richard Hirsch, was much more complicated. Hirsch believed that my only chance of success in my job was to follow his directions; perhaps that was his vain hope of turning me into a clone. Then again, I believed that I could carry out my mandate only if I could act without his involvement and along very different lines. The details that constituted the dispute are too trivial to relate, but the effect was that the relationship soured. What once used to be a friendship between two couples now became a source of tension. Since leaving the World Union, Dick and I have maintained a relationship of civility and, I hope, mutual regard.

I regret it, for I've boundless affection and much admiration for Richard Hirsch. If only he had created a framework that others could build on; but perhaps that would have been inconsistent with his personality and with his way of getting things done. As of now, the future of the World Union, as Dick envisaged it, is in serious doubt. This must be very painful to him, as it is to all who are committed to the future of Progressive Judaism, particularly in Israel and in the former Soviet Union.

To continue the family metaphor, I also had to find a way of working with Dick's son, Ammi Hirsch. After serving for a number of years in a New York Reform congregation, he had succeeded Rabbi Eric Yoffie as the executive director of the Association of Reform Zionists of America (ARZA), when Yoffie went to the Union of American Hebrew Congregations. Ammi Hirsch is an extremely capable rabbi with a flair for politics and public relations. ARZA, as it then was, was the ideal place for him.

But when his father retired, the lay leadership of the World Union seems to have panicked and, pushed by Eric Yoffie and other American Reform leaders, decided to merge its North American Board—the potentially principal source of fundraising now that Dick was no longer on the scene—with ARZA. As a member of the governing body of the World Union at the time, I was opposed to the merger—on the grounds that I knew of no mergers, only takeovers—but I was in a minority. By the time I arrived as the interim executive director, the merger was signed and sealed. I now know that it was never delivered. Not long after I left the World Union, the partnership was dissolved.

But as long as I was in charge, I was determined to do all I could to make the merger work, for I believed then that the future of the World Union depended on it. This was no time to say "I told you so." Even before I formally assumed the position, I went to New York to consult with Ammi Hirsch, and remained in frequent contact with him as long as I was in office. Unlike many of my colleagues in the World Union, I was opposed to the belligerence toward ARZA and its executive director, which often reflected frustration at not receiving the money that was expected and blaming the New York office for wantonly withholding funds. Instead, I counselled civility and mutual respect as the only way forward, even if I had to fend off Ammi's efforts to establish himself as the real ruler of the realm, his and mine.

Thus, when in March 2001 the World Union was to hold its first ever convention in the United States—in Washington, D.C.—I made sure that the event would become something of a celebration of the merger, with Ammi Hirsch as the principal speaker at the opening plenary session. If this was somewhat hypocritical, I consoled myself with the notion that in this case, the hypocrisy might serve a good cause.

Nevertheless, already it was clear to me that the new organization couldn't provide the necessary funds. It wasn't even sure that it could meet its negotiated original commitment to the World Union. The expectation that Ammi Hirsch would raise the money was unrealistic. Though he had inherited many of his father's qualities—including a reluctance to be a team player—fundraising may not have been one of them. To the consternation of the lay leadership, I made it clear from the very outset that I had neither skills nor experience as a fundraiser and didn't see that as my task during the transitional period of my tenure. Instead of looking at a different structure of the World Union, now with Dick Hirsch no longer at its helm, the lay leaders were also looking for a clone in the belief that all the problems of the World Union would be solved if there was more money and if the executive director would be able to raise that money.

Contrary to the expectations of some, I had set myself three very different tasks, with which Austin Beutel agreed: (1) to look after the day-to-day business of the World Union; (2) to make it possible for a new permanent executive director to be appointed; and (3) to create a new structure, or modify the existing one, to ensure a successful future of the organization.

Looking after the day-to-day affairs of the World Union entailed many meetings and a fair amount of travel abroad. One of my earliest steps was to create a framework for decision-making that involved lay leaders by asking the president to appoint a management committee. The committee met in person when circumstances permitted, but mostly we discussed matters in hand at conference calls. I'm not sure whether the lay leaders appreciated it. They seemed to have got used to the executive director making the decisions that allowed others to grumble in private, especially when the decisions turned out to be wrong. The new system I tried to bring in involved shared responsibility, and there may have been some who didn't like it. For me, however, such a process was essential for the good of the organization.

I also tried to meet with as many "stakeholders" as possible. This included not only Reform leaders who were visiting Israel, but also the various branches of the Israel Movement for Progressive Judaism. I also discussed matters with my two colleagues in the office, Menachem Leibovich, at the time in charge of the budget and of our operation in the former Soviet Union, and Rabbi Joel Oseran, who was responsible for contacts with constituents, arranging the convention and related tasks. When I arrived on the scene, neither Menachem nor Joel had a clear job specification, for they were hired to be at the beck and call of their boss. It took some time before I produced one for each of them, with their prior approval and with the agreement of the management committee. In the course of the year that I worked for the World Union, I also greatly encouraged Leibovich to cease to act as the unpaid executive director of the Israel Movement. I was convinced that the Israel Movement had to be an independent constituent of the World Union, not an attachment, as I surmise Dick Hirsch saw it. I maintained that the Israel Movement needed its own profile and its own spokespersons. The situation as I found it created unhelpful confusion between the two organizations. This may have been useful in earlier administrations, but it was destructive now. My approach, then, was radically different from that of Dick Hirsch, and I wouldn't have been surprised to learn that those who didn't like it reported to Dick on a regular basis. I don't know if as a result, he tried to undermine my efforts, but it surely felt like it at times.

Running the day-to-day affairs of the World Union also entailed visiting constituents to represent the Union and strengthen the commitment of constituents to the central organization. It was in the course of such visits, particularly to more isolated places like Costa Rica, Australia, South Africa and several European countries, that I realized how important the World Union is to our non-American constituents. However, as virtually none of them have the resources to contribute much to the overall budget of the World Union, the Americans pay relatively little attention to them. The fact that the president of the World Union who succeeded Austin Beutel—Ruth Cohen—and I as its executive director were not Americans further eroded the standing of the World Union in the eyes of the Americans.

Altogether, there was little evidence that our American constituent, the merger notwithstanding, was very engaged in the affairs of the World Union. Though we held a most successful convention in terms of the program in Washington in March 2001, attendance by American participants was sparse. Most of the leaders of the World Union's largest and most powerful constituent, including Rabbi Eric Yoffie, were always ready to tell us what we did wrong, but there wasn't much evidence of a readiness to help us to put it right. No surprise, really, for the attitude of the Union of American Hebrew Congregations has always been ambiguous. Many of its leaders seem to have been relating to the smaller constituents the way Stalin is said to have related to the Vatican when he asked how many divisions the Pope had. Many Americans wanted to know how much money the other constituents could raise and judge their status accordingly. There seems to have been very little appreciation for the heroic efforts of relatively few individuals in Europe and elsewhere to establish Progressive Judaism in the midst of hostility from the Orthodox establishment and indifference from almost everybody else.

The second item on my interim agenda was to pave the way for the appointment of a permanent executive director. It was quite obvious that to open a general search once again would be costly and yield nothing. The few possible candidates interested in the position had applied at the time that Rick Block was appointed, and the World Union leadership seems to have no particular interest in offering it to one of the previously rejected candidates. Therefore, an incumbent had to be identified in some other way.

Already at the time of the original search in 1998, I had asked someone to inquire whether Rabbi Uri Regev was interested in applying. The message came back that he was not. I regretted it, because I've always considered Uri Regev to be one of the most gifted and successful Progressive rabbis in Israel. As the founder and leader of the movement's Religious Action Center, he became a force in the struggle for justice and equality in the country and something of a household name in Israel. As an articulate and passionate speaker in both Hebrew and English, he was well known by the World Union family all over the world.

Virtually as soon as I took over the position, I brought up the possibility of approaching Uri Regev again. This time Regev showed much greater interest. Not long thereafter he was shortlisted for the position of president of the Hebrew Union College–Jewish Institute of Religion, and this further enhanced his standing in the United States. Some of the lay leaders of the World Union, disappointed with my inability and my refusal to be a fundraiser, assumed that Regev, having raised money for his Religious Action Center, would be able to solve this most pressing problem in the World Union. As a result, Rabbi Uri Regev was appointed as the new executive director. I did all I could to make sure that Regev could start work as soon as possible. On January 1, 2002, he assumed his duties and I could resume my retiree status. His sense of adventure and anticipation was matched by my sense of relief.

I still believe that Uri Regev is one of the few people who can turn around the World Union. Unlike most others, however, I believe that a turnaround will not be due to more fundraising but by creating a different kind of structure for the World Union. The notion that the World Union can only grow by having a larger budget is fallacious, not only because the prospects of a larger budget are slim, but also because the existing setup makes success unlikely. The way Dick Hirsch did things is no longer possible. A radically different approach is needed.

Which brings me to the third task I set myself as the interim executive director. Though I feel that I had been quite successful in dealing with day-to-day matters and in helping to find a permanent director, I know that I didn't get very far in changing the structure of the organization. Let me suggest a few reasons for it.

Since I was only going to be in charge for a short time and the lay leaders and staff alike were interested in maintaining as much of the status quo as possible and delaying radical decisions to a later time, or perhaps hoping that they'd never have to be taken. But more significant was the need to retain the old system, because the new one would entail a "paradigm shift" and, as is well known, when an old paradigm is about to collapse, as this one definitely did, those who created it go out of their way to keep it going long after its "best before" date.

One of the things that needed shifting was the role and the status of the two buildings for which the World Union was responsible, Beit Shmuel and Mercaz Shimshon. The former was in a state of disrepair and stood empty most of the time. The latter hadn't been completed yet and accusations and counter-accusations flew in different directions; whoever wasn't in the room at any particular meeting was usually blamed for all the woes. The responsibility for replenishing the repair fund for Beit Shmuel and completing Mercaz Shimshon had, understandably, remained with Rabbi Richard Hirsch. He had a long-standing personal relationship with the contractor, the project manager and the architect, for that was how he worked: the professional and the personal were frequently interconnected. This meant, of course, that I had no authority in their eyes.

Structural changes of the World Union were greatly hampered, perhaps even made impossible, by the merger with ARZA. In theory the merged ARZA–World Union North American Board (ARZA-WUNA) was the arm of the World Union in North America. Its constituent was the Union of American Hebrew Congregations (UAHC). In practice it was different. Since ARZA-WUNA was a constituent member of UAHC and since it was charged with the task of raising the bulk of the World Union's money, both from individuals and organizations, it saw itself as the World Union's constituent *and* paymaster. The UAHC seemed to have condoned it. This made the situation untenable, because the executive director of the World Union not only had no authority over the executive director of ARZA-WUNA, but was also dependent on the latter for funds and goodwill. I felt squeezed between Hirsch the father and Hirsch the son.

When Uri Regev was in charge of the Religious Action Center, he had countless occasions to express his frustration with ARZA-WUNA's failure to honour promised allocations and the way it thwarted the efforts of the Center. Now, as executive director of the World Union, Regev had to forge a new relationship. Whereas my aim was to keep the relationship on an even keel and not to identify with the many detractors of ARZA-WUNA, Regev had to make things work even better. There is no sign that he has succeeded. In fact, the merger has now been terminated and the two organizations are back to square one. Regev remains at the helm of the World Union and Ammi Hirsch has left ARZA. Shortage of money remains the most pressing problem of the World Union.

The achievements in Israel of Progressive Judaism, however slow in coming, have been quite remarkable in recent years. Though Orthodoxy continues to dominate public life in the Jewish state, religious alternatives have become a reality. Whereas once nobody in Israel heard or cared about Progressive/Reform Judaism, today there aren't many Israelis who are ignorant of it. Many take it seriously. Continued success depends on money raised abroad until the state itself comes to the support of non-Orthodox movements in Judaism just as it supports Orthodoxy—or better still, until there's a total separation between religion and state that would enable each denomination to compete in the free market of ideas and practices. In the meantime, however, Progressive Judaism in Israel will continue to depend on American money. Without it, an historic opportunity will be lost.

All major cities and towns in Israel, as well as a few smaller settlements, have Progressive (Israelis shun the term "Reform," for it smells of its earlier opposition to Zionism) congregations, mostly served by rabbis. In Jerusalem, where I now live, I can walk to Shabbat services in four Progressive congregations and I can drive to several others. The Hebrew Union College currently trains some three dozen Israelis for the rabbinate in the Jewish State. Though not all of them may end up as spiritual leaders of congregations, nevertheless, as teachers and public figures, they will greatly enhance the profile of Progressive Judaism in the country and thus further its growth. For there's little doubt that the combination of politicized Orthodoxy that seeks to milk the state on the one hand and the genuine search for Judaism on the part of a growing sector of the population that once described itself as secular on the other will bring many Israelis to Progressive Judaism.

A case in point: though Progressive and Conservative rabbis aren't recognized yet by the state to perform marriages and conduct funerals, many Israelis have circumvented the system. They travel abroad, often to nearby Cyprus, for a civil marriage that is recognized in Israel and then return for a suitable religious ceremony conducted by an non-Orthodox rabbi of their choice. Similarly many kibbutzim have cemeteries of their own that are outside the control of the hostile Orthodox authorities. Jews who wish to have a Reform burial service acquire plots in these places.

Despite meagre financial resources and petty harassment by legislation and functionaries alike, Progressive Judaism has truly progressed in past decades. This has been largely due to the efforts of the World Union.

But perhaps an even greater historic opportunity may be lost in the former Soviet Union, where the growth of Progressive Judaism has been spectacular. Again the potential is much greater, even though it'll take many years before the Jews there can pay for their own institutions. Person power in the form of Russian-speaking rabbis, now being trained in London, Potsdam and Jerusalem, and financial resources, also needed for the training of rabbis, will make the difference.

In the thirty-eight years that I served congregations in Britain and Canada, I came to think of myself as a successful rabbi. I worked hard to bring Jews closer to Torah and Mitzvot and to help them create viable and vibrant communities. I also tried to contribute to activities beyond my congregation as a writer, lecturer and social activist. As the interim director of the World Union for Progressive Judaism, I surmise that I was regarded, at least by Americans, as something of a schlemiel—because I didn't raise money. This wasn't the only reason I didn't enjoy my time with the organization. In the short period I tried to serve it, I also realized that I wasn't cut out to massage egos. I got used to speaking my mind without having to glance sideways all the time. What some would have regarded as the climax of a rabbinic career, I considered an irrelevant diversion.

This was particularly clear to me at the meetings of the executive of the World Zionist Organization, on which I had a seat by virtue of my position in the World Union. Each time I entered the building in Jerusalem where the meetings were held, I recalled the day we formed Arzenu in the Weizmann Room there. We had hoped that having a

Zionist presence in the Reform movement would help us to "Zionize" it, and by having a Reform/Progressive presence in the Zionist movement would enable us to testify to the ideals and values that our form of Judaism stood for. I saw little of that in the year 2001. Instead of serious debate with all members seeking to develop a common approach for the good of the Jewish people, all I heard were speeches made by department heads seeking more power and money for their corner of the enterprise. There were never any attempts at coming to decisions; after the speeches the chairman would move to the next subject. Throughout my time there I hardly opened my mouth, for I had no department to defend. When I once mentioned to the chairman that I'm not at all used to conducting business in this fashion, he told me that I'd get used to it.

I never did. It's possible that the presence of our movement at that table is important, and I'm glad that our representatives are there. But I'm relieved not to be among them. I've always seen my task as one of articulating the link between Reform Judaism and Zionism, the two manifestations of Jewish modernity, both seeking to create a Jewish future beyond the ghetto. I hope that those who participate in the affairs of the World Zionist Organization are confident that they are reflecting our ideals. I knew that I wasn't able to do it in that forum.

When Fredzia and I went to Jerusalem at the end of 2000, we rented an apartment in the centre of the city. We loved living in Jerusalem and in the course of the following year decided to establish a permanent home there. We found a small apartment in Jerusalem's German Colony and are happy there. Its being close to where Michael, Sarah and their family live greatly adds to the attraction. Though we missed the early childhood of our Israeli grandchildren Miriam, Nadav and Gaby, seeing them only for short spells during visits, we now feel greatly privileged to be around as they are growing up into loving and delightful human beings. We also find it easier to visit our family in England from Israel and try to spend as much time as circumstances permit with our daughters Viveca and Elizabeth, Elizabeth's husband, Anthony and their delightful children, Leone and Ethan.

To manifest our commitment, we became new immigrants and are now citizens of Israel. I had made three earlier attempts at aliyah, each time ending up in another country and each time embarking on a new life.

The first attempt was after returning from the Soviet Union in 1946, when my family assumed that we'd make our way to Germany and, presumably, Cyprus, to end up in Eretz Israel. But only months before Israel became a state we received papers to go to Sweden, and my parents decided to follow that route, at least as a start; if it didn't work out, we'd go to Israel from there. I'm not sure if it worked out for them, but they felt that they had found a place of refuge and that I had finally caught up at school and therefore shouldn't be uprooted again.

My second attempt at aliyah was with Fredzia. When in early 1957 we visited Israel for the first time, the implied hope was that we'd be able to go to live there. My failure to see the director-general of the Foreign Office, as my boss Yehuda Yaari had intended, coupled with my chance meeting with my Danish counterpart who had emigrated and now found himself set aside and frustrated by the Foreign Office were contributory factors to my decision to pursue rabbinic studies. So instead of going to Israel from Sweden, we ended up in England and lived there happily for over twenty-five years.

My third attempt at aliyah crystallized at the time of the Zionist Congress in 1982. Though I realized how frustrating it must be to serve as a congregational Progressive rabbi in Israel, I was ready for a change from my work in England and hoped that, perhaps, as Progressive Judaism was about to get a slice of the Zionist pie, I might be able to find a position in the World Zionist Organization or the Jewish Agency. In view of my subsequent experience of the World Zionist Organization, I've every reason to be grateful to the late Arthur Grant, who invited me to explore Holy Blossom Temple in Toronto. Thus, instead of moving to Israel from England, we moved to Canada.

Now at last, after my retirement from Holy Blossom, we could fulfill our ambition to live in Israel. We feel as if we've come home. But as the saying goes, you can take a Jew out of the Diaspora, but you can't take the Diaspora out of a Jew. Though we live happily about half the year in Israel, the rest of the time we spend in Toronto, where we still have a network of friends and activities, and where I still have the opportunity to teach and to contribute. For the time being it's an ideal arrangement.

Whenever I'm called upon to describe our double life in Israel and Canada, I not only state the obvious—that I feel privileged as a Jew to have witnessed the return of our people to our ancestral land and am keen to be part of this historic drama—I also refer to the American Protestant theologian Walter Brueggemann. In a book about the significance of the land he makes an important distinction between *place* and *space*. Place is where you find the roots of your people and where your people are at home; space is where you as an individual or a family or a community happen to be at any given time. The space of most other people is also their place, but not so for Jews.

As much as Jews insist that they're at home in the countries where they were born or to which they've immigrated, reality is different. It's less different in North America, where others, too, are immigrants, yet once you challenge them, most Jews will concede that they don't feel rooted in the United States or Canada. Their commitment to their faith and their people makes them different, the American Declaration of Independence and the Canadian Charter of Rights and Freedoms notwithstanding. Jews in Europe almost invariably see themselves, and are seen by others, as aliens, even though Jews in Britain are often offended by this assertion. Jews who come from Germany, where once they felt as much at home as Jews in America or Britain and were then destroyed only because they were Jews, know it best. Jews lived for the best part of a millennium in Poland, yet it took us only a few years to be rendered homeless.

Though I've happily occupied space in Sweden, England and now Canada, I know that my place isn't there but in Israel. Both Fredzia and I feel that there we're among our people. Our son and his family, as well as many of our friends, share that feeling. Yet the space we occupy in Canada has its memories and achievements, and we feel privileged that we can be part of that too. We also feel responsible for what's going on here. Hence my involvement in several projects that champion the cause of the powerless in Canadian society. It's not a matter of preference of one country over another but of a fundamental difference between our place in each. Much of what I've written about Israel and its relation to the Diaspora is an elucidation of this point.

Having found our place in Israel doesn't mean that we enjoy all the members of our people or are uncritical of our leaders. On the contrary. But being there entitles us, we believe, to express our criticism freely, for we are at home. In the Diaspora we always worry what effect our stance may have on non-Jews. In Israel we're free of such inhibitions. It's a very good feeling.

Since retirement I was able to see my mother more often than before. Especially after she was diagnosed with leukemia in 2001, I made a point of spending time with her, sometimes on my own, sometimes with Fredzia. The fighter that she was, she fought back as long as possible—in fact, she'd always tell me that life was a battleground—but gradually life became tiresome for her and she seemed more and more anxious to leave it behind. She remained totally lucid and as miserable as she had always been. Her fear, she said, wasn't death, but pain. Fredzia and I talked to her the last Friday in December of 2002 as we had talked to her every Friday for almost three decades. Since the death of my father in 1973, we would call her every Friday afternoon local time, from wherever we may have been in the world. She sounded particularly cheerful that Friday. Fredzia and I remarked afterwards about her fluent Polish, the language of her choice on that occasion. The following Monday morning, we were told by the home where she had been a resident for the last seven years that they had had to sedate her because of the pain that ever more frequent blood transfusions no longer could alleviate. Two days later, just before the year 2002 had come to an end in Sweden, she died.

The end was as easy as possible. She was ninety-seven years old, lucid until the end, spared the pangs of death. The funeral in Gothenburg, to which our daughters came from London—our son had visited his grandmother a few months earlier—was a kind of closure. We felt at ease in the knowledge that she was now at peace.

Uncannily, ten days later her sister Lola died in Brooklyn. She was one hundred years old, though her husband insists that she was only eighty-seven. The end of an era. I am now the old man of the family. There are days when I feel it, even though the air of Jerusalem is invigorating and even as I glance sideways to make sure that there are no suicide bombers in the vicinity. Writing this memoir in Jerusalem has given my life a sense of completion. I feel that I've come home.

Afterthoughts

For me, each move from country to country—from Poland to the Soviet Union and, after a brief interlude back in Poland, to Sweden; from Sweden to England, then to Canada and now to Israel—has been not just relocation but reorientation. Each country has given me a different life and a different language: native Polish followed by Russian, Yiddish and now-forgotten, Uzbekish of the war years, Swedish, English and Hebrew thereafter. Speaking many languages is often considered a sign of good education. In my case, it has had the opposite effect, for it has left me without a language that's truly my own. In her book *Lost in Translation*, Eva Hoffman, the Polish-born writer, describes a background not very different from that of Fredzia and myself. We, too, believe that somehow we got lost in translation and are still trying to find our way.

It sounds romantic when I tell people that I'd speak Yiddish to my mother but wrote to her in Polish, and that I speak Swedish to my wife, English to my children and Hebrew to my grandchildren. But my mother is no longer alive and nowadays Fredzia and I speak English to each other. Our Israeli grandchildren are bilingual and they always speak English within the family. But though English may have become the language in which I find it easiest to express myself, it's not really my language.

In addition to the burden of language, each country has put me in a different place in life and distanced me from the previous one. On the assumption that I'm still the same person, I ask myself what my worlds have in common. The attempt to respond is my way of summing up my life, perhaps also trying to understand it. What follows is, therefore, something of a confession.

The confession is grounded in confusion. For I still live in more than one world, this time dividing my time between Israel and Canada. Though I try to be at home in both places, in the end I may not belong to either, even though the chapter dealing with our time in Israel is called "Homecoming." Perhaps our coming to Israel is only homecoming in the collective sense, of having come to the place the Jewish people consider home, but even that may be illusory, as many of the Jews among whom I live in Canada regard that country as their only home and I spend at least half of each year with them.

Not being rooted in any language or any place has made me homeless in every country. That's probably why I feel best in the city. One must have roots to appreciate the countryside, whereas the city is the home of homeless people. In fact, I've seen very little of the countries in which I've lived. The occasional excursions have usually come about as by-products of some other pursuit: a conference, a vacation or a stopover on the way to some other big city. If I've seen more of Israel than of other countries, it's because for many years I used to lead tours, which compelled me to travel the country. I've had little desire to explore the Polish landscape, the beauties of Sweden, the richness of the English countryside or the vastness of Canada. I'm glad they're there, but like sport and recreation, I believe that they aren't for me.

The most persistent unifying factor of my life has been anxiety. For a long time it was fear. Fear is usually of *something*. In my early life it was the fear of perishing and even more, the fear of losing my parents. Many of my frequent nightmares in those days were about being taken alone to a place of execution or witnessing the execution of those close to me. Though I myself never experienced the Holocaust in German-occupied Poland, my parents and the people they mixed with talked of little else. As much as on a conscious level I lived in a different place, subconsciously I absorbed the ordeals of survivors and turned them into my own nightmares. To these I added my memory of being left without my parents while they were in a prison in Uzbekistan, when they refused to take Soviet citizenship, as well as the experience with the NKVD officer who, when taking us for deportation to Siberia in 1940, put his heavily shod foot on mine and made me too afraid to say that it hurt.

But having survived and having found a safe haven in Sweden, gradually the specific fear of extinction turned into an anxiety of existence. Anxiety doesn't require an object; one is anxious first and then finds something to be anxious about. It's therefore harder to bear than fear, perhaps because outer circumstances, viewed objectively, give little cause for it. So even when my life in Sweden became more or less normal, I remained anxious. I could have written this book solely from the perspective of first my fear and then my anxiety and now, perhaps, back to fear. It could have been titled something like Afraid of Living.

My fear started on September 1, 1939, when the Germans invaded Poland and my childhood came to an end. My anxiety was perhaps vindicated on September 11, 2001, when I realized that what I might have been anxious about since my early years was now demonstrated for the whole world, namely, that there's no haven on earth and that we're all vulnerable. The hope of *Pax Americana* after the collapse of the Soviet Union and her satellites has turned into the nightmare of global terrorism. Living in Israel reinforces the feeling of fear, for I feel compelled to constantly to look over my shoulder.

But here it's no longer myself that I'm mainly fearful for, but my children and grandchildren. What will their world be like? All I can do is to tell them something about my world in an attempt to show that as their grandparents survived to live a full and outwardly normal life, despite their bad experiences and haunting anxieties, then there's hope that the children will, too. That's why I've dedicated this book to them.

I think I feel so much better in Israel than in other places because here my anxiety has reverted to fear: I know what to fear and whom to fear. I know that my Israeli grandchildren and their parents need physical protection from identifiable enemies. Even though I'm not in a position to provide for their security, I still find fear much easier to bear than nameless anxiety.

The fact that people around me are in the same boat helps a lot. Many years ago the late Dr. Shammai Davidson compared attitudes of Holocaust survivors in Israel and California. His research showed that though the survivors in California lived more comfortable lives, their Israeli counterparts found life much easier, despite economic restraints and security concerns, because in Israel, unlike California, they could share their feelings and experiences with others. Instead of having to tell it to a psychiatrist, they could talk to each other and be part of the public discourses, and that was much more cathartic.

A friend of ours who was rescued to Sweden from a concentration camp and tried to tell Jews there of her ordeal soon gave up, because the locals told her that life wasn't easy in Sweden either. Shoes and other articles were rationed. Our friend left for England, but things weren't better there. Someone actually asked her once if it was *very* difficult to get kosher food in the camps. If your experiences aren't understood, your sense of alienation may become acute.

Though Fredzia is a concentration camp survivor and my childhood has been spent in the company of survivors, the Holocaust isn't at the centre of our lives. In fact, for all our understanding, or perhaps because of it, there are times we suspect that some of those who invoke the Holocaust to explain their foibles—or to justify their unyielding attitude toward Palestinians—may be abusing the collective Jewish trauma for cynical ends.

I've always understood the Holocaust as the end of a paradigm of Jewish existence that has been replaced by a new one that bases itself on the centrality of the State of Israel. In addition to being sacred memory to be preserved and cherished, the Holocaust is for me, not a justification of Israeli right-wing policies, but an additional reason for caring about all the downtrodden in the world, including the Palestinians. In this respect, Elie Wiesel has been something of an inspiration. He has moved, I believe, from the silence after the tragedy to stress on the survival of the Jewish people to solidarity with all who suffer. I try to emulate that path.

Anything good in life that has come my way has usually heightened my anxiety. I was so happy when Fredzia agreed to marry me that my anxiety turned into irrational jealousy. I was sure she would change her mind soon. I'm still amazed, and immensely grateful some five decades after I proposed, that she hasn't. It took me time to learn to trust even her. I'm not sure that to this day, I trust many others outside the circle of our immediate family. Fredzia is my best friend, perhaps my only real friend. I have her to thank for being able to control my anxiety and enjoy life. I don't wish to minimize my many other friendships, but inevitably they can't be as close.

Now that my mother is no longer alive, I fully realize that I'm more my mother's son than I'd like to admit. Though I was sufficiently alert to the circumstances of my life to have learned to be anxious on my own, my mother taught me that the world is replete with hostile forces, all of them nameless yet all of them poised to get me. When I first met Fredzia, my mother, having her own agenda and burdened by her own unsatisfactory marriage, warned me not to trust anybody, especially not a spouse. My mother also used to be visibly uncomfortable when she met the friends Fredzia and I made in Sweden, Britain and Canada, because she was sure that they'd let us down sooner or later, in one way or another. The Holocaust wasn't unique; as far as my mother was concerned, it's paradigmatic with no allowance for a paradigm shift. Perhaps she would have found life easier in Israel, where she could share her anxieties; in Sweden you had to keep such things to yourself.

I believe that it's my anxiety that has made me appear courageous in the eyes of some. People told me that it was courageous to abandon the prospect of a settled life in Sweden to go to London to study to become a rabbi, even though I had no religious background and no experience of the kind of life I was seeking; that it was courageous not to cave in to the demands of the Stockholm Jewish community but to hold my ground and speak my mind, even though that could have seriously endangered my career. Fredzia and I were told that it took courage to leave a thriving congregation in London, where we seemed to be very settled, and the Anglo-Jewry in which I was considered to be something of a force, and start afresh in Canada. In Canada I was often described as courageous for taking unpopular stands that brought me into conflict with the community, occasionally even with the congregation. But I knew that the driving force in each of my ostensibly courageous acts was the fear of being considered a coward, of missing opportunities or kowtowing to power or giving in to inertia or being seduced by a life of comfort. In fact, I know no other definition of courage than fear of cowardice.

This is related to what I perceived to be my father's lack of courage. It may have been prudent to appear weak in the eyes of the Soviets, but I was exasperated at his inability to stand up to my mother's bullying. On the few occasions that he did react, he would invariably pick an issue that led only to more defeat and humiliation.

He wanted me to be strong to protect him. At times he blatantly appealed to me for support against my mother. For many years I gave it, which poisoned the atmosphere at home and diminished him in the eyes of both his wife and his son. In retrospect it also diminished me and stunted my growth. When I left home in 1955 he felt defenceless and remained so until his death in 1973. Whenever he and I met he would try to unburden himself, but I was no longer able to help him.

I was determined, however, to appear tough and unyielding in my own life. I suspect that Fredzia suffered from this determination in the early years of our marriage. Later some of the people who worked for me complained of my unyielding ways. It hurt me greatly when I was told more often than I cared to hear that I intimidated people. Yet despite all the psychology I read and all the counselling in which I engaged, I didn't know how to act otherwise. It's a source of shame to me, and this is a feeble attempt at expiation. Mercifully my "strong arm" didn't seem to have reached my children. My relationship with them has remained warm, close and, at least from the way I see things, very non-hierarchical.

All the jobs I've ever had were offered to me. I was privileged never to have to write a résumé. (The two jobs I applied for but never got— rabbi in Stockholm and general secretary of the Reform Synagogues of Great Britain—didn't require a résumé since I was well known to those concerned.) Perhaps because of it, I've always feared that I'd be "found out" any day and sent packing, ending up driving a cab or selling ice cream because I didn't have adequate academic qualifications. My distance from co-workers and my toughness toward many of them may stem from this fear. My endeavours to act honestly and with integrity may not have been because I'm such a fine person, but because I couldn't bear the humiliation of appearing weak and indecisive. I may have been trying to expiate my father's ghost.

I don't believe, however, that it's fear or anxiety that brought me to religion. The common wisdom that fear is the beginning of faith doesn't resonate with me. Had this been my driving force I'd probably have ended up a rabid fundamentalist as so many "born again" religionists do. Fear as a motivating force in religion may be relevant to those who in their early years were coerced into believing, but that doesn't apply to me. Religion was totally absent from my childhood. If I encountered it, be it among the men in our hut in Uzbekistan or in the few Muslims I'd occasionally see prostrating themselves in prayer, it never occurred to me that it had anything to do with me. I didn't seem to have been even curious about it. When my friends in the Uzbek village were circumcised, I heard prayers recited, but they meant nothing. I didn't even perceive my bar mitzvah as a religious occasion.

The school I attended in post-war Poland was totally secular, as were the people we mixed with. Though my aunts, when we met them upon our arrival in Sweden in 1948, appeared to be Orthodox, it was obvious even to me that it was just their way to conform and had no religious significance. I recall that I tried to please them and for a few weeks said the traditional prayers every morning. I even donned the phylacteries that the Jewish Joint Distribution Committee provided me for my bar mitzvah. My parents weren't pleased and as I didn't feel much when I did it, I soon gave up.

My way to God was primarily the outcome of, first, a search for structure and, later, a quest for meaning and purpose. I needed to know what it was all about, and the only people who seemed to offer guidelines were religious people. I didn't find any Jews who might help, but Christian teachers in my school helped, particularly one. I felt that if these people whom I had great respect for believed, there must be something to it. Perhaps had not Ove Nordstrandh, my homeroom teacher who taught Christianity, encouraged me do a paper on Judaism, I might have sought myself within some Christian group, but once I began to learn about my tradition, I was hooked. Judaism has not given me security or peace of mind, but it has given me direction. All stumbling blocks notwithstanding, I feel that I know where I'm going. Looking back, I discern a purpose that has bestowed upon me much blessing and filled me with endless gratitude.

But I was never "born again," because what attracted me to Judaism was its rational manifestations. I was in search of conviction. My Judaism has never been emotional. To the extent that the Jewish world is still divided between the pious and the rationalists, I most decidedly belong to the latter. But my theology may have been influenced by my psychological makeup. In retrospect I realize that my stance was authoritative, even authoritarian. Even those who came to me for pastoral guidance tended to do so, not because they wanted me to hold their hand and cry with them, but because they wanted to be guided toward a goal.

It's only in recent years that I've come to relate to God as *Harachaman*, the Merciful, and realized that, even more than the strength of God, it's the caring nurturing God who really speaks to us. I now also know that, though I may have learned much Judaism, it's Fredzia who's the real believer. So I no longer agonize over why God allows evil in the world. Instead, I seek God's comforting presence. I believe that the essence of holiness is to be found in this search. I've learned much from those exponents of Judaism who stress this dimension of the divine.

My Jewish practice, on the other hand, may have its roots in anxiety. Though I wasn't brought up to regard Orthodox Jewish practice as natural, and though my theological outlook makes relatively little room for it, I'm a very structured person, perhaps even obsessively so. I know of no better definition of happiness than the sense of having done my duty. Though on intellectual grounds I cannot accept the traditional notion of Halakhah, Jewish law, as binding, I believe that mitzvah, commandment, is essential for Jewish life. I believe that as Jews we've been commanded by God and that the sources of Judaism, both biblical and rabbinic, testify to the nature of the commandments. There are different ways of responding to them; my way is that of Reform Judaism. I've tried to live by it as best I can. My life isn't *halakhic* (Orthodox), but it's Jewishly structured. Sanctification of time, prayer and the study of our tradition are central to it. It's one of several ways in which I seek to bear witness to my commitment to God.

I've often framed my appeal on behalf of Jewish practice in terms of "incremental Judaism." It's my way of recognizing that for many Jews, especially those to whom I've ministered over the years, maximal and consistent observance isn't possible. As it's not really possible for me, I wouldn't try to impose it on others. But I believe in an experimental way to God. It implies a widening of the range of religious experiences in our daily life by adopting more and more aspects of traditional conduct. I've therefore urged congregants to embrace "one mitzvah at a time" and thus enrich their Jewish lives.

As important as individual conduct is in this scheme of things, the primary way in which the testimony will be effective is by making room for the collective. I see Judaism not only, perhaps not even primarily, as a private matter, but as a public concern. The *minyan*, the quorum needed before certain prayers can be said, is an important category in Judaism. It speaks to me. That's why, whenever possible, I'd rather pray with a congregation than by myself.

Perhaps, again because I don't think very much of myself, I find it impossible to look at the universe as if it were created with me in the centre. I get impatient with those, many of them rabbis, who try to persuade audiences that the seeming coincidences in their lives have cosmic significance and thus explain their being religious leaders. My religious outlook makes for humility and gratitude for being, and for being able to act as a witness to God's presence in the world. I see myself as a tool and regard the rabbinate as the privileged way of acting as such. Teaching is a way of testifying. With Abraham Joshua Heschel I believe that a sense of awe and wonder is the root of religious faith. I try to reflect this sense in everything I do.

My commitment to duty goes far beyond personal observance. Most of my work has been shaped by my sense of obligation, including pastoral work. In retrospect, I'm not at all sure that I enjoyed much in the rabbinate beyond teaching and preaching, yet I tried to be as conscientious as possible, because to be negligent would have made me unbearably uncomfortable. The thought of being accused of having failed an individual or a task filled me with enormous anxiety, so I did what I had to do in order to sleep at night.

Though I've never known how to measure success, one great source of comfort and reassurance is that I've parted on the best of terms with all three congregations I've served. I'm also gratified that virtually all the presidents of these congregations and many other leaders have become more intimate friends at the end of their term of office than they were in the beginning. Despite my awkwardness, they seem to have come to appreciate my commitment and my devotion. I feel truly blessed.

Though my religious commitment has other sources, I'm well aware that to the extent that I've been a successful rabbi, it's not due to a natural talent for scholarship and interaction with people, but out of fear of being a failure. I worked much harder than I had to. I overprepared most sermons, lectures, articles and even minor talks to assure myself rather than impress others. As a result, often my presentations lacked spontaneity and didn't go down as well as I hoped. Whatever I did achieve, however, wasn't to satisfy some burning desire to be a success, but out of a burning fear of being a failure. In the same way as my alleged courage is the result of my fear of cowardice, so is my alleged professional success the result of being afraid of idleness that might precipitate failure. Appearing tough became something of a protective shield in the pursuit of both courage and success.

In my efforts to show strength, or at least an absence of weakness, and do the right thing, I often appeared ambitious, arrogant and immodest. Now I'm better able to express genuine humility, which in earlier years I would hide lest it be taken as a sign of weakness. My theological path, from seeking to fathom the power of God to yearning for divine comfort, has influenced this process. Whereas in the past I've often been critical of others, not suffering fools lightly, I'm now able to be more generous to people, because I'm more tolerant of myself, even less anxious about myself. I remember how difficult it is to discharge one's responsibilities in any context and to live up to the expectations of others in the helping professions, of which the rabbinate is one. I'm not sure that others find me a nicer person nowadays, but many have said that I appear more relaxed. I feel that I'm able to live with myself with much greater serenity than before. I cherish the thought that for God, being caring is more important than being powerful, and I see holiness (imitation of God, as described in Leviticus 19) as a noble human pursuit.

This has made retirement so much easier. Because I no longer have to carry out duties that I either imposed on myself or were imposed on me, my anxiety level has diminished. Combined with my unexpected, and perhaps unwarranted, greater sense of security that comes from living in Israel, I'm surprised that I'm enjoying retirement. While many of my retired colleagues are trying to fill their days with all kinds of pseudo-rabbinic activities, I'm quite happy to read a book, go for a walk, watch television or sit in front of a computer reflecting on my life and on the circumstances around me.

If I miss anything in my present existence, it's a platform that would allow me to express myself. The pulpit was a most congenial outlet. Though I have no desire to return to it, I'd welcome a column in some publication, however obscure. So far, apart from a monthly 450 words in the *Canadian Jewish News*, nobody has made me an offer and I haven't approached anybody, for as "cured" of anxiety as I may appear to be, I'd rather not ask than ask and be turned down. If I hadn't been fortunate in getting all the jobs I've had without applying for them, I'm not sure I'd apply for anything.

The need for a platform may, of course, be a manifestation of the old need to prove myself. However, it may also be a need to formulate thoughts and ideas that I'm working on, both about Judaism in general and Jewish life in Israel in particular. My outlook on both has changed over the years and continues to do so, and I need opportunities to interact with others so that I can formulate my thoughts and test them. That's why I inflict on friends listed in my e-mail file frequent letters with my reflections.

The change in my thinking may be illustrated, for example, by the belief, described earlier in this volume, that the term "Reform" in Reform

Judaism isn't a verb that demands constant change but an adjective that seeks to present Judaism in a particular key and from a perspective of the two-hundred-year-old tradition of Reform Judaism. My emphasis has shifted from "Reform" to "Judaism," where the former defines the latter, not the other way around. The shift may have come with age and its increased stress on continuity and permanence. But there may have been other factors, too.

It's possible, for example, that being a rabbi in the Diaspora requires one to bend with the wind. There, Reform Judaism is a way for many to adapt their Jewish heritage to the culture in which they live. That culture is usually the decisive factor. I laboured in that milieu, both in Britain and in Canada, for some four decades, trying to be among those who rescue the essence of Judaism without alienating adherents from their environment. Despite serious efforts to conform, I was often culturally maladjusted, especially when I tried to persuade those to whom I ministered that Judaism should serve as a corrective to the surrounding culture, not its slave. This was often the underlying agenda of my preaching and writing. Much of the time both were dismissed as alien and "intellectual." Often it was only in retrospect, that is, when I left the congregation I served, that my stance was appreciated. This, too, has been one of the rewards of retirement: I can look back on having made a contribution to the way a number of Jews now perceive their Judaism.

Unlike in the Diaspora, in Israel, despite strong American influences in most dimensions of public life, the culture and the religious heritage of Judaism are still of one piece. Here, the constancy founded on traditional Jewish norms may be easier to uphold. To adapt to the mores of Israel is to embrace the totality of the Jewish experience and to affirm the continuity of the Jewish people. I'm persuaded that, for all the strength of Diaspora Jewry and the influence of Reform Judaism within it, the future of Judaism is linked to the future of the Jewish state. I fear that those who say otherwise are assimilationists and if we depend on them, Judaism will not survive. Their arguments that the domination of hard-line Orthodoxy threatens to turn Israel into a pre-modern Levantine state are valid. However, we won't counteract this menacing trend by distancing ourselves from Israel. On the contrary, the threat of Orthodox fundamentalism makes the presence of liberal religious Jews—the label includes, apart from Reform Jews, the adherents of Conservative Judaism and of modern Orthodoxy— especially important. Should we seek to remove Israel from the centre of our Jewish consciousness, both Israel and our own Judaism will be greatly diminished.

The link between Zionism and Reform, the two most powerful modernist movements in Judaism, is to my mind of historic significance. It has brought back to Reform Judaism the dimension of *k'lal Yisrael*, the Jewish people, thus purging Reform from its earlier dangerous assimilationist tendencies. Zionism has alerted Reform Jews to the primacy of the public sphere of Jewish life, in addition to the private expressions of Jewishness it usually cultivates among adherents. We've been reminded that the Torah commands us to be holy (*kedoshim*), a holy people (*goy kadosh*), not a community of saints.

The fusion of Reform Judaism with Zionism also exposes Israelis to an alternative to Orthodox Judaism, which many of them—on modernist grounds—have rejected. Without Reform Judaism, Israel may become a theocracy like Iran or a secular state like all other states. In either case Israel will cease to be significant for contemporary Judaism, and as a result, the survival of Judaism as a witness to the world, not only the practice of isolated groups, will be in serious jeopardy.

Living in Israel has also made me aware of another challenge for Reform Judaism, perhaps even more important than providing an alternative to Orthodoxy: it is to confront the secular majority to make it affirm the treasures of Judaism as part of its cultural heritage. This was indeed the case in the first few decades of the existence of the State of Israel. It's much less so nowadays. Americanization hasn't meant only the prevalence of American secularity but also of many aspects of its religiosity. New Age religion has become a powerful factor among Israeli secularists. Because they still associate religion with Jewish Orthodoxy, which they reject, and are ignorant of non-Orthodox alternatives, they've become alienated from the wealth of Jewish teachings. Like their counterparts in other countries, many Israelis will say that they aren't religious, are perhaps even anti-religious, but that they're "spiritual." In addition to building congregations and challenging the Orthodox establishment, Reform Judaism also has to shoulder the task of seeking to inform, and thus influence, Israeli secular culture.

That's why Reform Judaism is so vital for the future of the Jewish state. Its growth in recent years has been a source of great encouragement. It's also a source of boundless joy and pride to me that my son, Michael, is in the forefront of that process. As the dean of the Hebrew Union College–Jewish Institute of Religion in Jerusalem, he oversees not only the training of American rabbis and other Jewish professionals who come to Israel for their first year of training, but also some three dozen Israeli students who study there full-time. I believe that at least some of these may come to influence the cultural climate of the country as a whole. In addition to providing whatever services individuals may need and will not have, or cannot get, from the Orthodox, these Israeli Reform rabbis may have a recognizable role in the overall cultural debate. Michael has turned my theory into his practice. For much of my writing, particularly my book, *The Star of Return*, is about the fusion between liberal Judaism and Zionism. But alas, like all my other books, it has had virtually no impact. As it was written several years after my son's aliyah, I can't even claim him as a disciple. Perhaps I am *his* disciple.

Wherever I may be, Israel is as close to home for me as anyplace can be. I wasn't long enough in Poland to have Polish roots, even though, inexplicably, I occasionally seem to hanker for them. I left Sweden before I could regard the country as my own. Though I lived in England for more than a quarter century, I never really felt at home there; Fredzia and I didn't even become British citizens. The two decades in Canada marked me as an outsider in American Reform— because I lived in Canada and because I had European baggage—and I wasn't enough of a Canadian in Canada.

While in Canada I'd often start a speech or a lecture by "explaining" what brought me to the country. I said that though I was born in Poland, there I was always regarded as a Jew. Growing up in Sweden, I was always considered a Pole. In England I was always a Swede. So I came to Canada to fulfill a life-long ambition to be an Englishman.

When I told this once to a Presbyterian audience, a Scotsman heckled me, "You're not very ambitious, sir, are you?"

The real reason my writings have had so little impact may be because they aren't very original. I'm aware of the many thinkers who have influenced me, even though experts may say that I've misrepresented them. In any case, I've not found it possible to be a disciple of any of them. I may have learned much, but ultimately I've turned away from them and moved on—not necessarily to my advantage.

The teacher I turned away from first was Ignaz Maybaum. Soon after I became a rabbi I realized that his version of liberal Judaism belonged to a bygone era. Though he had been a Zionist in his earlier years, in England he became the spokesman of a kind of exclusive Diaspora existence, believing that the British bourgeois lifestyle provided an authentic model for all of Jewish life. He even implied that the Holocaust made this more possible than it would have been otherwise. To the extent that he was committed to Israel, it was for the same reasons that non-Zionist Orthodox Jews care about Israel: because Jews lived there and it was our responsibility to care for them. I could not inhabit his world and left it, despite my admiration and affection for him and his family.

I recall Maybaum's irritation when I told him that I was reading the works of Gershom Scholem, arguably the greatest Jewish scholar of the twentieth century, and Martin Buber, that century's most influential Jewish thinker. Scholem's chosen field of research was mysticism, and Maybaum had no time for that. Buber's fascination with Hasidism was equally unacceptable. Yet it was Buber, more than any other Jewish thinker, who helped me to link my commitment to God with my commitment to other human beings, thus helping me to meet the challenge of every contemporary religious person: how to combine a notion of a transcendental God with acceptance of post-Enlightenment humanism. Buber made me realize that, in his own terminology, though God cannot be *expressed*, God can be *addressed*. Not abstract theology, but concrete encounters with human beings, and through them with God, faith is made possible. In this scheme of things, belief in God and commitment to human beings are compatible.

I tried to learn that, despite my propensity to explain and challenge, preaching may be much less important than praying. That's how Buber saw the biblical prophets and that's how he also perceived the exponents of Hasidism. My attempts at changing the liturgies of the congregations I served, particularly that of Holy Blossom Temple, have their origin in what I tried to learn from Buber and his followers, notably Abraham Joshua Heschel in his writings on the place of prayer in the contemporary synagogue.

I still recall the day when on my way back from Leo Baeck College, I stopped at a bookshop and on impulse bought a copy of Buber's seminal little book, *I and Thou*. I began to read it while waiting for the bus, but couldn't tear myself away from the book and stood for a long time reading, ignoring the buses that stopped. I didn't understand what I read and perhaps I still don't understand the book, but I knew that it was important to my quest for God. I believe that my interest in linking religious experience with interpersonal relations, which subsequently manifested itself in my joining the marriage guidance movement, stems from this. I may not have been the pastor who held the hands of congregants and wept with them, but I believe that I was an *I* who worked hard to encounter and thus affirm the *Thou*.

What I learned from Buber has remained with me to this very day, even though I'm no longer as involved in lay psychotherapy as I used to be. In fact, I'm often impatient with colleagues who try to reduce theology to therapy and reduce commitment to the Jewish people to the needs of individual Jews. But I believe that my interest in the writings of Emmanuel Levinas arises out of my interest in Buber. Levinas's teaching about ethics' preceding ontology and metaphysics resonates with me and helps me to understand the traditional Jewish emphasis on holiness as the this-worldly commitment to God's creatures and a way of reaching out to God, and being touched by God.

The thinker who helped me to move further along my path was Emil Fackenheim. Though judging by his pre-1967 writings, he had seen the Diaspora as normative, the Six-Day War and the events leading up to it had changed his mind. He now became the exponent of the call to Jewish survival in order not to give Hitler a posthumous victory. For Fackenheim the Jewish state has been the greatest guarantor of Jewish survival. He left Toronto for Israel soon after I went to Israel and I had many opportunities to invite him to speak at Holy Blossom Temple, where he had been an important presence for many decades. We were neighbours in Jerusalem, but I didn't see much of him, mainly because his near-obsession with the Holocaust coupled with a right-wing political outlook made it impossible for me to learn from him. I always had the feeling that my attempts to argue with him simply irritated him. Shortly before we left Israel in May 2003 Fackenheim came to dinner, along with some Christian friends who live in Jerusalem. It was a splendid evening. He died a couple of months later. I'm glad to remember him at that last encounter, and I spoke about it at the memorial service I organized at Holy Blossom Temple after the customary thirty days of mourning.

I began to move away from Fackenheim's position as early as 1982. My book *Beyond Survival* testifies to it. When I got to know him later, I urged him repeatedly to formulate a Judaism *beyond* his commandment not to give Hitler a posthumous victory. I begged him to move from the negative and defensive to the positive and affirmative, especially when he lectured at Holy Blossom Temple. He agreed on the topics I suggested but refused to speak about this particular subject. On one occasion he began his lecture by saying, "Dow Marmur wants me to speak about the topic as advertised, but I intend to speak about. ..."

I'm in fact much closer to the teachings of David Hartman, the other significant Canadian Jewish thinker, now living in Israel. But unlike several Reform rabbis, I've never sought to enter Hartman's circle, even though I live only minutes away from the magnificent institute he has built in Jerusalem and meet him from time to time. Perhaps it's because I don't know how to be a real disciple.

Hartman's affirmation of Israel as the start of a new paradigm in Jewish life that urges for us to move from Auschwitz back to Sinai on our way to the Promised Land speaks to me. My book *The Star of Return* is really about that. Hartman's open almost "trans-denominational" approach to Judaism appeals to me too. It's consistent with my non-sectarian understanding of Judaism in which *k'lal Yisrael* takes precedence over institutional interests.

Yet, for all my maladjustment, I've remained within Reform Judaism, and as the rabbi of one of its largest Reform congregations in the world, I did my best to promote its institutional interests. In my writings I often cite Eugene Borowitz, the principal theologian of American Reform. His structure of modern Judaism around the idea of covenant has helped me greatly to formulate Judaism in its collective dimension. It's not a coincidence, I believe, that Hartman, too, puts the Jew's covenant obligations in the centre of his structure of contemporary Jewish thought. However, over the years, I've found it more and more difficult to follow also Borowitz in his insistence on autonomy as the basis for Reform Judaism. As modernists we'll always put people before principles, but by making personal choice the decisive factor in matters of Jewish belief and practice, we've come to promote the anarchic side of Reform Judaism.

It's one thing when members of congregations, Reform and others, make their personal selections. It's something much more ominous when rabbis begin to "make Shabbas for themselves" and encourage their congregants to do likewise in an effort to promote self-expression and "spirituality." As unsatisfactory as I find it, for example, to worship in congregations that follow normative Orthodox practice, I find it at times even more difficult to attend the various attempts to turn worship services of whatever denomination into song-sessions. Michael Chernick, a professor at the Hebrew Union College in New York, calls this "warm fuzzies spirituality."

And though I find the company congenial in the congregation in which I normally worship in Jerusalem, I cannot discern any sense of the sacred there. Theology has been turned into sociology and the therapeutic has taken the place of the holy. Words of Torah spoken there are of the same ilk. My problem is that, to date, I haven't found an acceptable alternative. Many of the lectures I've given since retiring have been about the quest of the sacred in the collective experience of the Jewish people. Perhaps one day I will be able to develop these thoughts into a coherent stance.

Which brings me back to the search of a platform from which I can articulate my views, particularly as they apply to contemporary Reform Judaism. I've come to realize that, though I continue to learn from many teachers and thinkers, Jewish and non-Jewish, I cannot follow any of them. And I'm not sure that I've the intellectual wherewithal to formulate a credible alternative. I'm trying to adjust to the fact that I won't leave behind a lasting legacy and that much of my effort to give the impression of an intellectual is a way of compensating for my lack of academic credentials.

Perhaps my involvement in what's known in North America as "social action" is for a similar reason. I'm a Zionist because I'm in search of a homeland. I've in some modest way been involved in Canadian public life because of my desire to belong. I've been active in interfaith work as a way of trying to break out of my isolation as a person and as a Jew. I was particularly conscious that my earlier efforts on behalf of German-Jewish understanding were ways of making up for my disdain for Germans, for it was their Nazi regime that shaped much of my fragmented life. My sympathies with Israeli movements that demand rights and dignity for Palestinians are of the same ilk: an attempt to overcome an inbred fear of the other. Much that I've written in these fields arose out of a need to persuade *myself* before I could speak to others. Often it has worked; I feel that my efforts in this realm have shaped me as a person. I'm grateful for the opportunities to confront my demons and, in many cases, exorcise them. Mine has indeed been a rich and rewarding life. I thank God for it daily.

Coda

"My Luck" by Fredzia Marmur

I could not believe my luck when I met Dow Marmur. Having survived the ghetto of Lodz and the Ravensbruck concentration camp, my mother and I arrived in Sweden in the last days of the war, among those rescued by the Swedish Red Cross. My father survived in another concentration camp and we were later reunited.

I knew I was very lucky to have survived the Holocaust and that I should be extremely grateful to Sweden, but I felt bewildered and sad. I felt that somehow I did not deserve my good fortune. I couldn't speak to anyone about it, not even to my parents, who were preoccupied with trying to rebuild their own shattered lives. The friends I had made in my new country were too removed from my experience to possibly understand how I felt.

So I pretended to live a normal life in Stockholm. One year I was even chosen by my school to be Santa Lucia, the Queen of Light, celebrated with great rejoicing on December 13 every year. It reminded me of a Swedish-Christian-pagan version of Hanukkah. I could not refuse such an honour, especially since I knew that my teacher's wish to make a stranger feel at home had prompted the school to choose me. Usually it was the girl with the blondest hair who was selected. I vividly remember how totally alien I felt when the Queen of Light's crown of candles flickered over my dark hair.

Coda

One day my teacher at the religious school the Jewish community ran asked the class which Jewish festival we liked best, and the consensus was Hanukkah. When he asked me why, I said that it was because the Jews had won and had been made free in their own country. He looked at me, winked and said, "Don't tell me that's why you like Hanukkah," implying that the real reason was the fun and the presents. His implication devastated me, and again I felt lost. No one, including my Judaism teacher, could understand how I felt about the Jewish people.

I tried to *shadchen* (match) a friend with a boy from another city with whom I corresponded. Unsure of how to ask him to write to her, I suggested a kind of correspondence club, as there were so few Jewish people in Sweden. I gave him my friend's address and he gave mine to a young man named Dow, whom he had met at a conference a few months earlier.

Dow wrote me a long letter about himself and his background, which happened to be very similar to mine. I wrote a reply, but I spilled coffee on it, so I never posted the letter. As luck would have it, we later met. In the summer of 1954 we both attended a camp run by the Scandinavian Jewish Federation. Within ten days after the camp ended, we had decided to marry. It seemed the most natural thing to do.

Invigorated by the support we found in each other, we began to make plans for the future. Dow thought of becoming a rabbi. I wanted a large family and many friends, and the rabbinate would provide a family on a large scale. It would also offer the kind of validation for my survival that I had been seeking all along. For me religion had always been an expression of trust and of shared responsibility.

So it was that in 1957, a year after our marriage, we moved to London for Dow to enrol at the Leo Baeck College. We were ill-equipped for the English weather. Never before or since have we been as cold as we were that first winter in England, especially indoors. We found accommodation in a lovely house that lacked adequate heating. Being anxious not to miss classes, Dow once got up in the middle of the night, thinking it was already morning. I was able to put him right because my feet were still ice-cold and I knew that they only got warm in the morning.

201

After our initial shock at the small size of the Leo Baeck College in those days, we tried to adjust and got to know the teachers and the students. Our good fortune was to have Rabbi Ignaz and Mrs. Maybaum as our role models. They sort of adopted us, and we benefited greatly from their care and guidance.

Bent Melchior, for the last three decades the chief rabbi of Denmark, was a student at Jews' College at the same time. We became close friends with the Melchior family. At the time Bent's father was the chief rabbi of Copenhagen. Thanks to the Maybaums and the Melchiors, I saw rabbinical homes close up, and I liked what I saw.

After many stillbirths and miscarriages, our lovely daughter Viveca was born. She is now a palliative care specialist in London. Michael, our second child, is now a rabbi in Haifa.

Between pregnancies, I took courses at the college with Dr. Ellen Littman, the lecturer in Bible studies, as one of my teachers.

A few months before Dow graduated he became the minister of the South-West Essex Reform Synagogue, then still Ilford. There I was gently eased into the *rebbetzin's* role. It was a wonderful congregation. Its members took us in with open arms. Now for the first time the children had uncles and aunts, even a "grandpa" and "grandma," as they called the late Harry and Rosa Isaacs.

We were part of the real community. I will never forget the enthusiasm when we decorated the first *huppah* in the congregation's modest premises, a converted Victorian house. A rug and some vases were brought from our homes in an effort to add warmth and colour to the ceremony.

Our home was open to the congregation. We had study groups and meetings and dinner parties, and Dow saw people in his study at home. Once Michael opened the door to a woman in a hat and said, "Dad, there's a witch to see you." I hope Michael's children are more tactful when members of his congregation come to see him.

In those days my challenge was to keep at least one room tidy and a cake ready to be served. But Viveca complained, supported by her brother: "Strangers you let into the lounge and give them nice cakes, but your own children are not allowed to play there and are not offered cake." She was right. After that I took the risk of visitors sitting on toys and sometimes only having biscuits with their tea.

South-West Essex was then a new and still-small congregation. That meant the rabbi and his wife were expected to go to all the functions. We did. It was often hard to leave crying babies to be on time for a wedding reception or a bar mitzvah party. Children always know when you are in a hurry.

In our seven years in Ilford, we had our share of sadness. When my father was dying in Sweden and I went with Viveca to be with him, I left Dow and Michael for several months in the care of kind congregants. Then I had a spell in hospital before the birth of our daughter Elizabeth, now an actress in Toronto.

The only hostility I encountered at South-West Essex was when it became known that we were moving to the North-Western Reform Synagogue, Alyth Gardens, in London's Golders Green. People would say, "You won't want to come to our bar mitzvahs now, for you will be going to the posh ones in Golders Green."

The children were upset at having to leave their cozy world in Ilford. Alyth Gardens was a larger, more formal congregation. It took me longer to find my bearings there. But our home remained open— for Shabbat afternoon *shiurim* as well as for Talmud classes, Torah study groups, meetings and receptions during the week, in addition to numerous social occasions to which members were invited.

Without much help at home, I had my hands full. My role has always been a supporting one. I do not begrudge it, for otherwise I do not think Dow would have been able to do his work adequately. My greatest contribution to the congregations he has served has been enabling him to give unstintingly of his time.

I created support groups around me. Only recently did the wife of a much younger rabbi remind me that I taught her to take one afternoon a week off for herself. Apparently I did not tell her that my "afternoon off" started with delivering Meals on Wheels in the East End of London.

When I think back on those years, it is the rushing from one event to another that I remember most. I still have my black *rebbetzin's* suit with tiny multicoloured dots that would take me from a stone setting to a wedding to a funeral to a bar mitzvah party in one day. We often started evenings with a shiva service before going on to a dinner party.

A new chapter in our lives began when we moved to Canada. Moving is always easier for a rabbi, for she or he has a set agenda to work with. As for me, it took a while before I could find my own way in the new environment. Yes, life is more comfortable here—but the view from the window is not as nice as the one in London.

I found that it is more prestigious to be a rabbi's wife in Canada, especially the wife of the senior rabbi at Holy Blossom Temple. But that has its drawbacks. After chatting happily to somebody for a while, that person discovers who I am—then shakes my hand enthusiastically again, as if the previous chat didn't count.

It does not take much to be viewed as eccentric in Canada. My eccentricities include the fact that I do not drive a car, that I wear hats, and that I do not refer to Dow as "the rabbi." But I have made many new friends and feel at home in Toronto now. People are very nice to me. They stop to offer me rides and invite me to lunch. I appreciate their kindness. The members of Holy Blossom are devoted to the Temple, but do not come much to services, except on High Holy Days. And it does not occur to them to feel guilty about it, unlike their British counterparts. They even think me odd because I always attend Shabbat morning services.

My role is made easier because Dow is respected in the community. The worst hostility to which I have been subjected came from a neighbour who said, "I've heard that your husband is quite religious and talks a lot about God." I can cope with that.

When I look back on the years as a "rabbinical spouse," the term used here, I am still amazed at the tightrope I walk every day between responsibility and privilege. The privilege is getting to know people on a deep level and sharing their lives. The responsibility is keeping their secrets safe and knowing when to be there to help.

It is often difficult to know what matters to people and what is being ignored. Sometimes a simple telephone call to congratulate someone on a birthday or to inquire about her or his health is appreciated out of proportion to the effort. At other times, however, I have travelled across the city to visit someone in hospital only to be greeted with "Oh, it's you—I thought the rabbi would be coming."

I still worry about getting telephone messages right and about expressing condolences and wishing mazel tov to the appropriate congregant. Dow shields me from more serious unpleasantness in the congregation, for he knows that I brood on it.

I still find it hard to be public property, always expected to be on parade and to perform. I still spend long boring evenings with people, but there are no shortcuts to relationships.

My wish to be part of an extended family did indeed come true. By now its members are all over the world, including grandchildren, our own and those of our friends. We try to keep in touch. As in all families, you have the power to hurt and to be hurt, and nobody can quite avoid either. You can always do better and do more for others and may feel badly for not having done enough.

Yet I still cannot believe my luck.

Since this piece appeared, Bent Melchior has retired as Chief Rabbi of Denmark; he recently celebrated his seventy-fifth birthday. Our daughter Viveca is no longer working in palliative care nursing. Michael, our son, is now a dean of a rabbinic school in Jerusalem. Our youngest, Elizabeth, is still an actress but now lives in London. She and her husband, Anthony, have two children.

Index

Index

Index